Kingston

Cities of the Imagination

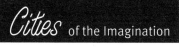 of the Imagination

Kingston

A cultural and literary history

David Howard

Interlink Books

An imprint of Interlink Publishing Group, Inc.
Northampton, Massachusetts

First published 2005 by

INTERLINK BOOKS

An imprint of Interlink Publishing Group, Inc.
46 Crosby Street, Northampton, Massachusetts 01060

ISBN 1-56656-420-4

Drawings by Wendy Skinner Smith
Cover Design: Baseline Arts
Cover Images: David Howard; Institute of Jamaica; courtesy Perry Henzell
Printed and bound in Canada by Webcom

Contents

CHAPTER THREE
UPTOWN

CHAPTER FOUR
THE GHETTO

CHAPTER FIVE
HEROINES AND HEROES: THE CITY'S NATION-BUILDERS

CHAPTER SIX
CITY SOUNDSCAPES

CHAPTER SEVEN
City Visions

CHAPTER EIGHT
Roundabouts

In memory of
Mos
(1968-2001)
wordsmith, freethinker, father, friend

Foreword

Like a beloved relative or friend who has fallen on hard times, you keep wanting to say of her, "you should have known her then." You should have known her then, the Kingston where I was born as Kingstonians say, "under the clock", over half a century ago, for if she was not the city of lights she was certainly the city of life, the promised land to which thousands of people like my parents had come from country to "make life". In this book David Howard does a remarkable job of presenting Kingston as a fascinating place of stark contrasts, a city which has for centuries affected visitors in powerful ways.

> *Kingston today storms to the mind as a confused cocktail of rum-soaked tropical sunsets and the more violent images of political and personal street vendettas. Myth abounds and reality lies in the popular imagination. Or, reality lies in a halfway house, perched precariously between the muzak-filled shopping malls and stratified suburbs of uptown Kingston and the rumbling, charred social landscapes of downtown.*

I was born at Lineen, Jubilee, which makes me a bona fide Kingstonian. For the first eight years of my life, Kingston, from the seaside at Victoria Pier and the stuffed "alligator" in the Institute of Jamaica on East Street to the pastoral splendor of Hope Gardens where we went to play on public Holidays, was "the Kingdom of my world". Although staunch Anglicans, my parents felt free to send my siblings and me to Roman Catholic schools—Convent Infant school and St. Aloysius Boys school on Duke Street. We were dressed in our best clothes and sent to church and Sunday school at All Saints Anglican Church on West Street, where one of Edna Manley's finest carvings, a life-sized black Christ, was hung behind the altar. On every street corner we passed pocomania and revival meetings where the deities of Africa and Europe were engaged in power sharing, for, as Howard writes, "the city's alleys and yards are places of religious intensity where spirits and Kingstonians cross paths in a myriad of daily performances and experiences."

Kingston was and is, as David Howard notes, a place where music and dance rule. And O if you could have been there when my brother Howard kept a dance at the Jubilee Tile Gardens, 21 North Street, one August night in 1954. To see all the men, who in daily life were just ordinary labourers, messengers, yard boys and such; and the women who by day were store clerks and maids, who had no last name, just "the girl", or "cookie" and "nursy" or "washy" to their well-off employers, you should have seen them transformed into important gentlemen and ladies in formal dark suits and fabulous net-over taffeta dresses, who danced till the break of dawn in what was original dance hall.

My family lived for eight years on Orange Street, where we became witnesses to the birth of modern Jamaican music, for Orange Street was the sound system and record shop capital of the island. The home of Tom The Great Sebastien. And who can forget the day when the news ran up and down the street that Tom, like the handsome tragic hero he was, had taken his own life for love of a woman? Orange Street would in later years come to be known as "Beat Street". Bob Marley's original Tuff Gong shop, Jack Taylor's Hardware and Record Shop, Prince Buster's Musical Empire, and the musical establishment of Sir Coxsone Downbeat, as well as Rupie Edwards' Record Shop and Beverley's Records, which produced the early Jimmy Cliff hits, were all founded there.

One of my brothers, Karl, who is a social worker, once said that he had no idea that we lived then in what people now call the ghetto. To us it was just "home"; and even if the buildings were, as so many visitors to the island remarked, shabby and ugly, what was more important to us as children then was the non-stop excitement of the city, the never ending parade of street characters like Elephant, who was a big tree man; and Bag O Wire, who had betrayed Marcus Garvey; and Bun Down Cross Roads, who used to own the property on which the original Carib theatre was built till he was arrested for arson and his name became "Bun Down Cross Roads Build Up Carib". All these characters, including "Pearl Harbour", Kingston's most infamous fallen woman, have helped to inform the sensibilities of poets, artists and songwriters of my generation, from Burning Spear to the Sistren Theatre Collective.

Who would not consider themselves fortunate to have had their first theatre going experience at the Ward Theatre? Or to have been taken by my sister Barbara who was then a "cub-reporter" at the *Daily Gleaner* for lunch at the Myrtle Bank Hotel, which was as grand a hotel as you ever saw in films? And sure, all this was this stuff of dreams available only to the privileged; but every Kingstonian felt that they too stood a good chance of getting through, one day one day, for Kingston was filled with stories of little people who had "made it" and who had made the move uptown. Until then, as one of our great statesmen said, "the poor were kept alive by the generosity of the poor," and many Kingstonians of my acquaintance recall learning about compassion and generosity through being sent by their parents to carry covered dishes of food to neighbours in need.

> *Barely four miles, but a great gulf separate uptown and downtown Kingston, Oxford Road severs Cross Roads from New Kingston, invisibly slicing apart the city's social spheres... But the drive uptown from Harbour Street via Slipe, Half Way Tree, and Constant Spring Roads to the neat neighbourhoods of Arcadia Gardens, Aylsham and Cherry Gardens conjures up images beyond even the most lucid of imaginations.*

Howard's acuity of vision leads him to comment on the great divide between uptown and downtown. Many of his observations, about downtown Kingston call to mind "The Town I Love So Well", which the Irish songwriter Phil Coulter wrote in 1969 about the troubles afflicting his beloved Belfast.

Maybe you should have seen my Kingston during the nineteen-seventies, for while Howard catalogues much of the horrible effects of the political tenor of that time, it was a great thing to have witnessed the powerful changes that took place in the lives of the maid, cookie, nursy, washy, the girl, the yard boy and the common labourer, when life-changing legislation like the minimum wage act, the law authorizing equal pay for men and women, and the law which banished "bastardy", were passed. And how somewhere in the ferment of that time what Professor Rex Nettleford is fond of referring to as the "Smaddytization" of the average poor black Jamaican came about.

As Howard points out, the questions surrounding race and class in Jamaica are extremely complex. For while there are people willing to bleach their skins and swallow "fowl pills", it has always been my experience that many black Jamaicans possess a level of pride in their skin colour and appearance that has survived capture, enslavement and colonialism with a remarkable degree of self confidence and wholeness. I consider myself lucky to have come under the influence of a number of these people as a child growing up in Kingston, where I was encouraged to see myself as inferior to no one, for, as I once heard one facety Kingstonian say to another who had insulted him, "Yu see mi poor, black, short, bruk and ugly ya? Me is an important smaddy!"

Buried deep in this book is a cautious note of optimism that Kingston, that is downtown Kingston, will one day take on new life There are several references in this book to driving through deserted and dangerous downtown streets at night, which bring to mind two of my most recent experiences. A year ago my husband Ted Chamberlin and I were staying with a friend, who was then living in the Ocean Towers in an apartment with a breathtaking 180-degree view of Kingston Harbour. We were running the red lights after midnight on our way back from dinner uptown, when we turned by Harbour Street and came upon a tall blonde woman carrying what looked like a large cauldron. It was the stuff of mythology. Who was she? Annie Palmer the white witch of Rose Hall on a visit to Kingston? Or a duppy accustomed to dining at the Myrtle Bank who had not heard that the fabulous hotel was no more? When we drove up close, what we saw was a live woman tenderly feeding the stray dogs of Kingston from a large pot.

And if you could have been there in 2003 when Marcus Garvey's newly restored Liberty Hall was reopened on King Street, largely through the efforts of a committee led by cultural activist, Elaine Melbourne. You should have been there to see the little children from the streets and lanes all dressed up in their Sunday clothes—for some things never really change and Kingstonians have always had a sense of occasion—come to hear about the great Marcus Garvey. Among the guests was the fine architect Patrick Stannigar, who has had his office in the heart of the "ghetto" for years, an office that also functions as an oasis of calm and security and a homework centre for neighbourhood children. May such centres of light and calm multiply and multiply. Last summer, as we drove past the dilapidated buildings on Orange Street, my husband would look over at me and say "Cheer up. The town you love so well is going to live again." From his mouth to God's ear.

Lorna Goodison

Preface and Acknowledgements

I first came to Kingston in 1998, to attend a conference and to take the first steps in gathering census data for a research project, which sought to plot Kingston's progress from colonial city to independent capital. Fiscal concerns and stubborn inquisitiveness kept me out of taxis and on the buses, or on foot, in search of people, places and elusive publications for the study. On many occasions ignorance can be bliss; I happily, but reasonably warily, headed off uptown and down. Kingston has a reputation as a rough town in certain places, at certain times. By the third day, I had walked into an armed argument, avoided a bus hijack by an hour and managed to lose my wallet.

But that was all, my nearest brush with bad times and the dangerous stereotypes that haunt much of Kingston's urban mythology. I had found my forgotten wallet stowed in a safe spot the following day. Like any place, and perhaps more than some, the city has its share of incidents and skulduggery, but none that common sense and sporadic doses of taken-for-granted good fortune will not help to avoid. As in any town, behind the closed front doors of polished mahogany and brass or corrugated tin and cardboard, household wars are waged. On the streets, social inequality or bad governance can intermittently bring simmering tensions to the boil.

One of the things to do in Kingston, however, is to wander. Be safe, but wander. While many of the well-heeled writer-visitors of yesteryear, whose nuggets of wisdom appear in the following pages, strolled colonial streets to the tune of that earlier age, the city today remains a place for walking or catching the bus. Suburban sprawl has covered Liguanea Plain and vast flows of new houses have spread to the west, but neighbourhoods still have their say. Whether it be a new mall in Portmore, a shopping joint uptown or street stalls off the Parade, Kingston's localities make up the city proper—a mix of money, politics, nights out and sounding in to the hustle around. The majority of travellers to Jamaica miss the trip to Kingston. But the tour routes are progressing and heading to town more often, and so too the capital and its varied attractions change.

Many friends have helped to write this book along the way, and slanted me in the right direction. Colleagues in the world of academia have done more than their fair share. Foremost, Colin Clarke must be thanked wholeheartedly. After enduring my efforts as a student, he provided my first full-time wage cheque as a research assistant on the project, which led to the following chapters. His book, *Kingston, Jamaica: Urban Development and Social Change, 1692-1962*, published in 1975, remains the most informative text to be written on the city. While I was being paid to follow up six decades of census data, I began six years of moonlight reading about the capital in the yellowing or freshly printed pages of writers who knew Kingston's places and people. I am very lucky to have been able to combine the two tasks. At the University of the West Indies, both Elizabeth Thomas-Hope and Dave Barker were helpful beyond the call of duty when I first visited the Mona campus. Kathleen Grant and David Dodman have both provided great and welcome buzzes of Kingston while I have been writing away from the city. In Edinburgh, Karina Williamson has been good company and a truly encyclopedic source of Jamaican letters. It is hoped that the numerous libraries which house these manuscripts and books in Jamaica, the United Kingdom, France and the United States will receive adequate state funding to maintain their literary treasures.

I first met this book's editor, James Ferguson, in Oxford with the late David Nicholls. Both have dramatically shaped what I do today. The latter's commitment, energy and insight on Caribbean matters helped to fuel my own interests, while the former has sustained and tolerated a textual gestation period with a continent's worth of patience. After encountering Kingston, I met Abi who has lived with the city and the scribing of this book for the course of our time together. Deep thanks and love indeed are due for her illuminating enthusiasm and endless support.

Publisher's Acknowledgements

The publisher would like to thank the following for permission to reproduce extracts from:

Salkey, Andrew *Jamaica*, 1973 (by kind permission of Mrs Patricia Salkey)

Zephaniah, Benjamin, *City Psalms*, 1992 (courtesy of Bloodaxe Books)

Craig, Christine, *Mint Tea and Other Stories*, 1992 (courtesy of Harcourt Education)

Goodison, Lorna, *Guinea Women: New and Selected Poems*, 2000 (courtesy of Carcanet Press)

Gunst, Laurie, *Born Fi Dead*, 1995 (courtesy of Canongate Books)

Kennaway, Guy, *One People*, 1999 (courtesy of Canongate Books)

Leigh Fermor, Patrick *The Traveller's Tree: A Journey Through the Caribbean Islands*, 1984 (Reproduced by permission of John Murray Publishers)

Spence, Vanessa, *The Roads Are Down*, 1993 (Reproduced by permission of Greene and Heaton Ltd. Copyright © Vanessa Spence, 1993)

Glass R, *Clichés of Urban Doom*, 1989 (courtesy of Blackwell Publishing)

Coward, Noël, *Collected Verse*, 1984 (courtesy of Methuen Publishing Ltd. Copyright © The Estate of Noël Coward)

Chris Salewicz, *Rude Boy: Once Upon a Time in Jamaica*, 2000 (courtesy of the Orion Publishing Group)

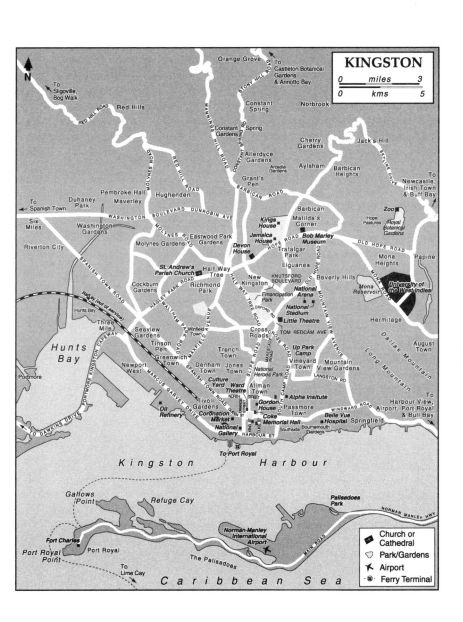

KINGSTON

	miles	
0		3
0	kms	5

To Castleton Botanical
Gardens
& Annotto Bay

Orange Grove

STONY HILL RD

Constant
Spring

Norbrook

To Sligoville,
Bog Walk

N

Red Hills

RED HILL ROAD

RED HILL ROAD

MANNING HILL ROAD

Constant
Gardens

CONSTANT SPRING RD

Allerdyce
Gardens

Cherry
Gardens

Jack's Hill

SKYLINE DRIVE

Arcadia
Gardens

Aylsham

Barbican
Heights

To
Newcastle,
Irish Town
& Buff Bay

Grant's
Pen

BARBICAN ROAD

Pembroke Hall
Maverley

Duhaney
Park

Hughenden

Barbican

To
Spanish Town

WASHINGTON   BOULEVARD   DUNROBIN AVE

Matilda's
Corner

Zoo

Hope
Pastures

Royal
Botanical
Gardens

Papine

Six
Miles

Washington
Gardens

MOLYNES ROAD

Eastwood Park
Gardens

Kings
House

HOPE ROAD

Bob Marley
Museum

OLD HOPE ROAD

Riverton City

Molynes Gardens

Jamaica
House

Devon
House

Trafalgar
Park

Mona
Heights

SPANISH TOWN ROAD

Hunts Bay

St. Andrew's
Parish Church

Half Way
Tree

Liguanea

Beverly Hills

Three
Mile

HAGLEY PARK ROAD

Cockburn
Gardens

WALTHAM PARK ROAD

Richmond
Park

HALF WAY TREE ROAD

New
Kingston

KNUTSFORD
BOULEVARD

Mona
Reservoir

University
of the West Indies

Railway (out of service)

MAXFIELD AVENUE

Emancipation
Park

OXFORD RD

National
Arena

MONA ROAD

Hermitage

Seaview
Gardens

Winfield
Town

National
Stadium

MOUNTAIN VIEW AVENUE

Tinson
Pen

SPANISH TOWN ROAD

Little Theatre

Dallas Mountain

August
Town

Greenwich
Town

Trench
Town

Cross
Roads

TOM REDCAM AVE

Up Park
Camp

Mountain
Gardens

Long Mountain

Newport
West

MARCUS GARVEY DRIVE

Denham
Town

Jones
Town

SLIPE ROAD

Vineyard
Town

Mountain
View Gardens

Podmore

Culture
Yard

National
Heroes Park

CAMP ROAD

LANGSTON RD

To
Harbour View,
Airport, Port Royal
& Bull Bay

PORTMORE KINGSTON CAPEWAY

Ward
Theatre

Allman
Town

Alpha Insitute

NORTH ST

Tivoli
Gardens

Gordon
House

Passmore
Town

Belle
Vue
Hospital

WINDWARD ROAD

Springfield

Oil
Refinery

Coronation
Market

Coke
Memorial Hall

Southside

Bournemouth
Gardens

TO DAWKINS DRIVE

National
Gallery

KING ST

HARBOUR ST

To Port Royal

Kingston   Harbour

Gallows
Point

Refuge Cay

Palisadoes
Park

NORMAN MANLEY HWY

Fort Charles

Port Royal

MAIN ROAD

Port Royal
Point

Norman Manley
International
Airport

Church or
Cathedral

To
Lime Cay

The Palisadoes

Park/Gardens

Airport

Ferry Terminal

Caribbean   Sea

INTRODUCTION

Accidental Capital

"Kingston, a city created to serve a great natural harbour, nestled in a side pocket of a distant plain, where it looked oddly practical beneath the virgin mountains. In the distance the encircling sea stretched like the island's imagination."

Rachel Manley, *Drumblair* (1996)

"But then I realized, very soon, that I had never before been in any place in which history is so overwhelmingly alive as it is in the Caribbean islands."

Ruth Glass, *The Listener* (1 February 1962)

The first steps in Kingston paint your imagination with indelible colours of past and present. Kingston once stood as the Caribbean's English-speaking capital. It stands now as a capital for all that is right in the world, and much that is wrong. Reggae graces the musical landscape with perhaps the clearest trademark that any city can offer. Political and group conflict, edged to extreme during the 1970s, etched a reputation of violence upon downtown Kingston that lingered beyond the first blows of political conflict to the follow-through of turf wars and the dubious culture of personal patronage.

Kingston lies on the southern, leeward coast of Jamaica, sheltered from the trade winds by the looming Blue Mountains, while wrapped in a crescent running from the Red Hills to Dallas Mountain. Today, the majority of Kingstonians live on the Liguanea Plain, which slopes down from the mountains to the natural harbour and delta of the Hope River. Kingston's upstart western neighbour, Portmore, began as a commuter suburb during the 1970s and now claims its right as a satellite city. This fledging urban development, for all its concrete brashness, is rapidly becoming the pulse of Jamaican urban culture, where the past and in-your-face presence of today combine to reveal a city of contradictions. Stately colonial mansions in uptown New Kingston back onto contemporary shacks of cardboard and scrap, while downtown has developed into a "no-go" zone for many of the suburban middle classes. The radical political waves of the seventies, which carved up social and physical spaces, have receded to reinforce the lasting poverty of the present.

This book sets out to discover Kingston, a city entwined by colonial legacy, contemporary chaos and a future determined as much by external as by internal plans and powers. The following pages will unveil Kingston's historical roots and the lively hubbub of today, as highlighted by writers, residents and reggae stars. The chapters journey northwards, beginning with the relics of piracy at Port Royal and the crumbling jetties of Kingston harbour up to the surrounding mountains and across to the former rival Spanish Town.

First Impressions: A Beautiful or Beastly City?

"One is particularly struck also by the ugliness of the buildings."
Anthony Trollope, *The West Indies and the Spanish Main* (1859)

Bleached by sun, dusted by breeze, Kingston presents the visitor with an array of challenging, sometimes harsh, scenes. Commentators have long wrestled with the contrasting elements of the city's aesthetics. In the mid-nineteenth century the celebrated and often pompous English writer, Anthony Trollope (1815-82), guardedly admired the city's merits, "Kingston on a map—for there is even a map of Kingston—looks admirably well. The streets all run in parallels. There is a fine large square, plenty of public buildings, and almost a plethora of places to worship. Everything is named with propriety, and there could be no nicer town anywhere. But this word of promise to the ear is strangely broken when performance is brought to the test."

Twenty years later, the Scottish traveller Charles Rampini (1840-1907) wrote of the pleasures of Kingston in similarly ambiguous terms. His first sight of the city, on arrival by sea, led him to confer that "owing to the unmodulated flatness of the site, Kingston, from the water, presents the appearance of a mere confused mass of sun-baked buildings." His journal *Letters from Jamaica: the Land of*

Streams and Woods (1873), describes the nineteenth-century visitor's opening panorama:

> *These cocoa-nut trees, and these white rocks, these crumpled mountains, and this gently-curving bay, was 'that wondrous isle in the western seas' which we had come five thousand miles to explore. And truly our first view of the island, seen from the deck of the steamer as we steamed slowly past the long coral reef called the Palisades which guards the entrance to the harbour, in degree belied our expectations. Not that Kingston itself, as it stretched along the shore with its dingy wharves and its low-lying dilapidated wooden houses, added much to the beauty of the landscape. But behind and above rose the magnificent range of the Blue Mountains, clothed, up to their very summits, with verdure, their green sides furrowed into many a fissure and gully by the impetuous rains which in spring and autumn sweep down the mountain sides and find their way to the sea in innumerable rivers and torrents.*

At the beginning of the following century, novelist and journalist Herbert de Lisser (1878-1944) penned an influential and detailed account of his country and hometown. His evident national and civic pride still failed, however, to veil the limited attractions of Kingston's built environment compared with its lush surroundings: "The dull grey of the metal strikes a most inharmonious note in a country of vivid greens and blues; and iron as a covering, with a thermometer normally over eighty degrees in the shade, does not give one the impression of being the coolest thing imaginable." Nevertheless, the capital retained a unique urban allure: "This handsome island has not a handsome city; yet, to me at any rate, the city has an eternal fascination. I never weary of it."

Kingston today storms to the mind as a confused cocktail of rum-soaked, tropical sunsets and the more violent images of political and personal street vendettas. Myth abounds and reality lies in the popular imagination. Or, reality lies in a halfway house, perched precariously between the muzak-filled shopping malls and stratified suburbs of uptown Kingston and the rumbling, charred social landscapes of downtown. One hundred years after Trollope's description of the city's "equally ragged, disreputable and bankrupt appearance," Jamaican writer and academic, Orlando Patterson elaborated a vivid picture of Kingston's market and sidewalk scenes in his 1964 novel, *The Children of Sisyphus*:

> *The street is called the Spanish Town Road. Sketches of a long and narrow pandemonium. But colourful. Never forget the colour. Of their faces, of their hands, of their ragged skirts, of their naked, gleaming torsos bleeding with sweats of scalding chocolate, of their buttocks peeping out. Black and brown and hardened, impure touches of white. Churned with the steel-grey of the majestic factory chimneys. Trucks, cars, bicycles, big chi-chi white buses and the wheels of urchins. Avoiding each other only by the satanic power of some unseen hand.*

The handcart sellers still plough their sinuous paths and ply their wares through Kingston's hectic downtown mêlée. Visitors to Kingston, more frequently arriving by air than sea, are immediately struck by the island's busy roads and streets. In the 1940s Patrick Leigh Fermor described his frenetic welcome at Kingston airport:

> *A stupendous and echoing dome of metal swallowed us up, and the roar of aeroplanes landing and taking off was replaced by a babel of English, American, Spanish, Portuguese, French and Dutch as the swarm of travellers from Europe and North and South America and from every point in the Caribbean Sea were slowly churned through the formalities of departure and arrival. Jamaica is in the very heart of the heart of the Central American waters, and every air line seems to cross there.*

Jamaican author Anthony Winkler's experience of his arrival at the same airport forty years later in *Going Home to Teach* (1995), is similarly chaotic:

> *We are immersed in a throng that has just deplaned, and all around us in the cavernous terminal are piles of luggage, boxes, cartons, attended by a milling crowd of passengers. My brother isn't supposed to be in the customs hall, but he has an influential friend. The customs officials, wearing the hardened look of the bored—the trademark expression of West Indian civil servants—are pawing through the open suitcases, filling out*

declaration forms, and levying fines as the mood takes them. Here and there passengers bicker with a customs officer, and sometimes a peal of derisive laughter rings through the room as bystanders react to one of the many raging debates.

An initial impression of Kingston by Zenga Longmore, however, during her look-see voyage from Brixton through the Caribbean in the 1980s was far less full of life: "Kingston town itself seemed unbearably hideous to me that first night. Street after street of dilapidated houses, empty shops and vile refuse. Buildings that had obviously once been grand and gleaming now stood peeling and filthy. In the town centre, no one walked the streets so late at night, which produced a rather terrifying effect. An eerie ghost town where man has not walked for centuries, crumbling away to dust."

Despite the buzz of excitement that greeted his arrival forty years earlier, Leigh Fermor's eloquent prose similarly elicits a more downbeat view of the Jamaican capital when compared with the island as a whole:

It would be idle to pretend that Kingston is an attractive city. It is bigger and uglier than any other town in the British West Indies. The centre resembles the nastiest of London outskirts, and the outskirts are equal to the most dreary of West Indian slums. It was a relief to discover, after a few days, that it is quite unrepresentative of the rest of this beautiful island. The evil streets, the red brick Victorian Gothic, the Chinese general stores, the goitrous and stunted statues, the rusty field guns and howitzers of the First World War placed as memorials in meanly conceived squares, the profusion of chapels dedicated to depressing sect –all these dismal adjuncts told us nothing of the country that we were to encounter outside its walls. But even Kingston had its compensations.

One of these was the obsolete splendour of breakfast, a sparkling still-life that could have only fallen from the volutes of a tropical cornucopia: paw-paw, sour-sop, mango, pineapple, and ice-cold mandarines peeled and impaled on forks were the merest forerunners of a multiplicity of eggs, kedgeree, sausages, bacon, fried banana, a cold wing of fowl, hot rolls, a week's butter ration, and marmalade. It was a breakfast fit for a tropical potentate or a Regency prize-fighter.

First Tastes

This book is not about food, but to taste the intricacies of life in Kingston, it may be as well to begin at the breakfast table. Like Leigh Fermor, many writers have contrasted the opulence of a luxury Jamaican breakfast with the desolate urban poverty beyond the gates of the hotel or uptown mansion. Food critic Poppy Cannon leapt with relish at her five-star start to the day in the 1950s:

> *First, fresh tangerine juice and slices of pawpaw sprinkled with lime. Next, bowls of cornmeal porridge, thickened with condensed milk and topped with grated nutmeg. After this, plates of fried eggs and ham home-cured over pimento-wood fires, cold roast pork garnished with country peppers and thyme, and fried plantain. Finally, slices of hard dough bread and guava jelly, pots of coffee grown, dried and ground at the property, and mugs of milk, still warm from the cow, spiced with nutmeg and white rum.*

Many examples like the above can be found to counter Ian Fleming's (1908-1964) slightly downbeat jibe at island cuisine: "Food is delicious and limitless, but the cooking uninspired and 'English' unless you fight against it." The author of the James Bond spy thrillers certainly feasted on the culinary and cultural highlife at his home on the North coast, and good food abounds for those who can afford it. Even the more simple tastes may inspire. During times of slavery, sugar brought much wealth to a few and misery to the many on the sugar plantations. Today, the island produces over 2 million tons of sugar per year and the related industries employ around 15,000 people. Sugar still leaves a poignant aftertaste from its former role as the island's "king" commodity, not least on the taste buds: "How many visitors have ever tasted the big, soft, glittering, molasses-scented, almost chocolate-brown richness and lingering sweetness upon the tongue, of [even] the cheapest grade of Jamaican sugar?" wrote Poppy Cannon, en route perhaps to a second pot of breakfast coffee.

Jamaican coffee, although produced in small quantities compared with other states, holds it own in the world's cafés. Governor Sir Nicholas Lawes planted the first island coffee beans in 1728. Less than a century later, six hundred plantations, fuelled by enslaved labour and high commodity prices, produced coffee for export. Today, coffee is produced largely by smallholders, whose beans are marshalled and marketed by the state Coffee Industry Board. Jamaican Blue Mountain, harvested above 1,800 feet in the namesake ranges east of Kingston commands high prices and praise.

Few visitors, perhaps, will shirk a cup of fine coffee, but many have wondered at the three bright yellow bulbs and swollen jet black seeds of the ackee, which guards its poison before the pod bursts open, like a safety valve, and renders the fruit edible. After surgical removal of a red membrane, a process of heating and reheating delivers a scrambled egg lookalike ready to eat. Saltfish and johnny cakes—crisply fried dumplings of wheat flour or cornmeal—accompany the breakfast treat. This may explain why "Salt fish and ackees are a cult amongst many Jamaicans—a taste which not too many tourists develop." For those who find poisonous vegetable excision at dawn too hard to handle, Walkerswood proudly present their tinned Jamaican ackee.

Given the challenging range of local produce, from cho-cho to callaloo; pepperpot, gungo pea, and mackerel run-dung (a coconut and vegetable stewed fish) to curried goat and mannish water (a souped-up version of the animal's head, feet and entrails), culinary travellers may wish to seek catering advice, in personal or published form. The roadside jerk chefs stoke pimento wood barbecues, or more often charcoal-filled drums, while spicing up meat and fowl. Every corner shop will have a glass display cabinet of beef, shrimp or chicken patties, to be revived with a dose of "Picka-peppa" sauce.

The family cookbook of John Pringle, one-time head of the Jamaican Tourist Board, found its way into the published scribblings of the highly impressed food writer, Poppy Cannon. The pages soon turned to the speciality of turtle. One can imagine that today's tourist chief would be less willing to reveal a zeal for an endangered species. The prize recipe begins: "A good family soup is to be made by stewing down the day before you make your soup two parts of turtle stewmeat or a little less." The fat and gristle is then cut off, and cloves, cinnamon and spices added. A day passes, then more turtle meat, with salt pork or beef, are added and fused by boiling and boiling again with onions, herbs and tomatoes. After Worcestershire sauce, lime, salt, cayenne and an additional bucket of spices (as available) are added, the concoction is ready for further disfigurement: "Pour this over the fat and gristle diced in the tureen and serve, adding just before serving, a wineglass full of sherry." The emasculated turtle should now be totally unrecognizable and you may pass off the traumatic brew to your unsuspecting guests as a favourite and charmingly benign home-made broth.

The friendly food critic, wishing to further the readership's admiration for the Pringle prowess at turtle consumption, helpfully informs that the family has a head start in this specific culinary course, since "their ears are tuned from babyhood to hear the particular blast blown on the conch shell to announce to the hungering countryside that turtle has been beached." Somewhat overawed by the seemingly magical skills of this gastronomic dynasty par excellence, Cannon contents herself with the more practical social skills of "how one should go about sucking the fruit of the egg [turtle, of course] out of the shell with some measure of efficiency and gentility."

Turtle may be less common fare these days, but its consumption is clearly part of the island's culinary history, and not a topic for exoticizing as part of another Caribbean odyssey. Michelle Cliff's poem, "Make it Your Own" (1985), rails against the essentializing of her island roots, particularly by inquisitive others:

> "And your food is so interesting.
> I didn't know people ate goats. Or turtle either.
> What does turtle taste like?"

Healthy bones will always be helped by pickled fish, known as escabeche or escoveitched fish, which is fired in a sauce of hot red peppers, spices and vinegar and fully accompanied by dasheen, plantain, tannia, sweet potato, scotch bonnet peppers and okra. Few will, or should, last long in Kingston before being fed yam, rice and peas, and of course bammy or fried cassava bread.

On the fruit front, as expected, the tropics prove to be fine hosts. The custard apple provides, with gratifying little diversion from its job title, a custardy pulp in a thin skin marked with flat honeycomb clusters. The rose apple, favouring a thicker skin, places its weight behind a rich aroma. Bananas, oranges, green coconuts, mangoes and pineapples roll off street fruit stalls, while Busha Browne's guava jelly prefers the stability of a shop shelf.

A century earlier, mangoes were the fruit of choice for a visiting gastronome. And academic James Anthony Froude (1818-1894), during an otherwise largely derogatory account of late nineteenth-century Jamaican society, waxed lyrical about the delightful, celebrated 'Number Elevens' for sale in Kingston:

> *[T]he famous Number Eleven of which I had heard such high report, and was now to taste... it is too delicate to bear carriage. It must be eaten in the tropics or nowhere. The mango is the size and shape of a swan's egg, of a ruddy yellow colour when ripe, and in flavour like an exceptionally good apricot, with a very slight intimation of resin. The stone is disproportionately large. The flesh adheres to it, and one abandons as hopeless the attempt to eat mangoes with clean lips and fingers. The epicures insist that they should be eaten only in a bath.*

While natural delights abound, technology has not failed to advance culinary frontiers during the twentieth century. Amid the high street run of rapidly fried and fast forgotten chicken chains, technical simplicity bites home with the popularity of "bun and cheese"—a flawless combination of processed cheese and white spiced bun.

Drinking Denizens

Ian Fleming continued his gastronomic advice with some alcohol-related thoughts, though without a shaken martini in sight. In Jamaica, there is "plenty of heavy drinking, particularly on Friday and Saturday nights, after pay-day, and there is some smoking of Indian hemp, or marihuana or ganja as it is called locally... (If you are caught at this, or at cockfighting, you will get severely punished.)" For those who manage to refrain from the latter two sins, liquids provide quite enough scope for exploration. The well-connected or well-to-do may arrive at one of the city's social clubs, although late nights cannot always be expected if experiences related in Alec Waugh's *Island in the Sun* (1956) are to be believed: "Rum-swizzles and whisky-sodas had only been served for an hour; West Indians need two hours of sundowners before they are ready for the dinner which will be succeeded by a direct and immediate retiring for sleep."

This twentieth-century tale varies markedly from James Stewart's *View of Jamaica*, written in 1823, which relates the decadence of upper-class soirées: "On these occasions no expense is spared to render the entertainment costly and splendid; every luxury is catered up for that purpose, and copious libations of various wines and other liquors are poured forth to the jolly good of fellowship. On these occasions, it is rather to be apprehended that there is a greater risk of the sacrifice of health than a certainty of enjoyment of rational pleasure. Excess is commonly the order of the day, and that may be of serious consequence to those indulging in it in such a climate as that of Jamaica."

Over one and a half centuries later, on the cusp of the Western world's swinging sixties, Fernando Henriques looked back censoriously, half in admonition and half in awe, at the ribald lives of the male planter class: "Sex, food, drink, and dancing are the themes which are interwoven to form the backbone of the planter's life. Many died early as a result of a surfeit of all four. The practice of drinking heavy wines in vast quantities in the tropics must have hastened the end of many an aristocratic young sprig."

These exploits, of course, were fed by slavery, derived from the profits of the sugar plantation and the concurrent physical and sexual exploitation of the slaves. Edward Long (1735-1813), in his classically detailed and thoroughly racist account of eighteenth-century Jamaica, recounts the indentured and enslaved labourers' nutritional experiences on the estates: "Maize, palm oil, and a little stinking fish, make up the general bill of fare of the prince and the slave; except that they regale themselves, as often as they can, with *aqua vitae*, and palm wine."

Having jettisoned slavery, the happier legacy of Planter's Punch remains. The much touted brew may be concocted by following a deceptively simple rhyme, mixing lime juice, sugar, dark rum and crushed ice in quantities as the drink-maker feels fit, or as the day has been long:

One of sour
Two of sweet
Three of strong
Four of weak.

A suitably sharp dash of angostura bitters and a quick shake should conclude the cocktail's preparation. Experts, or those with little else to do, will wish to explore the garnishing possibilities of the maraschino cherry. Other may wish to fill their tall glasses with less fanfare. Many Jamaicans prefer a straight white rum to the cumbersome preparation of a fancy cocktail.

At the end of the nineteenth century, most sugar estates operated their own mills and distilleries. Today, fewer than half a dozen distilleries fill the country's barrels of "kill-devil". Of those who have led national rum production, one name stands out. In 1825 John Wray opened an inn next to the popular Theatre Royal at the north-east corner of the North Parade in Kingston. Catering for thespians and a thirsty public, several of whom may have sought respite from the pulpit's boom in the parish church opposite, Wray aptly called his new venture the Shakespeare Tavern. As tankards clinked and liquor was downed, his business interests flowed more deeply into the lucrative area of distilling. Two years before his death in 1862, he brought family into the business and so J. Wray and Nephew was born.

The new partner, Charles James Ward, channelled his dynamism not only into establishing a formidable rum-producing operation, but also to civic duties. The company's headquarters soon moved to 24 Port Royal Street, but in later years it was the now Colonel Ward's financial muscle that rebuilt the earthquake-shattered Theatre Royal on the Parade. The company's original Appleton Special is known throughout the region, as is Wray and Nephew's lively over-proof rum. For those not wishing to be spirited away, Desnoes and Geddes' Red Stripe lager provides a locally produced and globally drunk brand. Alternatively, for the abstemious, a tin of Irish Moss seaweed drink will make alcoholic abstinence memorable.

Travelling Light
Fighting dehydration is a noble and necessary pursuit, given the daily heat on the streets. Visitors to Kingston can reasonably prepare for a range of weather, from humid, hot, to very hot. The heat, according to Edward Long, the eighteenth-century chronicler, could have quite unexpected redeeming features: "Aged persons on coming hither find themselves renewed as it were in youth; their exhausted vessels full again; the wrinkles become less conspicuous; and the emaciated form of their bodies is changed to plumpness." Championing the open-air sauna, he dubiously enthused, "a free and constant perspiration, and the dilatation of all the bodily tubes enabling the circulation to be carried on with ease and regularity, are effects naturally produced by the temperature of this atmosphere."

To escape the heat, Long advised his wealthy compatriots in the 1770s that, "About the dawn of day the air is the most agreeable: this is the time for pleasurable exercise, and it is generally taken, here either in wheel-carriages or on horse-back." Modern travellers without horse or carriage may need to settle for car air-conditioning when the temperatures soar. Failing such assistance, the contemporary tourist may then wish to turn to Long's tried and tested remedy to remain in health:

> *A merchant who was here at the time, assured me, that having dined with an intimate acquaintance one day, and left him in the evening in seeming perfect health, he was summoned the very next day to attend his friend's funeral. He accordingly went, with five others, as a bearer; and in a few day's time he was left the only survivor of the whole company, the other five having caught infection from the corpse, as they accompanied it to the burial-place. He imputed his escape to the precaution he took of chewing tobacco, and carrying some in his hand, which he frequently applied to his nose.*

While sun and heat are constant factors in Kingston's climatic equation, the more threatening possibilities of tropical storms are apparent, particularly during the hurricane season, which lasts from September through to November. Andrew Salkey (1928-1995) conjures up vivid images in his poem commemorating the famous hurricane of 1951, which devastated much of Kingston:

> *I remember the night,*
> *black with slack rain,*
> *flaccid when it first began*
> *but with brick drops beating later on*
> *like jump-Poco drumthumps,*
> *beating back the coming morning,*
> *beating with purpose,*
> *routine, rhythm and ritual,*
> *beating like the bounce of batter hide,*
> *hide battered on a shoemaker's block,*
> *batter hide, hide battered,*

pane shatter, shattered pane,
batter hide, pane shatter through to dawn.

Given the potentially diverse weather conditions, packing light might not be the best option. Anthony Trollope assures us of the minimum travel requirements for a mid-nineteenth-century English gentleman. He wrote, "I found four horses to be necessary, one for the groom, one for my clothes, and two for myself. A lighter weight may have done with three." The more sceptical, but equally well-heeled, diarist Charles Rampini advised on only slightly less opulent baggage: "… if we had acted on all the other recommendations we received, we should have carried with us, in addition to the host of unnecessary rubbish which we did take, such useful articles as a photographic camera, a mountain-barometer, a Norwegian kitchen, wading-boots, a bull's eye lantern, a large ham, a complete set of ice-buckets, a boot-jack, and a fishing rod." Even the best-equipped and intrepid traveller may fall prey to the smallest, most predictable hazards. As Trollope is quick to point out, "Your Kingston musquito is the craftiest of insects, and the most deadly."

Despite these grumbles, the city retains a certain affection in the heart of most visiting writers and residents. Trollope concluded that he "never met wider and kinder hospitality than I did in Jamaica," while Patrick Leigh Fermor reflects soberly on the city in the middle of the last century: "Kingston is not altogether to blame for its unpleasant appearance. It was intended to be neither the principal port nor the capital of the island. History, the exigencies of trade and the violence of nature have turned it into both." It is to these roots that we now turn briefly.

Introducing Kingston's History
Kingston, indeed, was never meant to be the capital city of Jamaica. Subsequent chapters will outline the rivalries associated with the former capitals of Port Royal and Spanish Town. The former was bedevilled by pirated wealth and natural misfortune; the latter left to quarrelsome rifts between councillors and countrymen. Ruth Glass in her collected essays of the late 1980s, *Clichés of Urban Doom*, outlines the tortuous trail of Kingston's colonial struggles brought to the

present: "There is not a single feature of that society that is not stamped in the past." While the streets echo with the steps of previous citizens, free persons and slaves, it is the robust cultural and social strides of today which "lively up" Kingston's modern urban mosaic.

Reliance on the written word precludes much contemporary knowledge of Kingston's pre-Columbian and pre-literate indigenous cultures—a society generated by immigration and consumed by subsequent emigration. The first settlers in Kingston, as far as we know, arrived 13,000 years ago via the American mainland and the archipelago of islands that now form the Lesser Antilles. They established a community in a cove on the southern coast of the island. It was their pathways that first criss-crossed Liguanea Plain and the shelving shores of the bay. Several hundred years later, the same bays were to house Spanish, and subsequently British, outposts seeking to impose European rule in the name of mercantile and evangelical advance.

The Arawaks, originating in South America, had established themselves by 500 BC and were the true residents of the islands when Columbus's fleet arrived in 1494. Many modern accounts of indigenous life idealize a bucolic, peaceful existence. Patrick Leigh Fermor exemplifies these romantic views:

Their life was one of blessed indolence. Dancing and singing, to the accompaniment of a drum and small timbrel, and a game called bato, played with an elastic ball, were their passions. One can easily picture them lying in hammocks strung between these shady trees, talking to their tame parrots and smoking through branching calumets, or wandering into the woods with their bows and arrows... Their dwellings were beehives of timber and wild cane clustering among the trees. The floor was strewn with palm leaves. Sometimes the houses were surrounded by a little garden, and the hut of their cacique would slightly overtop those of his neighbours. They never quarrelled amongst themselves, and the Spaniards, when they arrived, found them pathetically docile. Their life in these dreamy hills and savannahs must have been akin to that our first ancestors in the Garden of Eden, a prelapsarian existence evolving without land-mark or history until the steel-clad Christians, with their armoured horses and fire-breathing culverins… suddenly irrupted into this private paradise.

This bubble of presumed innocence burst by accident in 1494. Columbus, on his second voyage in search of the Indies, was blown off course while charting the southern coast of Cuba. His helmsman sighted Jamaica, but with other matters on his mind, he returned to Cuba without landing. Only later that year did the Spaniards explore the island, and scribble down their first impressions. Andrés Bernaldez, a companion of Columbus, wrote:

And the island Jamaica is the most lovely that eyes have seen… It is a very mighty land, and beyond measure populous, so that even on the seashore as well as inland, every part is filled with villages and those are very large and very near one another, at four leagues distance.

Initial hostilities were subdued by gifts of bread, fish and fruits to the island's residents, although subsequently sixty thousand were to fall to the Spanish sword and diseases over the next hundred years. Bernaldez recounts that expressions of dissent were clearly not negotiable, unlike the limited amount of gold which Columbus and his entourage extracted from the island:

The Admiral saw that it was not reasonable to allow them to be so daring without chastisement, in order that on other occasions they might not be so bold… that they might become acquainted with the arms of Castile, they approached close to them in the boats and fired at them with crossbows and thus pricked them well, so that they became frightened. They landed continuing to shoot at them, and as the Indians saw that the Castilians were speaking with them, they all took to flight, men and women, so that not one was to be found in all that neighbourhood. And a dog which they let loose from a ship chased and bit them, and did them great damage, for a dog is the equal of ten men against the Indians.

Edward Long, writing three hundred years later at the height of the slave trade, lamented the barbarity of the Spanish colonizers and heralded the indigenous resistance, which African enslaved populations would later continue against the British rulers:

> [*W*]*hen the Spaniards had resolved upon the extirpation of the Indians, they made use of dogs of a peculiar breed, large, bold, and very fleet. The poor Indians having for some time been obliged to take refuge in their woods, these animals were constantly employed to hunt them out. The Spaniards by this means caught a great number of them; and were content at first to kill several, quartering their bodies, and fixing their limbs on the most conspicuous spots in terrorem, that the rest might take warning by their fate, and submit at discretion. But this horrid cruelty, instead of intimidating or reducing to friendly terms, only served to embitter them more against their savage invaders, and affected them with so inveterate an abhorrence of the Spaniards, that they determined to fly their fight for ever, and rather perish by famine or their own hands, than fall into the power of so merciless an enemy.*

And so began the Spanish conquest. African slaves were initially imported in 1509 by Juan de Esquivel, the first governor of Jamaica, to replace the indigenous workers. He created his seat of government at Santo Jago de la Vega, later to be known as Spanish Town, following its ransacking by Cromwell's expeditionary force in 1655.

Edward Long gave due recognition to the Spanish colonial style: "The Spanish ecclesiastics (however blameable in other respects) must be allowed some merit in having cultivated the elegances of architecture in these remote parts of the world." Of Spanish Town, he writes, taking a side swipe at the contemporary British built environment: "… it is better laid out than most of those in England. That a West-India town should be irregularly planned is, indeed, almost inexcusable, not only on account of health, which ought to be principally regarded, but because it is formed as it were at once." Indeed, on the British conquest of the city and colony he outlines the destruction of such "magnitude and opulence", which boasted "two thousand houses, sixteen churches and chapels, and one abbey… English soldiers exercised their powers against these edifices with so furious a zeal, as to leave only two churches and about five hundred houses undemolished."

Henry Whistler in his *Journal of the West Indian Expedition, 1654-1655*, enthused more fully over the island's wealth of flora and fauna: "The Island as it is naturally the best in all the Indies: it hath a great deal of level ground, and many brave savannas full of cattle, and abundance of brave horses, but they are all wild: and many hogs: and wild fowl an abundance: a many parrots: and monkeys: and plenty of fish: here are the abundance of alligators and many large snakes."

English Conquest

Despite the enthusiasm of the chroniclers, the conquest of Jamaica was more the afterthought of a failed attack on the main Spanish colony of Santo Domingo than a masterstroke of empire building in the Caribbean. The disgraced expedition leaders General Robert Venables and Admiral William Penn were thrown into Tower of London on their return for their failure to conquer the then major prize. General Venables, in particular, was hounded for military incompetence. During the failed attempted to take Santo Domingo, his troops were ambushed after landing in the wrong place and being forced to marched twelve miles in heat with no water. On encountering the Spanish forces, he promptly hid in a tree. Henry Whistler recounts this day, 17 January 1655, in his journal:

> *General Venables being one of the foremost, and seeing the enemy fall on so desperately with their lances, he very nobly did run behind a tree; and our sea regiment having this day the forlorn hope did fall on most gallantly, and put the enemy to fly for their lives, and coming from where General Venables was got behind a tree he came forth to them. But he was very much ashamed, but made many excuses: being so much possessed with terror that he could hardly speak...*

At the time, Oliver Cromwell, Protector of England, remarked in Parliament, without due ceremony: "Our fleet have possessed themselves of a certain island called Jamaica, spacious in its extent, commodious in its harbours and rivers within itself, healthful by its situation, fertile in the nature of the soil, well stored with horses, and other cattle, and generally fit to be planted and improved, to the advantage, honour, and interest, of this nation." This particular isle was to become the most profitable colony in Britain's empire throughout the following century, exporting sugar, tobacco and cocoa to an expectant and insatiable European market. But at the outset, the lustre of this territorial jewel was far from clear, not only in the eyes of Cromwell, but also in the opinion of an anonymous roundhead soldier, whose letter from Jamaica, dated 5 November 1655, remains as a testament:

> *Never did my eyes see such a sickly time, nor so many funerals, and graves all the town over that it is a very Golgotha. We have a savannah or plain near us where some of the soldiery are buried so shallow that the Spanish dogs, which lurk about the town, scrape them up and eat them. As for English dogs, they are most eaten by our soldiery; not one walks the streets that it is shot at, unless well befriended or respected.*

British forces had based themselves initially not at the present site of Kingston, but at the former inland Spanish stronghold. This capital thus came to be known as Spanish Town under British rule, and remained so until the 1870s, when the eager citizenry of its burgeoning coastal rival took over governance. Seafaring activities centred on the natural harbour at the estuary of the Hope River, which was shielded by the sinewy arch of the Palisadoes. Port Royal, located at the tip of this curving sand bar, emerged during the seventeenth century as the Empire's regional hub, and as the privateering capital of the Caribbean. The latter role had been nurtured by British colonial tolerance and greed, but was ultimately laid to waste by nature's, some said divine, wrath.

The destruction of the port by an almighty earthquake and tidal wave allowed Providence to lay the foundations for what was called King's Town: "After the repeated desolations by earthquake and fire, which drove the inhabitants from Port Royal, this town was founded in the year 1693, on the North side of the harbour, which, next to Port Royal, appeared the most convenient port for trade." Kingston's early history was precarious at first. Edward Long records that "the uncertainty of property in a town liable to such mutations at the arbitrary will of the governor, reduced its inhabitants to the utmost distress: some quitted it; and many persons were deterred from purchasing land, or occupying houses in it; while all those, who subsisted in its neighbourhood by supplying the market were agitated with the dread of inevitable ruin."

Shattering Times
Kingston has weathered more that its fair share of disasters. The destruction of Port Royal set the pace at the end of the seventeenth century. Hurricane season annually threatens the humid tranquillity of late summer months. Half a dozen or more have hit the city with full effect each century. The most severe in recent times was Hurricane Gilbert in 1988, which caused wide-scale destruction and misery. Four particularly bad storms, however, lashed the city in the 1780s, giving residents hardly time to recover or rebuild in the intervening years. The first hurricane in 1780 devastated the town of Savanna-la-Mar and much of the south-west of the island. Popular folklore placed the blame for this earthly fury on the curse of Plato, a famous Obeah man, or spiritual go-between, who was helped into a drunken stupor, then arrested and sentenced to death shortly before the storm. In advance of

his final hour, he issued a curse for malevolent spirits to spite the island and its population.

Three violent earthquakes in the 1700s followed the path previously set by events at Port Royal; one shook Kingston's foundations in 1812, but by far the worst in modern times was that of 1907. The devastation and legacy were comparable in part to the spectacular levelling of the former port. The city's sins were perhaps not as notorious as that of its piratical predecessor, but the main difference was that the catastrophe ushered in the dynamism of urban renewal, rather than whitewash and removal. The seismic destruction and post-shock fires, however, were exhaustive. Stumbling through the city soon after the event, Sir Frederick Treves described a sombre city in ruins:

> *Almost as strange as the silence was the greyness of the scene, the absence of all colour, the sense of a desert of pale stone. With it too was the unwonted light, for as all the roofs and upper stories had vanished, and as many of the houses were left no higher than a garden wall, the city seemed bared to the heavens, bared to its very bones and whitened ribs.*
>
> *There hung above the town at the time a mist of dust, horrible to breathe, and with it drifted, now and then, a loathsome smell which was not merely that of smouldering débris.*

The violent tremors that rippled and ripped apart the city's floor lasted no more than twenty seconds. Within twenty minutes, scattered firebursts had erupted in all parts of the central city. The 46,000 residents received no portent of the coming hell, save the ominous hissing crescendo of a terrific gust of wind. Treves reproduced a survivor's account for his journal: "Those who speak of it compare it feebly to the rumble of a crowd of waggons tearing on at a gallop, to the rush of uncountable horsemen, to the hollow roaring of a train in a tunnel, to the bursting of a great river."

Four days of fires scarred the central city beyond recognition and emotionally severed the populace. Andrew Salkey's novel *Earthquake* (1965) devises a tale around Gran' Pa's eyewitness account from Princess Street on that terrible day. Retelling the events to his grandchildren, he remembers with some pain the transformation of the breeze which clattered the shutters and slammed doors into a violent gust. This then fell to an unnerving stillness, but was followed immediately by groaning which "sounded like a giant engine, buried in the ground, revving up to get loose and trying to break through and blast its way to the surface... Our house shook violently and the movements continued, mixing and overlapping, jarring, bumping, swelling, rumbling, rushing and rocking. They came all together, and it was hard to believe that so many different movements were just one solid movement coming out of the bowels of the earth."

Following the violent ground spasms, those able to do so made their way to the open space of the old racecourse, now known as Heroes' Circle. Crushed bodies lay beneath mangled zinc sheets and shattered stone, as fires began to consume straining girders and collapsed beams. The devastation left over 800 people dead and thousands homeless. Subsequent natural events, such as Hurricane Charlie in 1955, have caused similar alarms, but less damage. Building codes post-1907 had ensured, in part, a more resistant Kingston.

Colonial City

Just as the destruction of Port Royal gave the go-ahead for the original King's Town to be built, so another disaster had brought in a new era. The 1907 earthquake transformed the city. New buildings were erected and damaged edifices repaired. The landmark tower of the Parade's parish church was almost cleaved in two, but still pointed heavenward above the charred rubble. The latter half of the twentieth century heralded the all-out development of Liguanea Plain, spurred on by the motor car. The business and government hubs moved north away from the sea. Wooden jetties and docks were removed during the 1970s. Eyeing the rum shops, ruins and old bricks of merchant houses, many of which came from the earliest ships' off-loaded ballast, Mona Macmillan looked into the future from her 1950s viewpoint: "No doubt before long these spaces will be filled by streamlined modern buildings; already the waterfront is in process of being morally and physically cleaned up, the streets are swept and smart policeman patrol the lanes as well as controlling the traffic with much style."

From a shaky, earthquake-derived start, Kingston's population had grown in substantial numbers. Within fifty years of its original foundation, the local inhabitants numbered five thousand citizens, five thousand slaves and a further one thousand slaves who had been granted their freedom. Edward Long could begin to extend an early civic pride: "In propriety of design it is, perhaps, not excelled by any town in the world. The plan is a parallelogram, one mile in length by half a mile in breadth, regularly traversed by streets and lanes, alternately crossing each other at tight angles, except in the upper part of town, where a large square is left." The gentle slope of the Liguanea Plain, he continued, prevented "the lodgement of water in the heaviest rains," but here his zeal faltered, since it "is attended with one great inconvenience; for it admits an early passage to vast torrents, which collect in the gullies at some distance towards the mountains after a heavy rain, and sometimes rush with so much impetuosity down the principal streets, as to make them almost impassable by wheel-carriages, and cause a shoal-water at the wharfs, depositing accumulations of rubbish and mud."

During the nineteenth century, when torrents abated, city life for the colonial elite had adopted more a sedate rhythm. Rampini described a typical house belonging to a wealthy Jamaican:

The ordinary arrangement of a Jamaica house is something like this: Entering upon the piazza, which is fitted up with rocking chairs and ottomans, you pass to the drawing room, off which the bedrooms diverge on every side. The dining room is generally on the ground floor, and to reach this you have either to descend by a trap stair or by the same outside staircase by which you gained admission to the drawing-room... In 'old time' houses the only room of anything like decent dimensions is the dining-room—a striking instance of the social habits of the colony in its so-called palmy days.

Within these homes, Rampini found time to celebrate the quality of the local press in the absence of parlour pastimes:

Killing time in the tropics is no easy matter; and how we should have spent this long weary day we know not, had not good luck placed in our way a file of Jamaica newspapers. The general tone of these journals— of which we afterwards learned the colony supported no less than seven—

was one of extreme animosity to each other and to all the world besides, except the favoured class which they called 'our readers.'

Today, the oldest and most popular newspaper, *The Daily Gleaner*, remains as strong and opinionated as ever but the readership has expanded in numbers and type.

Colonial hangovers also endure and form a significant influence in Jamaican society, in which the past is ever-present. William Makin described a fancy dinner at King's House during the 1930s as though it were a scene from the eighteenth century. Women in frilled finery and long white gloves chatted over cocktails with heavily uniformed male officers:

In the cool of the evening the spacious grounds with their close-cropped lawns, lush trees and dark vistas presented the appearance of a lost canvas by Watteau. One was quite prepared for satin-clad shepherdesses to come frisking from those blue-black bushes, with slant-eyed fawns playing on pipes and gazing lustfully at their loves.

Michelle Cliff, one of Jamaica's leading contemporary authors, describes a twentieth-century Jamaican town house in which the variegated décor still reeks of the Old Empire:

Her small house was a cliché of colonialism, graced with calendars advertising the coronation of ERII, the marriage of Princess Margaret Rose, the visit of Alice, Princess Royal. Bamboo and wicker furniture was sparsely scattered across the dark mahogany floors—settee there, table here—giving the place the air of a hotel lobby, the sort of hotel carved from the shell of a great house, before Hilton and Sheraton made landfall. Tortoise-shell lampshades. Ashtrays made from coconut husks. Starched linen runners sporting the embroideries of craftswomen.

Suburbs Come to Town

The concreting of Liguanea Plain happened to full effect during the second half of the last century. Kingston Metropolitan Area swallowed up much of the neighbouring parish of St. Andrew. Half Way Tree, once the mid-point rest stop for troops marching between Spanish

Town barracks and the military station in the mountains at Newcastle, was soon the centre of suburbanization as cars, buses and trams ferried people across the urban sprawl. Mona Macmillan, having commented on the sleaze to be found in the old harbour-side streets, basked in the suburban contrast: "The gardens with their very green lawns and flowering trees make these suburbs of Kingston among the most lovely places in the world." William Makin, who started a doomed newspaper in the 1930s, wrote a lively account of his time in Kingston from a quite different perspective. Despite the journalistic flop, he gained extensively "in experience, new scenes, and some queer human contacts." On the subject of suburbs, he chided:

> *St. Andrew is, in fact, the reality of that place in Alice in Wonderland where it is always afternoon. The suburbanisation of St. Andrew is more terrifically suburban than anything in England... Life begins at four o'clock in the afternoon. Cars begin to meander the lanes, insert their sun-glistening snouts between trim, poinsettia hedges, and deposit those etiquette-minded people who would consider it only right to leave their cards on God as a proper introduction to Heaven.*
>
> *There is a ritual to be observed. There are those who call, and those who are called upon. The latter are either at home, or not at home. If they are in the latter state, there is a distinct relief among the callers. But the collisions occur, and sometimes the callers find people at home. It is then the duty of these people to talk social nonsense for exactly fifteen minutes—no longer, no less. It is not considered good form to offer or accept a drink. A cigarette may be puffed, however. At the end of fifteen minutes there is an apologetic scraping of chairs on the veranda, a life-less handshake, and the polished snout of the car moves off in search of further prey.*

James Bond, Ian Fleming's agent of action, remains, unsurprisingly, not stirred by the residential finery of New Kingston during his hunt for *Dr No* (1958). Here, the elite financiers and government officers lived in "big withdrawn houses", cut-off by moats of velvet lawn, crunchy gravel and the micro-fauna of well manicured gardens, weighted by the "heavy perfume of night-scented jasmine":

Richmond Road is the 'best' road in all Jamaica. It is Jamaica's Park Avenue, its Kensington Palace Gardens, its Avenue d'Iéna. The 'best' people live in its big old-fashioned houses, each in an acre or two of beautiful lawn set, too trimly, with the finest trees and flowers from the Botanical Gardens at Hope. The long, straight road is cool and quiet and withdrawn from the hot, vulgar sprawl of Kingston where its residents earn their money, and, on the other side of the T-intersection at its top, lie the grounds of King's House, where the Governor and Commander-in-Chief of Jamaica lives with his family. In Jamaica, no road could have a finer ending.

Much has changed in recent decades as uptowners live in fear of hungry muggers or resentful ne'er-do-wells, and seldom venture far from the "fortified" territory of home. The Jamaican sunset soirées have diverted to Miami, L.A. or New York. When Bond was about, much of the dusk cocktail traffic would roll only as far as 1 Richmond Road, "a two-storey house with broad white-painted verandas running round both floors… This mansion is the social Mecca of Kingston. It is the Queen's Club, which, for fifty years, has boasted the power and frequency of its blackballs." In unexpectedly radical—but surprisingly optimistic—words, the author added:

Such stubborn retreats will not long survive in modern Jamaica. One day Queen's Club will have its windows smashed and perhaps be burned to the ground, but for the time it is a useful place to find in a sub-tropical island—well run, well staffed and with the finest cuisine and cellar in the Caribbean.

The social arrangements of Kingston's chattering classes have long been underpinned by a ubiquitous supply of underpaid domestic workers. Up to a fifth of the city's working population is employed in some form of domestic service. Men guard gardens, while women and girls wash, bake, scrub and relieve their employers of home chores. Michelle Cliff, continues her tale of the Kingstonian homeowner, Charlotte, and her servant, Columba, in the collection of short stories, *Bodies of Water* (1990):

*There was, of course, someone responsible for cleaning the house, feeding
the animals, filling the carafes and emptying the chamber pots, cooking
the meals and doing the laundry. These tasks fell to Columba, a fourteen
year-old from St. Ann, where Charlotte had bartered him from his
mother; a case of condensed milk, two dozen tins of sardines, five pounds
of flour, several bottles of cooking oil, permission to squat on Charlotte's
cane-piece—fair exchange.*

A century ago, Anthony Trollope held a begrudging respect, of
sorts, for his servants in Jamaica: "They are not absolutely uncivil,
except on occasions; but they have an easy, free, patronising air. If you
find fault with them, they insist on having the last word, and are
generally successful." Arguably, one of the lasting impacts of slavery
and colonialism is resistance, or the ability to subvert inequality to
create bearable living conditions. Despite an earlier glance over the
barricades, Ian Fleming unfortunately fails to apply the history lesson
to his own staffing circumstances: "Servants are plentiful but varied.
They require exhortation and a sense of humour, which the majority
appreciate."

Falling for the Place

Errol Flynn in his autobiography *My Wicked, Wicked Ways* (1976)
revealed how he was forced to take shelter on Jamaica's shores during a
storm, which rooted his desire to return and live on the island: "Never
had I seen a land so beautiful. Everywhere there is a blanket of green so
thick that the earth never shows through." The herbivorous and
hedonistic plenty brought him back to Jamaica as a resident in the
1950s. Similarly enamoured, the playwright and wit Noël Coward also
found such a decadent tropical lifestyle irresistible and settled just west
along the North coast at about the same time. "Jamaica" (1984),
published after his death, sings his light-hearted praise:

*In fact every tourist who visits these shores
Can thank his benevolent Maker
For taking time off from the rest of His chores
To fashion the Isle of Jamaica.*

Coward's close friend, Ian Fleming, first visited the island's North coast in 1946 and eventually built his own house, "Goldeneye", on a barren former donkey racecourse. From there, perched behind a red bullet wood desk, he found the inspiration to pen the first dozen best-selling thrillers: "I wrote every one of them at this desk with the jalousies closed around me so that I would not be distracted by the birds and the flowers and the sunshine outside until I had completed my daily stint."

It is unlikely that Coward and his immediate circle provided copycat examples of the daring precision of 007's tasks. When Ian Fleming married in 1952, Noël Coward and Cole Leslie were witnesses. In the excitement, the famous wit tied the time-honoured old shoe to the bumper of his own car by mistake. Jamaica, however, did provide a great deal of inspiration for Fleming's writing, not least the namesake of his famous protagonist. The "real" James Bond was the author of the much-respected ornithologist's tome, Bond's *Birds of the West Indies* (1936), which was perched on the novelist's bookcase. James Bond, the bird watcher, seemed to give more delicate attention to his subject's plumage than is evidenced in his harsh generalization of local knowledge about natural history: "It is well to bear in mind that a West Indian when asked the name of a bird he does not know is apt to conjure up one that he think suitable." This leads ultimately to the open conclusion that "the number of local names of birds in the West Indies is infinite."

Back in the secretive world of international espionage and skulduggery, *The Man with the Golden Gun* (1965) brings our hero to 77 Harbour Street after following a lead from an auctioneer's announcement in *The Daily Gleaner*. The legalistic colonial jargon of perches and chains of land for sale had enticed him with the "old-fashioned abracadabra" of Jamaica and "the authentic smell of one of the oldest and most romantic of former British possessions". He thus set out across town on his next mission. Even James Bond, however, when negotiating Her Majesty's business under the glare of a pursuing car, can get caught in the crush of Kingston's traffic as he discovers during adventures with *Dr No* (1958): "They came into the stream of Kingston traffic—buses, cars, horsedrawn carts, pannier-laden donkeys down from the hills, and the hand-drawn barrows selling violent coloured drinks." Advice from Mona Macmillan in *The Land of Look Behind* (1957), would have pre-warned the secret agent: "Many people, especially in business, get frustrated by the inertia and confusion of Kingston."

Kingston clearly sends mixed messages. The concrete bulk of the city on first sight does less to excite than even the repetitive blandness of travel book descriptions of turquoise waters and cocktail sunsets. Yet, as Cynthia Wilmot exclaimed after migrating from Canada to live in the city, "here was a pepped-up, super-charged, hot-rod kind of beauty that even the most inspired copy writers could hardly overrate." Mona Macmillan suggests a lightly sexualized lure to the city's attractions: "Kingston does not lay herself out to chase the visitor, she squats like a Jamaican market woman among her wares with a take-it-or-leave-it air." Her wanderings along the quietly sloping streets of Kingston during the 1950s convinced her that "the real beauty of the town lies in the deep blue sea visible at the end of the road as it comes into it, and the mountains closing the vista as one looks away from the sea." Unguided roving on foot brings into view the often ramshackle and sharp edge of the city. Hot, dusty, Corolla-filled streets are a common sight today, but so too, as Macmillan added earlier, is the "the unexpected elegance of wrought iron, the lacy bits of fretwork that decorate the eaves and the balconies of modest little wooden houses—these are wisps of finery on an old lady who has come down in the world."

Having skirted downtown to the waterfront and then turned around away from the sharp glints of the sea's crests harbouring the low, hazy outline of the Palisadoes in the near distance, the first impression is of the enclosing hills. A dramatic, craggy crêpe-veil of blue-green peaks pushes the horizon up above the grey-tanned sloping lowlands of the city. To the west, Hope River leads dryly up to Jack's Hill and the affluence of stilted villas amid more humble hillside homes. Stony Hill and Red Hills Roads carve residential routes across the skyline. The Eastern hills, bleached brown-beige at the height of the long summer months, line up as Long Mountain, its lower slopes sprinkled with the glitter of the Beverley Hills mansions, its upper slopes scarred by an ugly development dubbed "uptown Portmore". This towering outcrop then shoulders Dallas Mountain to the east and the distant folds of the Blue Mountains behind.

The following chapters illuminate these cultural and architectural traces apparent in today's downtown Kingston, roaming through squares, markets and along the harbour. Kingston is full of striking contradictions, a love-hate medley of old and new, stasis and rebellion. Its enchanting allure of difference is captured by Rachel Manley in her anthology, *A Light Left On* (1992):

> *Before these cities*
> *came to look the same,*
> *truth had its own shape,*
> *magic was magic.*

CHAPTER ONE

Port and Harbour

"Southwards the plain slides into the white rose-dusted city and the cloud-reflecting blue of the harbour, on which the Palisadoes float like the green stem and leaves of some placid water-plant... The wonderful bay of Old Harbour, azure, flawless, calm, five-fingered, shining, where the silken recession of the flats moves shapely to lift on either side of the water long, low, and violet bluffs, wears in its absolute repose that ideal radiance... Kingston lights flicker on like a field of Indian corn with lit ears."

Kenneth Pringle, *Waters of the West* (1938)

"The sun was setting. The Dakota banked sharply. When it straightened out there was land to port. It rose sheer out of the sea, misted and tinged with purple in the setting sun. Lower down, the coastal plain took sweeping shape, lush and green; and behind it were the hills, each succeeding one higher than the one before. The plane swept down to the Palisadoes. This was landfall: Jamaica."

Peter Abrahams, *Jamaica: An Island Mosaic* (1957)

Port and harbour have historically defined Kingston, both complicit in the prosperity and cruelty of its mercantile past. The dockside marked the point of arrival for thousands of slaves following their shipment from West Africa during the eighteenth century. By way of a return transatlantic passage, its piers and jetties supported the precious exports of sugar that would build the base of the British Empire. Once the 1739 Sugar Act had secured the West Indian monopoly of the imperial market, the course for Kingston's early riches was set. Colin Clarke observes in his comprehensive history of the city: "Kingston's role was the import, storage and despatch of slaves and British manufactured goods to the sugar estates and the collection, storage and export of sugar to Britain."

But the first port was not on the northern side of the bay, as it is now, but on the Palisadoes, a thin sinew of land that shelters the harbour's waters from southerly swell, so-called due to a palisade built across the spit as defence from land attack. The original port, founded in 1650 by Spanish settlers, but claimed for the English Crown in 1655, was the first seat of water-born wealth. At its peak during the seventeenth century, Port Royal was ranked with Santo Domingo and Havana as the one of the principal towns of a Caribbean awash with colonial booty and devilment. Of the three, Port Royal surpasses its rivals in tales of horror and infamy as the haven for the Brethren of the Coast, the pirates and buccaneers who laid siege to the surrounding seas, encouraged by the English state during the latter half of the seventeenth century. A monumental earthquake and tidal wave crashed down upon the booming town of Port Royal at the close of that century; thus began the rise to prominence of the replacement settlement of Kingston.

The waters are somewhat calmer these days, perhaps too placid for Kingston's port and tourist authorities. Yet many visitors, and writers, have been lured by the harbour's beauty and the tales of Port Royal's riotous past.

Coming Ashore

Few have landed on the shores of Jamaica with such literary pomp and sycophantic circumstance as Governor Lawes. An anonymous poet, who penned the earliest poem published in Jamaica in 1718, celebrated the arrival of the new officer of the realm with "A Pindarique Ode on the Arrival of His Excellency Sir Nicholas Lawes, Governor of Jamaica":

> *The painted Dolphins sport and glide,*
> *And court his gracious Hand in all their Pride;*
> *The fierce devouring tyrants of the Main*
> *Forget their Nature, for a while are tame;*
> *The Shark himself neglects his easy Prey,*
> *Swims to the Vessel and doth Homage pay,*
>   *Th' exulting harmess little Fry*
>   *Wanton before their Enemy*
> *Secure in Innocence whilst LAWES is by.*

A later governor of the island, Lord Olivier, while not possessing such a seemingly magical hold over the bay's residents, recounted a more subtle yet equally colourful arrival by sea two centuries after his predecessor's landing:

As you steam into Kingston Harbour you have on your left hand a desolate mass of hills that at sundown stands black-purple against an incredible glory of crimson and orange and ochre and delicate apple-green; and ahead of you, where the bluff dies out at Port Henderson, that glory drives broad shafts of level colour across the banana-flats and the salt-ponds. The emerald of the mangrove fringe of the beaches is drenched with floods of scarlet; the opal of the huge lagoon, dead calm between day breeze and night breeze, is burnt into its depths with strange, dull lilac tinctures: the folded ranges beyond are olive and lake, seen clear through ruddy haze; and over the shelving plain of Liguanea, eastward, the great whale-flank of the stranded mountain shows, where it sinks towards Mona, a long, low, flaming scar of rust-stained limestone rock.

Kenneth Pringle, also writing in the 1930s, was equal to Lord Olivier's kaleidoscopic account of the bay, but his gaze was caught primarily by the sensual energy of Kingston's portside:

Picture the rich drench of dark blue and purple sea, the raffish plumage of the black-brown palms, the filth wooden shanties crazily tipped on the irregular inshore, the perfect blazing sweep of the white sands, the red and green sheds running out on crude iron piers, the crackling gauze of wind-rippled heat, the macadamised road glaring through the façade of gaudy one-storey shops, the rickety bars with painted doors and frowsy girls on the steps, the more pretentious wooden billiard saloon with dark, cockroach-ridden bedrooms upstairs where the planters have high-jinks, the rolling odour of rum, the clouds of wasps, the scarlet bushes of hibiscus, the spruce, whitewashed law court with its gravel bed of coleas... Then picture Monday or Tuesday, which are banana days. Picture the enormous trucks driven furiously by hell-drivers rocking with produce down from the hills. Picture the wild scenes on the wharves; the men and women and girls and boys rushing along the platform each with a dark-

*green bunch of bananas borne on the head... Picture a sudden quarrel
for precedence and a man lashing a lad with a cowhide whip. Picture a
man suddenly dropping his load to crush a girl in his arms... When you
have these images clearly fixed in your mind's eye and the sense of this
activity in your blood, you have grasped what considerably elaborated is
also the essence of Kingston.*

Travellers arriving by air for the first time will realize just before
landing that the straggly bit of land beneath them, surrounded by
water, and not the solid bulk of land on the near horizon, is their
immediate destination. The Norman Manley airport is perched on the
Palisadoes peninsula, described by Anthony Winkler as bending "across
Kingston harbour like a claw, giving it a sheltered anchorage. The
peninsula is a thin strip of land; you stand in its middle and hear the
surf thundering against the windward side that faces the open sea, and
see the same ocean licking peacefully at the brown sand on the
sheltered shore." Kingston rests across the bay, a distant haze of heat
during the day and a low smudge of light at night. The sinuous main
road takes you to town, a much-improved option than that offered
during the mid-nineteenth century, when Anthony Trollope advised:
"Those who are geographically inclined should be made to understand
that the communication between Port Royal and Kingston, as, indeed,
between Port Royal and any other part of the island, is by water. It is I
believe, on record that hardy Subs, and hardier Mids, have ridden along
the Palisades, and not died from sunstroke in the effort. But chances
are much against them."

Today's route, less arduous although no more fetchingly
described by Winkler, "winds down the centre of the peninsula, past
the ruins of an old blockhouse that was once part of the Port Royal
fortress but now lies half buried in sand, past foetid swamps whose
mangroves tiptoe out of darkness on thin, knobbly roots. After that
it plunges down a flat spit of land where the wind and surf bleat
endlessly."

The chain of cays around the peninsula offer immediate glimpses
of deserted isles, albeit framed by the hulk of a passing container ship.
The most popular, Lime Cay, is a stunning splash of mangrove and
white sand in the bay's waters, the "candour and simplicity" of which

clearly captured the imagination of Kenneth Pringle in *Waters of the West*: "Jamaica was the music of an orchestra, but Lime Cay a single pure note on a flute." Whilst the fanciful flautists have moved on, weekend crowds bring their own sound systems or share those of ferried visitors and weekend boat folk who inhabit the islet's slim strips of beach. During the 1940s, Lime Cay was the scene of a more brutal meeting, when police finally caught and shot the infamous Kingstonian gangster Rhygin. Louise Bennett, "Miss Lou", the popular oral poet whose work is now recognized as literary treasure, wryly comments that Rhygin's ghost, or duppy, might prove to be as wily and troublesome as the killer himself. In "Dead Man", she wonders if he will have one more trick for the morgue's photographer:

> *But ah wanda wat would happen*
> *To de picture-man miss Sue?*
> *Ef wen him dah-tek de picture*
> *Rhygin duppy did sey "boo"!*

Port Royal: Pirate Capital

Rhygin, the romanticized rogue of twentieth-century Kingston, would have found many-like minded colleagues among the seventeenth-century inhabitants of Port Royal, the most famous privateering stronghold in the Western Hemisphere. Strategically placed for attacking ships journeying the Windward Passage and supported by Jamaican governors, most notably Sir Thomas Modyford, the pirates and buccaneers of the region clustered in Port Royal in the latter half of the seventeenth century. While some of the wealthier planters had houses in the town, the most notable entrepreneurs were the privateers and buccaneers. The former held Crown commissions or letters of marque authorizing the capture of Spanish vessels, but all engaged in the same freebooting activities.

On 10 May 1655, British forces landed and overran a weakly defended Spanish colony of around 3,000 inhabitants of African and Spanish descent. Earlier Arawak-speaking communities had already succumbed to the advent of new diseases and harsh treatment from the unwelcome invaders. The new colonists anchored off what was later named Passage Fort, and established themselves at the existing capital of Santiago, now called Spanish Town, ten miles west of present-day Kingston.

The English colony did not originate as a planned acquisition, but more as a face-saving afterthought on the part of Admirals Penn and Venables, who sought a consolation prize following a bungled invasion of Hispaniola. Oliver Cromwell's puritanical desire to rid the Western Hemisphere of Roman Catholicism spurred on the Western Design, his plan to seize the Caribbean islands for British interests. Penn and Venables, equipped with a dubious fighting force of ne'er-do-wells, were sent forth to capture the large island of Hispaniola. On their departure, Sir Charles Firth disparagingly remarked, "No worse or ill-prepared expedition ever left the English shores." After the foreseen defeat at their first choice of conquest, the poorly defended island of Jamaica seemed a more appropriate target for the would-be invaders.

This secondary prize turned out to be a rough diamond for British imperial and economic plans. Captured while Cromwell held office, Jamaica was finally and officially ceded by Spain to the reinstated English Crown in 1670 by the Treaty of Madrid. The slave-based sugar plantation system would shortly become the mainstay of the Jamaican economy, but the initial hub of activity for this nascent, mercantile colony revolved around the fierce, seafaring exploits of Port Royal's residents.

Founded in 1657 by General Brayne, the location's potential was clear to all. Goldsmiths, tradesmen, inn-keepers, seafarers and speculators filled the town, while ships hugged the harbour-side with cargoes of tobacco, spices, sugar, beef and wine. Embracing mercantilism, either via the roughshod route of piracy or more formal avenues of trade, the town became the centre of moneymaking.

The excellent anchorage in the road, where a thousand ships might lie secure from all winds except hurricanes, and the depth of water, insomuch that the largest vessels used to lay their broadsides to the wharfs, and load and unload with little trouble, made it so desirable a seat of trade, that it soon became celebrated for the number of its inhabitants, the extent of its commerce, and amazing treasures of gold and silver.

Thatched buildings of mortar, rough wooden sheds, solid counting-houses and an unhealthy quota of inns spread out along the coastal scrub and marsh from the sand bar's westerly point. These drinking dens not only catered to residents, merchants and itinerant seafarers, but the front verandahs of the more "reputable" establishments which attracted the monied crowd, such as Baker's Tavern, were regular sites for barbaric slave auctions. In the swirl of money-grabbing, market-led morality and fiscal zeal, plots of lands were parcelled and purchased along the rapidly built-up Tower, Common and New Streets. Port Royal boomed. Ships great and small lined the freshly erected jetties, and the steady haul of legitimate and illicit treasures began to flow onshore to the port's gaping coffers and their expectant keepers. Edward Long, writing in 1774, recalled Port Royal's bustling trade and wealth during the latter half of the seventeenth century.

> *The revenue of the landholders was considerably increased likewise by the rising of rents of houses there, which in its flourishing area were let on as high terms as the best houses in the City of London... The town was inhabited by scarcely any other than merchants, warehouse keepers, vintners, and retailers of punch; the latter were very numerous, and well supported by the buccaneers, who dissipated here whatever they got from the Spaniards.*

The commentator was nevertheless clear that the spirit and skills of privateering fuelled the port and colony's early development: "But the principal supporters of the colony, by the torrents of money which they poured in, to the enriching of merchants and planters, and the introduction of new settlers, were the Bucaniers, an hardy race of seamen, and other bold spirits, united in firm league."

While the wealth flowed from ship to shore, the wicked reputation of Port Royal's population and its "crew of vile strumpets and common prostitutes" grew wider and more infamous. A contemporary traveller and chronicler, writing by the name of Henderson, observed the crass ostentation of its citizens:

The place was a gilded hades, and mammon held sovereign sway over its people. Bearded seamen, bronzed and weather-stained, bedecked with priceless jewellery and the finest silks of the Orient, swaggered along its quays and gambled with the heavy gold coins whose value no one cared to estimate. The drinking shops were filled with cups of gold and silver, embellished with flashing gem stones torn from half a hundred cathedrals. Each house was a treasure store. Common seamen hung their ears with gold rings studded with the costliest gems.

Irish writer Patrick Leigh Fermor similarly echoes the earlier epithet of the port as the "Babylon of the West". He imagined the tumbling riches off-loaded from ships to shore and cited an anonymous observer who recorded the seafarers' antiques and how they "bartered to all the races of the Caribbean for bars and cakes of gold... wedges and pigs of silver, Pistoles, Pieces of Eight, and several other Coyns of both Mettles; with store of wrought plate Jewels, rich Pearl Necklaces, and of Pearl unsorted and undrilled several Bushels... beside which... the purest and most fine sorts of Dust Gold from Guiney."

Wealth and self-congratulation were enjoyed in equally abundant measure. The contemporary historian John Esquemeling observed that the pirates "wasted in a few days... all they had gained, by giving themselves over to every manner of debauchery." Some, he continued, "will spend two or three thousand pieces-of-eight in one night... I saw one of them give unto a common strumpet five hundred pieces of eight on that he might see her naked."

The drink of choice in the taverns, according to Governor Modyford, was "kill-devil", a rough sort of rum. A supporter and beneficiary of the buccaneers' exploits, he also recorded their prodigious appetite for alcohol: "The Spaniards wondered much at the sickness of our people, until they knew the strength of their drinks, but then wondered more that they were not all dead." The hapless clergyman who arrived to minister to the lost souls of Port Royal no doubt felt similar sentiments. He returned to England immediately on the same ship, expressing his horror and resignation: "Since the majority of its population consists of pirates, cut-throats, whores and some of the vilest persons in the whole of the world, I felt my permanence there was of no use."

Blackbeard and Company

Savagery and ill-gotten riches accrued in like measure among the pirate community. A host of violent characters fill the pages of contemporary tales. Roche Brasiliano, a Dutchman who had spent much of his life in Brazil but later relocated his activities to Port Royal, was among the most barbarous residents. He recruited his shipmates amid scenes of raging drunkenness in the waterfront drinking dens, expressing his furious temper to captives by roasting them alive on spits.

One of the most notorious pirates to chase booty throughout the Spanish Main was Edward Teach, a hell-raiser born in Bristol around 1680 and more commonly known as Blackbeard. Captain Charles Johnson's *A General History of the Robberies and Murders of the Most Notorious Pirates, and also their Policies, Discipline and Government* (1724) records him drinking aboard ship with first mate Israel Hands. During the course of the evening, the notorious seaman shot his crew-member in the kneecap, exclaiming that "if he did not now and then kill one of them, they would forget who he was." If his actions did not already terrify those about him, then his appearance certainly caused alarm. His dark beard was plaited and tied with ribbons; three pairs of pistols were strapped across his chest, while fuses in his hat—short lengths of hemp cord dripped in saltpetre— belched black smoke about him in battle. Blackbeard's buccaneering tallies were not the most bounteous, but his ferocity remained to the bitter end. In 1718, he was hunted down by Lieutenant Robert Maynard, receiving twenty cutlass wounds and five pistol shots before collapsing. His head was cut off and then hung from the bowsprit of his vessel.

Gallows Point, a low promontory to the east of Port Royal, was the scene of serial hangings between 1680 and 1830. Many men and women caught crossing the law of the land or high seas met their end on this shore. Two cross-dressing buccaneers, Mary Read and Anne Bonny, were among the few who were convicted yet escaped execution. The former was born in Plymouth, England, during the 1690s. From birth, her mother had raised her as a boy to claim an inheritance. Aged thirteen years, she went into service as a boy servant, then left for sea, before joining a foot regiment in Flanders and marrying a male officer. The historian Johnson writes of the encounter that "she found a way of letting him discover her sex… He was much surprised at what he found out, and not a little pleased." The marriage did not last, and with no financial support she resumed men's clothing and deserted the army to join a ship bound for the Caribbean. The tale twists further after buccaneers captured her en route. At this stage, she met Anne Bonny, the illegitimate daughter of a lawyer from County Cork. Anne had married a sailor, then left him for a pirate's life with Calico Jack, so-named for his taste for calico cloth. The new alliance formed, the British navy then captured their ship and crew at Negril Bay in 1720, allegedly in the midst of a drunken beach party. Male crew-members were sent to the gallows, but both women were spared, supposedly due to their pregnancies. Mary Read later died of fever in Spanish Town, while nothing more is known of Anne Bonny.

Henry Morgan

Of all the buccaneers stationed in Port Royal, the most celebrated was Henry Morgan, who was rated as "equal to any the most renowned warriors of historical fame, in valour, conduct and success" by the historian Edward Long. His skills as a pirate, military strategist and *bon vivant* are legendary. He carried out raids with the full approval of the Council of Jamaica, while holding office as the respected leader of the "Brethren of the Coast", an association of buccaneers whose common aim was to loot the vessels of the Spanish Main. Among his celebrated exploits were daring raids on Havana and Portobello in the 1660s, which so impressed Charles II that he was knighted, and later appointed deputy governor and then lieutenant governor of Jamaica. He died in 1688 of dropsy, being "much given to drinking and sitting up late."

While Morgan has inspired countless colourful tales of piracy, his legacy has also launched famous literary journeys, most notably that of John Steinbeck, whose first novel, *Cup of Gold* (1929), charted the buccaneer's roguish ways. Typical of many swashbuckling accounts, *Sir Henry Morgan, Buccaneer* (1931) was rousingly written by Merritt Parmelee Allen for "any boy who wants a stirring story and a true picture of those exciting historical days." The testosterone-laden tale plots the highs and lows of the pirate's life as an active Gentleman of Leisure.

After a few months of ease, restlessness began to stir his blood. He sniffed the sea air, as it blew in across the green hills, and it brought him smells of tar and camp-fires and burning gunpowder. He fell to pacing the gallery of his house, as he used to pace the quarter-deck. With sudden revulsion he noticed that he had grown fat and soft. His hands were white and the old cutlass calluses were gone. Bah! That was not "Harry Morgan's way" at all.

Less bewitched by the buccaneer's bravado, the celebrated botanist and physician Sir Hans Sloane (1660-1753) recorded a meeting with Morgan in 1688, who was then an ailing alcoholic, describing him as "lean, sallow-coloured" with yellowish eyes and a prominent belly. He prescribed him a series of purges and scorpion oil-based diuretics, but Morgan opted for an obeah-man who offered "clysters of urine", then "plastered him all over with clay and water, and by it augmented his cough." Morgan died shortly after, and was buried in the churchyard at Port Royal, only for his grave to be consumed by an earthquake four years later. In one of many twists to his life story, the allegedly reformed pirate, facing the stark proximity of a perhaps less decadent after-life, donated his silver beer tankard to the church as a communion cup.

A one-time physician at Port Royal, Sloane's set of travel journals, *A Voyage to the Islands* (1707), recounts many incidents of the time. This first of two volumes was one of the earliest English descriptions of life in Jamaica, being written after the author spent a year on the island. Recording his sojourn in Port Royal, a few years before the earthquake hit, he joined others in criticizing the decadence of the residents: "The Passions of the mind have a very great power on mankind here, especially Hysterical women and Hypochondriacal men." On his welcome return to London, Sloane increased his personal fortune by marrying the widow of a wealthy Jamaican planter. His meticulously collected books, plants, fauna, gems and curios later formed the nucleus of the British Natural History Museum, while his name today labels a range of Chelsea addresses.

The romance and wretchedness of Port Royal's pirates has not escaped the silver screen. Idealized heroes of the high seas and exotic isles starred in many of Hollywood's early adventures. Douglas Fairbanks Senior and a thousand-fold cast of cutlass-wielding ruffians led the way in *The Black Pirate*, an experimental two-tone Technicolor film produced in 1926. Errol Flynn, himself a lover of Jamaica, starred in the 1930s remake of the silent film *Captain Blood*. The story is based on Rafael Sabatini's novel, in which a falsely accused surgeon joins the buccaneers' ranks, naturally becoming governor of Jamaica, with Olivia de Havilland as his bride. Of all the pirates' tales, J. M. Barrie's *Peter Pan* (1907) is the best known. Captain James Hook, Blackbeard's former bosun, "and many another ruffian long known on the Spanish Main" have captured imaginations as the story's devilish seafarers.

Judgment Day

Visitors hoping to trace the path of pirating jaunts amid the streets of Port Royal will be hard pressed without scuba gear. A catastrophic earthquake in 1692 laid waste to much of the settlement, which was subsequently doused and drowned by a vast tidal wave. Two thousand buildings and up to 4,000 inhabitants perished. Eighty years after the disaster, Edward Long reconstructed the events: "All the principal streets, which were next to the water, sunk at once, with the people in them; and a high rolling sea followed, closing immediately over them… The harbour had the appearance of agitation as in a storm; and the huge waves rolled with such violence, as to snap the cables of the ships, drive some from their anchors, and overset others." The *Swan*, at anchor in the harbour, was washed by a colossal wave into the centre of town and left perched on the flattened rooftops.

Andrew Salkey puts Port Royal's past to verse in "Because of 1692", one of a collection of poems chronicling key events in Jamaican history:

> *Port Royal,*
> *I see you*
> *sweating*
> *in your wealth;*
> *I see your loaded wharves,*
> *waiting,*
> *lopsided*
> *with loot;*
> *Peru left*

with a slit throat;
Mexico maimed.

The disaster occurred on a tranquil Sunday morning, as the port's faithful few were returning from church. Jamaican writer and historian, Frank Cundall, retells in detail how the Anglican rector, Dr. Emmanuel Heath, was enjoying a drink of "wormwood wine as a whet before dinner" with Council president John White. As they sat in the churchyard following the morning service, the ground started "rowling and moving". It was 11.40 a.m. on 7 June 1692. A series of tremors roused folk from reverie or slumber, before buildings began to crash down around them. Brick and stone houses collapsed along the northern edge of town and two streets plummeted into the sea.

Published two centuries later, a secondary account based on the eyewitness report of a Captain Crocket indicates that the ground opened up in gaping cracks: "The sand in the street rose like the waves of the sea, lifting up all persons that stood upon it, and immediately dropping down into pits; and at the same instant a flood of water rushed in, throwing down all who were in its way; some were seen catching hold of beams and rafters of houses, others were found in the sand that appeared when the water was drained away, with their legs and arms out."

Two-thirds of the town slid beneath the sea during the catastrophe, which was viewed by some as God's judgement on "that wicked and rebellious place, Port Royal". An anonymous account published soon after, *The Truest and Largest Account of the Late Earthquake*, describes the after-effects of the calamity, in keeping with the port's nefarious reputation:

> *Immediately upon the cessation of the extremity of the earthquake, your heart would abhor to hear of the depredations, robberies and violences that were in an instant committed upon the place by the vilest and basest of the people; no man could call any thing his own, for they that were strongest and most wickedest seized what they pleased.*

The horror of the scene was complemented for days afterwards by the spectacle of the corpses of those recently killed and uprooted from the graveyard bobbing in the bay. Edward Long exclaimed, "What rendered the scene more tragical were the numbers of dead bodies which, after perishing in the shock at Port Royal, were seen in hundreds floating from one side of the harbour to the other." Writing two hundred years later, the British historian James Anthony Froude referred to the hidden, silted corpses of Port Royal: "There is proof enough, however, that in the sand there lie the remains of many thousand English soldiers and seamen, who ended their lives there for one cause or other. The bones lie so close that they are turned up as in a country churchyard when a fresh grave is dug." Salkey's poem "Because of 1692" continues the description of wrecked lives and haunting legacies:

> *I imagine the dislocated bodies,*
> *the float of shoals*
> *of destruction*
> *lying along the port;*
> …
> *I know those bruised knots*
> *in the wood,*
> *the upright post and arm*
> *on which the bodies dangled;*
> *I still see the raked sand.*

The destruction of property and livelihoods had meant that many left Port Royal to take refuge in "miserable huts" in that part of Liguanea where Kingston now stands. Although this tragedy did not herald the immediate demise of Port Royal, it spurred the colonists to consider developing a new settlement, that of King's Town across the bay. A devastating warehouse fire next to a gunpowder store and a violent hurricane thirty years later, however, finally terminated dreams of the old port's revival.

Physical destruction aside, Port Royal's standing and its buccaneering tradition were increasingly sullied by the end of the seventeenth century. In *A Trip to Jamaica: With a True Character of the People and the Island* (1698), Ned Ward lampooned the newly colonized island, with a particular dose of vitriol saved for Henry Morgan's old abode:

The Dunghill of the Universe, the Refuse of the whole Creation, the Clippings of the Elements, a shapeless Pile of Rubbish confusd'ly jumbl'd into an Emblem of the Chaos, neglected by Omnipotence when he form'd the World into its admirable Order. The Nursery of Heavens Judgements, where the Malignant Seeds of all Pestilence were first gather'd and scatter'd thro' the Regions of the Earth, to Punish Mankind for their Offences. The Place where Pandora fill'd her Box, where Vulcan Forg'd Jove's Thunder-bolts, and that Phaeton, by his rash misguidance of the Sun, scorched into a Cinder. The Receptacle of Vagabonds, the Sanctuary of Bankrupts, and a Close-stool for the Purges of our Prisons. As Sickly as an Hospital, as Dangerous as the Plague, as Hot as Hell, and as Wicked as the Devil. Subject to Turnadoes, Hurricanes and Earthquakes, as if the Island, like the People, were troubled with the Dry Belly-Ache… In short, Virtue is so Despis'd, and all sorts of Vice Encourag'd by both Sexes, that the Town of Port-Royal is the very Sodom of the Universe.

Rebuilding Port Royal

In the early 1970s David Buisseret and Michael Pawson described arriving at Port Royal by car from Kingston: "The visitor will normally approach Port Royal by land, driving along that Palisadoes road which was opened in 1936. Passing the airport, he will see on the harbour side extensive mangrove swamps, and on the sea side dunes covered with scrub and cactus; all this must look much as it did in 1655." Scrub and cactus hide the brief history of the Palisadoes as a coconut plantation, briefly established at the end of the nineteenth century. Midway along the road lies Plumb Point lighthouse, built in 1853 of stone and cast iron. You hear the rumble of overhead passenger jets carving their landing paths towards the Norman Manley international airport at the end of the narrow peninsula, but little else has changed over the centuries. A few newer hotels and bars lining the shore add a stroke of modernity, while the mangrove swamps could do with a spring tide flush to remove the plastic flotsam. Attempts have been made to clear up Kingston harbour, memorably described by Morris Cargill of *The Daily Gleaner* as "the world's most beautiful sewer", although an overall strategy has yet to come clean. Nevertheless, the straight narrow road, sandwiched between restless waters, is a beguiling drive for first-time visitors to today's Port Royal.

Crossing the bay by ferry is still an adventurous outing. Louis Simpson describes the trip to Port Royal in "A Fine Day for Straw Hats", highlighting the next stage in the settlement's history:

> *to Port Royal… sand and coconuts,*
> *a few houses and huts,*
> *and a low wall with embrasures*
> *for cannon. This was Fort Charles*
> *where Nelson used to stand*
> *gazing at the sun and the pelicans.*

Port Royal itself led a slow recovery from the traumatic events of the seventeenth and early eighteenth centuries. After the hub of activity moved across the bay to the new King's Town, the old port developed a significant military role following the decision to base the British fleet there, with the subsequent construction of a naval dockyard after 1735. Six forts were erected, housing 2,500 soldiers and seamen. Based at Port Royal, English Harbour in Antigua and Bridgetown in Barbados, British naval capacity in the region relied very much on these fortified havens. Yet victory at Waterloo reduced the need for such military outposts as the Napoleonic threat to Britain's Caribbean colonies receded.

Just as this armed menace was removed, the ever present danger of fire devastated the entire settlement in 1815, but again it was rebuilt as the docks and the town's role as a staging post remained important. Despite waning port profits and activity, the settlement was smartly redeveloped to such an extent that the historian James Phillippo could write in 1843 that, "It presents an imposing appearance from the sea; groves of cocoanut trees in stately columns, waving their verdant branches amongst the buildings." The streets remained narrow, jumbled, dirty and largely dependent on mercantile and naval activity to fill them with life, but curiously the town had also maintained its status as a "health resort" of sorts. The change of fresh sea air for Kingstonian visitors was much remarked upon, with a sojourn in Port Royal heading many doctor's prescriptions for those finding the stress of nineteenth-century city living too much for the system.

The naval buildings and forts remained a clear expression of British colonial power in the region, of its glories and scandals. Arriving with the English mail in the 1880s, a patriotic and pro-imperial James Anthony Froude was moved to remark:

I do not know that I have ever seen any scene more interesting than that which broke my upon my eyes as we rounded the point, and the lagoon opened out before me... At the back were the mountains. The mist had melted off, standing in shadowy grey masses with the sun rising behind them. Immediately in front were the dockyards, forts, and towers of Port Royal, with the guardship, gunboats and tenders, with street and terrace, roof and turret and glistening vane, all clearly and sharply defined in the exquisite transparency of the air. The associations of the place no doubt added to the impression. Before the first hut was run up in Kingston, Port Royal was the rendezvous of all English ships which, for spoil or commerce, frequented the West Indian seas. Here the buccaneers sold their plunder and squandered their gains in gambling and riot. Here in the later century of legitimate wars, whole fleets were gathered to take in stores, or refit when shattered by engagements. Here Nelson had been, and Collingwood and Jervis, and all our other naval heroes. Here prizes were brought in for adjudication, and pirates to be tried and hanged. In this spot more than any other, beyond Great Britain herself, the energy of the old Empire was throbbing... There were batteries at the point, and batteries on the opposite shore. The morning bugle rang out clear and inspiriting from the town, and white coats and gold and silver were passing to parade. Here, at any rate, England was still alive.

But dockside days were numbered. Lord Dundonald, writing in the 1840s, differs markedly from Phillippo's contemporary account. While the latter acknowledged that the port could indeed be viewed in part as "a miserable wreck of its former greatness", the former ripped forth: "Never have I seen a place so disgustingly filthy, or which could give so bad an opinion to foreigners of British Colonial Administration." A drastic clean-up or clear-out campaign was thus required to align one of the Empire's erstwhile premier ports with contemporary imperial aspirations.

Port Royal had ceased to be a separate naval command in 1836 and the dockyard was eventually closed in 1905. Yet two years after the dockyards were wound up, Jamaica's original Babylon was once again visited by natural misfortune. An earthquake ripped through the port and the new capital of Kingston, causing extensive damage. Today, a few of the naval buildings survive and form the focus for yet another proposed revival, this time under the golden banner of tourism. Walt Disney had allegedly seen the potential of Port Royal's colourful legacy six decades previously. During the 1940s, he drummed up enthusiasm for a "Pirates of the Caribbean" theme park. This was not to be, however, so he relocated his oddball idea for a so-called "Disneyland" to the United States. The later conceptions of Mickey Mouse and company were to be firmly rooted as creatures of Americana, without a hint of an earlier Creole twinkle in their patron's eye. In recent years, though, plans have resurfaced to recreate the port as a major tourist attraction with earthquake simulations, underwater explorations of the sunken city and a new pier to attract cruise ship passengers.

Ghosts and Ruins

Despite natural calamities, much endures of Port Royal's past. Approaching by road from Kingston, the first historical landmark is the naval cemetery that lies half a mile from the town. The eighteenth-century tombstones record the presence of military barracks, the common curse of yellow fever and early mortality. Little remains visible today of Morgan's personal legacy: a slab of stone on the esplanade mysteriously reads "Morgan's Line", while Captain Morgan rum is racked up at Morgan's Harbour, the club and hotel built by Sir Anthony Jenkinson on the site of the old naval dockyard. Although the British navy has long since set sail, the local waters still buzz with small craft and marlin-fishermen. Helicopters en route to the neighbouring barracks of the Jamaican Defence Force occasionally clatter overhead.

The town palisade, known as Morgan's Wall despite its eighteenth-century construction, lines Tower Street and leads to St. Peter's Church. Restored after the first earthquake, a tombstone records the miraculous escape of Lewis Galdy, who was swallowed up and spat out of the trembling earth's folds. On the edge of the bay, the cast-iron framework of the earthquake-proof Old Naval Hospital has fared less well against the more subtle ravages of time. In operation until 1905, the magnificent sun-bleached bulk of the building wastes away as plans for its regeneration as a new museum are mooted.

Fort Rupert lies ruined by a lagoon to the east. On the southern tip of the peninsula, Fort Charles, the oldest surviving monument to the British occupation of Jamaica lingers stolidly. On these battlements, the young Horatio Nelson gazed at the horizon, expecting French invaders. His lookout post, a wooden quarter-deck, survived until the hurricane of 1951. Since rebuilt, a nearby plaque states solemnly, "In this place dwelt Horatio Nelson, you who tread his footprints, remember his glory." He served at the fort for two years and returned a year later in 1779, suffering from fever and dysentery, to be nursed by Couba Cornwallis. Singularly disenchanted with his tours of duty in the Caribbean and with his marriage to Frances Nisbet in Nevis, Nelson's footsteps in the region are well recorded.

Originally built in the 1650s and named after Cromwell, the fort was swiftly re-titled in 1660 as the Royalist cause triumphed. Despite sinking three feet into the ground during the earthquake of 1692, it has undergone renovation and rebuilding and has weathered subsequent tremors. A small museum in one of two lodgings in the cockpit of the fort lengthens a glance at the past, and much more can be conjured up by images of freebooting buccaneers, shackled slave labourers, a war-ready fleet at bay and Nelson's pensive stride.

Giddy House, a former artillery store, just a short walk from the walls of the fort, adds to the visual sense of the past. During the earthquake of 1907, the small building slipped to a 45-degree angle and slumps in its contorted state, as if to be soon devoured by the surrounding sands. Also built in the 1880s, and underlain by a labyrinth of connecting subterranean tunnels, the Victoria and Albert Battery at the tip of the peninsula suffered more severe earthquake damage but similarly echoes the contrasting fortunes of the town. Time seems to have slipped by a sleepy Port Royal in recent decades, evidently a tourist and heritage honey-pot in waiting. In contrast, Kingston's harbour has been systematically chopped, changed and refashioned.

The Waterfront Past and Present

The modernized sea frontage of present-day Kingston cements over the fear experienced by the earliest forced migrants as they were unloaded from slave ships. Fifty years ago, visitors and cruise passengers were voluntarily retracing the slaves' footsteps in altogether different circumstances. Today cruise ship visits are on hold, pending the redevelopment of Port Royal, and the jetties and docks that witnessed the maritime beginnings of the Jamaican economy have receded beneath the waves. To the west, the older piers have been replaced by an oil refinery and the industrial complex of the aptly named Newport West.

Following the demise of the buccaneering brethren by the eighteenth century, the colony of Jamaica developed a reputation as a place where fortunes could be made through alternative channels of commerce, plantations and the professions. Undoubtedly, skulduggery and the evils of slavery eased the route to riches for many European sojourners and migrants, but their misdeeds were largely undertaken within the framework of colonial law. Kingston, and not Port Royal, was now the principal harbour and the focus of much activity.

The proximity of water was not always to the advantage of early residents. During the eighteenth century, Long reported: "The land Westward from the town, and confining on the harbour, is, for four or five miles, interspersed with lagoons, and in many places subject to be overflown by the salt-water... It was observed that the yellow West-Indian fever often reigned there, attended with most profuse evacuations of blood, by vomiting, stools, and even by every pore of the body." A source of much concern were the "salt-marshes and swamps, the putrid fogs or exhalations." The hospital at Greenwich Town, only a mile from the town centre, and now a busy downtown neighbourhood, offered little comfort as a sanctuary: "The effects of its unhealthy situation were, that, when a patient was sent thither with only a gentle or intermitting fever, this mild disposition was apt to be changed into either a malignant fever, a bloody flux, or some other mortal distemper." Clearly of great concern to Long, he continues on the theme of wretched waters:

Much of this water remains afterwards stagnant, and becomes highly putrid. It is impossible not to be sensible of it in travelling over this salina to Kingston, especially at an early hour in the morning, when the stench of the ooze is often remarkably foetid; and a vapour may be observed hovering over these lagoons and swamps of a most disagreeable smell. It may well therefore be suspected, that a Westerly land-wind... especially after a violent rain there, may impel these effluvia into the town of Kingston.

Out of these early troubles Kingston's port-side progressed and flourished. Victoria Pier at the end of King Street was a busy throng of sailors, merchants, slaves and servants, and for a century, the first footfall of visiting dignitaries. During much of the nineteenth and twentieth centuries, the Myrtle Bank Hotel on East Street, and to a lesser extent, the South Camp Road Hotel, were the mainstays of colonial and commercial gentility. Herbert de Lisser, advising on the significance of these establishments in *Twentieth Century Jamaica* (1913), informs visitors that "Balls are frequently given by them, and at some of these you will find hundreds of handsomely dressed people—Jamaica's best—one will get some idea of what a social function in the West Indies is like."

Near the Myrtle Bank Hotel, the former United Fruit Company

pier offered ready evidence of Jamaica's plantation and export-oriented economy. By the 1930s, the agricultural commodity markets had waned, although the extravagant colonial airs of the hotel survived downtown. Patrick Leigh Fermor records his visit during this time:

> *The strains of a brass band came panting through the air from the garden of the Myrtle Bank Hotel, and I hastened my steps towards that great centre of Kingston social life. The khaki drill of army officers' uniforms, the first, apart from the occasional police, that I had seen in the West Indies, interspersed the white-duck elegance of the swarms of English*

winter-visitors. Caps with the two sphinx-badges of the Gloucestershire Regiment lay about on tables. The Sam Brownes and shorts and swagger-canes and rumour of forgotten military terminology lent to this hotel a savour of Shepherd's, the Cecil or King David. But strangest of all were the musicians.

Harbour Street

While gentle promenades were the pastimes of many portside visitors, the harbour hosted a range of alternative activities. Harbour Street was once the focus for life by the docks: chaotic, bustling, where the ruffed and roughs crossed business and social paths amidst the port's mêlée. Today it remains a busy conduit for cross-town traffic, with some vestiges of the mid-nineteenth-century streetscape, as highlighted by Charles Rampini in his *Letters from Jamaica*: "Broken walls, charred beams, crumbling ruins meet one in all directions. Harbour Street, the main thoroughfare, is unpaved; and gutters to carry off the heavy rains which fall at certain seasons of the year are unknown."

Daytime events were no less frenetic, if less lurid and without such musical accompaniment. Rampini continues his description of portside Kingston, slightly bamboozled by the hectic flurry of new sights and sounds one early morning in Harbour Street:

Clerks and shopmen were hurrying to their respective offices and stores, some on foot, some in 'buses, and not a few in buggies. Handsome equipages were dashing past: this, with a merchant on his way to his counting-house; that, with a party of ladies going shopping before the heat became intense. Higglers of all descriptions were vigorously plying their trade. Coolies with baskets of vegetables on their heads; girls with cedar-boxes full of sugar cakes of every kind; boys with bundles of walking-sticks; vendors of tripe and "chickling"; men with trays of kingfish. At the corners of the streets, with little boxes by their sides, women were selling pins and tapes and braids. There stood one with a basket of parched maize on her head; here another tempted you with a heap of rosy apples which the ice-ship had just bought down that morning from the Newcastle hills; whilst another exposed some magnificent artichokes, which had also been grown among the mountains. Each had his or her spécialité.

In more recent times, Orlando Patterson projects the feeling of the neighbourhood at night, as a woman walks alone to her destination:

The night was dark and it threatened to rain. She hurried by the railway station, passed the warehouses, taking in the familiar smell of stored food, coffee and peanuts, sugar, rum and cod-fish, pimento and rice, all mixed up with the musty board dungeons, the raw, sordid smell of the murky sea and the stink disinfectant powder that the Chinamen used to clean out their wholesale groceries. Another ten minutes and she had passed the little Chinatown with the narrow alleys behind the shops, the mess of expensive-looking garbage in front of them and every now and the contrasting smell of pop-cheow. Cautiously now, she turned off Harbour Street so as to avoid the water-police station, made a semicircle among the nasty little back lanes where the only signs of life were the mangy mongrels with their heads buried in the garbage-boxes and every now and then the eerie, bellowing sound of an old condensed-milk can falling and rolling to the gutter which had the effect only of emphasizing the dark, musty, mean silence, and was finally back on Harbour Street.

Fermor disdainfully described the "smouldering" street during a similar era, in which "a dejected and unconvincing brothel-quarter damply blossoms. Here, on the balconies of bars and ramshackle hotels with jaunty names, strapping West Indian girls diffidently conjure the passers-by with their artless blandishments: a dumb crambo of soft whistles and inexpert winks."

Wallace Collins, on the other hand, was more enthusiastic about Harbour Street's energies during the 1920s. In *Jamaica Migrant* (1965), he engagingly recounts "the experience of his life" while doubling as a drummer for his father's band, "The Collins Brothers and Their Swinging Aces", at a once celebrated hotspot:

The Dirty Dick was a large cobwebby old bar where business men, teachers, Babylons, as the cops were called, and musicians gathered; while copious bearded men, swathed in coloured sashes of red, black and gold, stared disdainfully from outside the swing doors... The visiting sailors literally rolled through the doors in droves and groups and the place started to buzz with excitement. Bottles began to pop open, glasses clinked against each other. The fat barmaid greeted her foreign acquaintances endlessly, while the helpers, comically made up, gave shrill laughs and disappeared beyond drawn curtains for a few minutes, then breezed in again with triumphant smiles. The whores were darting from one sailor to another, making up to them, while we played our hearts out and no one listened or noticed us, at least not until the liquor soaked in.

The rough and always ready side of Harbour Street has been largely pushed into retirement, or more secluded venues and bars. Mona Macmillan happily, if somewhat naïvely, reported in 1957, "Whatever they may once have been, Harbour Street and the lanes about the Myrtle Bank have been reduced to outward respectability by a zealous police force, and a fine Seaman's Club helps to protect sailors from the consequences of cheap rum." Only a year later, and with his nib perhaps closer to the ink, Ian Fleming provided contrasting counsel: "I would advise you to give a miss to the stews of Kingston although they would provide you with every known amorous constellation and permutation. Kingston is a tough town—tough and dirty—despite all the exhortations of the *The Daily Gleaner* (my favourite newspaper above all others in the world) and the exertions of the quite admirable Jamaica police force."

Harbour life, however, has changed dramatically since Rampini's nineteenth-century account and the appraisals of fifty years ago. During the 1960s and 1970s, the hotels, bars, market and piers of the portside were smothered under the concrete of urban renewal. The Urban Development Corporation redesigned and rebuilt the waterfront as a commercial and financial showpiece. Contemporary blueprints, consisting mostly of concrete and steel, replaced ginnels, jalousies and gingerbread latticework. Banks, an international conference centre, the ubiquitous shopping mall and a fresh hotel, since converted to offices, now adorn the new Ocean Boulevard, a breezy grass and palm tree-lined strip, primed for loafing, liming and biding time. Much to the chagrin of the planners, Kingston Mall and the striking modernist monoliths by its side now seem similarly disengaged from the rest of the city, uptown and down.

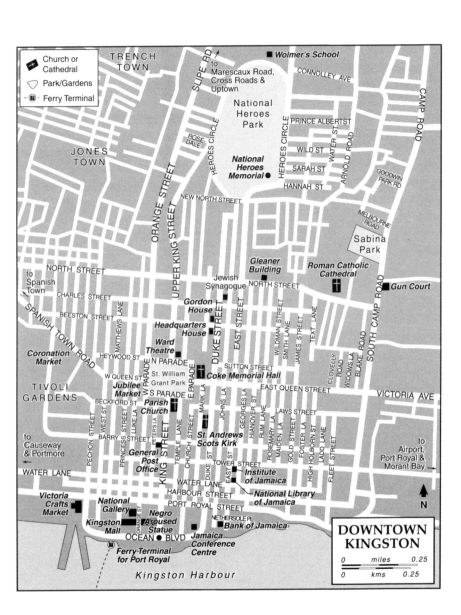

DOWNTOWN KINGSTON

CHAPTER TWO

Downtown

"Already the fascination of city life had seized her, and from that hour henceforward, no matter what hardships she might have to face in Kingston, that city was the place above all others in Jamaica that would most appeal to her."

Herbert de Lisser, *Jane's Career: A Story of Jamaica* (1913)

"It would be difficult to imagine a place whose general aspect depresses one so much as Kingston."

Charles Rampini, *Letters from Jamaica: The Land of Streams and Woods* (1873)

Kingston's clearest markers—literary and literal—are those of uptown and downtown. Socially and economically etched on the urban landscape, the different lifestyles of those who live south of Half Way Tree and those who live above, their residences fanning out through the foothills of the Blue Mountains, sharply divide the city into two. Pockets of poverty are found uptown, and a few, very few, affluent households may be found downtown, but by and large the city lives apart from itself.

The waterfront developments aimed to rejuvenate a flagging port area, but have been thwarted by the uptown moves of wealthier inhabitants, pulled by the social and business boom of New Kingston and pushed by the suicidal politics of turf war during the 1970s. The very poor majority, the sufferers of West and East Kingston, were left to scrap and scratch out a living in an urban economy nearing free-fall. During the final decades of the twentieth century, Kingstonians continued to live different lives in two seemingly separate cities, nominally banded together as Jamaicans. Writers and poets have delved deep into this apparent social and spatial partition, exposing the capital's energies, attractions, and simmering tensions.

The following pages move on from the former dockside to explore the surrounding downtown neighbourhoods; a source of wealth during the eighteenth century and a focus of fear for much of the twentieth. Two destructive earthquakes in 1692 and 1907 forced physical tremors through the ever-changing social and architectural fabric of Kingston. The first gave birth to the city itself, as Port Royal was swept away. The latter led to the widespread rebuilding of the commercial area and older parts of town, yet for all its turbulent transitions, the downtown area covers an intriguing labyrinth of corrugated-iron walled yards, crumbling ornate mansions and resplendent Victorian edifices.

Two Jamaicas
The city's beginnings were far from salubrious, and as much induced by the ill fortune of Port Royal as by opportunities of location. Colin Clarke's history of Kingston recounts the decision of the Council of Jamaica to investigate suitable sites on the Liguanea Plain as a replacement for Port Royal: "Having rejected Delacree Pen, where the ferry connecting Port Royal to the Liguanea Plain and Half Way Tree deposited passengers in a marshy, unhealthy tract, they settled for a hog crawl farther to the east which had access to the deep water of Kingston Harbour." The early days of the new settlement were fraught with civil rivalry. Firstly with Port Royal, whose remaining residents ably battled to rebuild the town until a fire in 1703 confirmed Kingston's primacy. Secondly with Spanish Town, whose citizens resolutely campaigned for its status to remain as the seat of colonial government, until finally relinquishing the title to the burgeoning trade centre of Kingston in 1872. The latter had been designated as the capital in 1755, only for Spanish Town politicos to reclaim the appointment in 1758. The expanding new town, however, proved an irrefutable lure for the Jamaican legislature.

During the seventeenth century Kingston's population increased six-fold. The growth of the town, fuelled by rural migration and a steady birth rate, was quite phenomenal. Although the motor of the colony's economy was plantation-based, emphasis on trade and the eventual demise of a rural-centred slave society meant that urban matters were of prime concern. The population doubled between 1920 and 1940, and again between 1960 and 1990. Today a third of the island's population of around two and a half million people live in the Kingston Metropolitan Area, which consists of the old parish of Kingston and much of St. Andrew parish.

Kingston's appearance has seldom inspired the fairest of literary visions or courted the most eloquent of penned praise. Anthony Trollope was sure that he would not live there if forced to choose.

> *Were it arranged by Fate that my future residence should be in Jamaica, I should certainly prefer the life of a country mouse. The town mice, in my mind, have but a bad time of it. Of all the towns that I ever saw, Kingston is perhaps, on the whole, the least alluring, and is the more absolutely without any point of attraction for the stranger than any other.*

Philip Curtin, writing one hundred years later, described the mid-nineteenth-century settlement as "a dirty, hot, bedraggled tropical town set at the foot of a long sloping plain against the backdrop of the Blue Mountains. It was the most important town in the British West Indies, but not in appearance." James Anthony Froude also lamented the town's limited attractions, placed squarely in comparison with alleged English virtues: "But there is nothing grand about the buildings, nothing even handsome, nothing even specially characteristic of England or the English mind. They were once perhaps business-like, and business having slackened they are now dingy. Shops, houses, wharves, want brightness and colour."

Beyond physical attributes, the enduring legacies in Kingston during the twentieth century were often those of British design, shaping the social and cultural mores of many inhabitants. Curtin was the first describe "two Jamaicas", as apt for Kingston as for the country at large, namely the separation between the European and African aspects of life in Jamaica. He placed much emphasis on the "Old Colonial System" with Kingston as the pivot for Jamaican high society, mopping up fashions fed through from London:

> *Just as the system as a whole centred on the Imperial trading centre in London, the life of the island centred on the island trading centre at*

Kingston. And by virtue of its economic supremacy Kingston was also the social, intellectual, and cultural centre of the colony. As the chief port, it was the window on the outside world—a world where most of the Jamaican ruling class would rather have found themselves.

Patrick Leigh Fermor's description of a social club in 1950s Kingston emphasizes the melancholic mentality of the colonial old guard:

The members on the verandah were all English, but most of them, it appeared from the conversation, had alighted in this little backwater after half a lifetime in India. Elderly ex-soldiers and civil servants meditatively contemplated the golf links over their whiskies and sodas, exchanging stories of Rawalpindi, Simla and Darjeeling and half a dozen outposts of empire that had cruelly pre-deceased them. They were joined in their reminiscences of khitmagars and khansamahs and the Saturday Club by an elderly mensahib, sadly dethroned and transplanted. The verandah was heavy with nostalgia. It was all rather moving and sad.

Victor Stafford Reid, author of *New Day* (1949), which recounts a nineteenth-century rebellion against British rule and heralds an emerging Jamaican identity, laments the cultural straitjacket that restricted new movements: "We danced the European quadrilles under the tropical sun, sang the European madrigals beneath the mango trees, sat at European afternoon teas belted and brass-buttoned in our woollen suits in the flaring heat."

The glance back to Europe or sense of colonial nostalgia has raised much literary ire. V. S. Naipaul criticized what he saw as the Caribbean's cultural dependence in characteristically dismissive tones: "Living in a borrowed culture, the West Indian, more than most, needs writers to tell him [sic] who he is and where he stands." Rachel Manley writes more subtly of the colonial legacy in her poem, "First World (for my father)":

Like memory
it kept us real, and it kept us back.

Remembrances can shape the present without obscuring the future. A walk through downtown Kingston cannot fail to evoke memories of the city's past, and impressions of its troubled present. Benjamin Zephaniah foretells a more ominous path for those not wary of history's injustices in "A Modern Slave Song":

Remember where I come from, cause I do.
I won't feget.
Remember yu got me, cause I'll get yu.
I'll mek yu sweat.

Colonial Remnants

Kenneth Pringle, writing thirty years before Jamaica gained independence, stirred up both past and present when he cuttingly exclaimed, "Jamaica is that pride of the orphanage, a Crown Colony." The ghosts of colonists past roam not only in the downtown buildings and streets, but haunt the descriptions of many writers' accounts of contemporary Jamaican life.

Jamaican patois or *patwa*, famously celebrated in the poems of Louise Bennett and the prose of Carolyn Cooper, is described by Anthony Winkler as "rich in idioms and aphorisms that crisply sum up social situations with an elegant economy, and its hybrid vocabulary of Africanisms and English is spoken with an inflection that invariably strikes the foreign ear as sing-song." Wryly, but pointedly, he comments on the constraints of formal English in a country where the vast majority speak Jamaica talk:

When Jamaica was under English rule, the colonial Englishman was as every bit a caricature of what bad Hollywood movies now imagine the nineteenth century Empire-bound Englishman to be, and his speech reflected eccentric mannerisms he had picked up on the playing fields of public schools. He spoke with a precise and rigid emphasis on enuncia-tion which included the rat-a-tat rattling of his "r's" on the tip of his tongue and the gusty aspiration of all initial "h's," said pardon inces-santly, observed picky and knee-jerk rules based on Victorian syntax, and sprinkled his words with colloquialisms that we now see as stuffy. Because he was our colonial master, the notion spread throughout

Jamaica that his English was the authentic and superior one, and that any departure from this accent, his syntactical patterns, his vocabulary, even his low-keyed and muted gestures, were barbarisms, corruptions, or simply uncouth.

British men and women, brought their linguistic and cultural predilections as accompanying baggage for what was primarily an economic mission. To make money; to make it fast and to retire across the Atlantic, leaving a manager to oversee properties and to forward the revenue. Jamaican plantations existed, by and large, to provide the upkeep for estates in the British Isles. Not all colonists were planters, and not all monies were easily transferred to overseas coffers. Many of the townsfolk and country squires built up debts at home in order to pick immediate profits from their colonial holdings or businesses. Barbadian Frank Collymore's poem "Triptych" runs deep into the make-up of Jamaica's social mix:

I see these ancestors of ours:
The merchants, the adventurers, the youngest sons of squires,
Leaving the city and shires and the seaports,
Eager to establish a temporary home and make a fortune
In the new lands beyond the West, pawning perhaps
The old familiar acres of the assured competence;
Sturdy, realist, eager to wring wealth from these Barbadoes
And to build trade, colonize, pay homage to their King,
And worship according to the doctrines of the Church and England.

Outside the elite, he also pictures working-class whites who migrated freely as indentured labourers or servants, and the slaves, twelve million of whom were transported across the Atlantic to the Americas:

I see them, these ancestors of ours;
Children of the tribe, ignorant of their doom, innocent
As cattle, bartered for, captured, beaten, penned,
Cattle of the slave-ship, less than cattle;
Sold in the market-place, yoked to servitude;
Cattle, bruised and broken, but strong enough to plough and breed.

While the majority of slaves worked on the rural plantations, many worked in Kingston as labourers or within the homes of the wealthy. A broad three-fold division was apparent on the streets of Kingston, in the work places and at the hotel bars, the legacy of which has been well charted by social commentators. Before emancipation in the 1830s, Jamaican society was legally divided between the citizens, freemen and freewomen, and the slaves. The middle group were the former slaves who had been granted or bought their liberty or were born from sexual relations between the owners and enslaved women. In downtown Kingston, the freed slaves lived in yards on Duke, Barry, East and Rosemary Streets. Despite their freedom from slavery, lives were harsh and remote from the hierarchical status of upper-class whites. In 1808, James Stewart commented that "vile hovels and sheds are inhabited by free people of colour who keep petty huckster's shops and by low white people who vend liquors and give rise to many disorderly and indecent scenes."

At the start of the nineteenth century, Kingston's population of 33,000 consisted of 10,000 "whites", 5,000 free "coloureds" and "blacks" and 18,000 slaves. With the demise of slavery, the legal strata of citizens, freemen and slaves slipped across to the socially recognized, and equally severe, colour hierarchy of white, coloured and black. While these categories had no formal or legal standing, such labelling opened and closed cultural worlds, allowing and denying access to livelihoods and lifestyles.

Downtown Worlds
Social separations transferred themselves readily to Kingston's landscape as the capital developed through the centuries. Today, uptown New Kingston lies worlds, but only miles, away from downtown. Up until the middle of the last century such a division was perhaps less evident, although during the nineteenth century, the wealthy classes increasingly lived on the Liguanea Plain north of the harbour area, their townhouses gathering around the governor's residence. At that time, the professions were still concentrated on King Street, Laws Street and Duke Street, with business offices also located amid the hubbub of Harbour Street.

The torpid crawl of contemporary Kingston's "rush-hour" traffic is notorious, as cars and buses jostle for road space in a slow-motion parody of the real thing. One hundred and fifty years ago, the commuters were also out in force. Anthony Trollope records their privileged movements, employing a strikingly bizarre comparison with a small town in England.

> *Indeed, the residents in the town, and in the neighbourhood of the town, never walk. Men, even young men, whose homes are some mile or half-mile distant from their offices, ride or drive to their work as systematically as a man who lives at Watford takes the railway.*

Trollope observed the to-ing and fro-ing of the affluent classes with access to horse and carriage (later transformed into Landcruiser and Mercedes). The pavements and streets of central downtown nowadays buzz with traders, spectators, shoppers and occasional tourists. Andrew Salkey sauntered through and savoured the contemporary scene of a Saturday downtown, surrounded by the echoes of the past and slices of the present:

> *I walked with my back to the whistling*
> *of the Harbour breezes;*
> *I stepped hard on history*
> *like a cool customer*
> *crunching down*
> *on dry calabash skins,*
> *and then I spun around*
> *and faced Victoria Pier.*
> *...*
> *I picked up scraps of conversations,*
> *customary monologues,*
> *calculated confessions,*
> *light lip-stick laughter,*
> *giggles about last night's party,*
> *happenings in a new American historical novel,*
> *incidents from the latest middle-class adulteries,*
> *more giggles, giggles of incidents*
> *that never occurred, wicked suspicions,*

evil overstatements, downright lies,
slanderous personal histories
and a gossip of assorted
Kong's Grocery gossip.

Amid the chatter and sights, physically close but socially distanced, exist those largely left behind by society. Olive Senior concisely catches those moments of separation and shock when unluckier lives are revealed during pedestrian encounters: "On King Street watching the legless/beggar on wheels/I counted my fortunes."

King Street

Leading up from the new harbour front, King Street is a medley of city life, a straight line through the government buildings, fast food stores, occasional offices and retail ventures. Covered in peeling paint-work, the colonnades, iron lattices and ornate decorations are often hidden by the glare of the sun, or conversely tucked into the shadows of the piazzas and shaded verandahs that cover the sidewalks. Much of downtown was rebuilt after the earthquake in 1907, most notably the elegantly frazzled Post Office, Treasury and Law Courts between Water Lane and Barry Street, remnants of a once grandiose design. Kenneth Pringle describes the street during the 1930s:

> *The centre of Lower Kingston is King Street, with its Government Build-*
> *ings of a cellular, efficient, uninteresting design in white concrete, and*
> *its big stores owned largely by Syrians (the dry goods stores) and the*
> *Chinese (who specialise in groceries)… West of King Street lies China-*
> *town, with its peaka-peow gambling dens and its rum-shops; and north-*
> *west the sheer slum of Smith Village, where outside their tumbledown*
> *cabins, often hardly more than old planks and sheets laid together, ladies*
> *in dirty dresses may usually be seen plucking poultry… Out of these*
> *slums emerge the energetic dock-workers and those crowds of coco-nut-*
> *sellers, orange-sellers, candy-sellers, toy-sellers, and agents of every descrip-*
> *tion whose street cries and vivacity give Kingston most of its life.*

The dockers have disappeared, as has much of Chinatown, but the mix of drabness and pomp still makes King Street the principal

thoroughfare downtown, connecting the central square, the Parade, to the sea.

The Parade

More correctly called Sir William Grant Park after a renowned political activist, this open space is still referred to as the Parade, central to the grid designed by John Goffe at the start of the eighteenth century, when the town was bounded by Harbour, Orange, North and Church Streets. A statue of Queen Victoria, which allegedly turned about to face directly away from the sea during the earthquake of 1907, inspired the square's name before the regal label was replaced by one more politically in tune with the times.

The Parade was planned for leisure, military manoeuvres and public executions—an eclectic combination of activities matched by today's diverse pursuits of selling, sleeping, chatting, commuting and begging. Former barracks to the north of the square quartered soldiers who regularly marched on the square, which is now tree-lined and decorated with statues and a seldom-flowing fountain. Waiting bus passengers and street traders or higglers form the current rank and file of the square's perimeter. Louise Bennett's "South Parade Peddler" catches the itinerant sales pitch of the higglers, perennially aware of attracting police attention:

One police man dah come, but me
Dah try get one more sale.
Shoelace! Tootpaste! Buy quick, no sah!
Yuh waan me go to jail?
Ef dah police ketch we, lize,
We peddler career done.
Pick up yuh foot eena yuh han.
Hair pin! Curler! Run!

Writers have consistently promoted the Parade's aesthetic merits. In 1774, Edward Long could write:

The parade is a large, handsome square; on the North-West side of it are barracks of bricks for the troops quartered here; a very well-designed and convenient lodgement for the two hundred men and their officers. The front, which contains apartments for the officers, makes a good appearance. The soldiers' barracks stands detached behind, in a square court walled round; in which are proper offices; and at one angle a powder magazine belonging to the town. On the South side of the parade is the church; a large, elegant building of four aisles, which has a fine organ, a tower and spire, with a large clock. The tower is well-constructed, and a very great ornament to the town.

Over a century later, Herbert de Lisser highlighted the Parade's attractions in a drab and dusty urban landscape, while adding disparaging comments about some of the people who could be found enjoying its benefits:

The appearance of Kingston more or less suggested poverty. The sun played havoc with the paint upon the houses, and the dust assisted the sun in its work of destruction. With one or two exceptions, every street was covered in an inch-deep carpet of dust, and when there was wind the dust swept along the whole length of the street like a mass of vapour, but infinitely more distressing to the eyes and lungs. There were paved sidewalks in the city's business area; elsewhere the sidewalks were unpaved, and a short hardy grass grew upon some of them. In the centre of Kingston, an oasis in the desert of brick and wood, was a park with plenty of shade trees and a large number of benches. This park was the rendezvous of loafers mainly, who, hour after hour, discussed such matters as the composition of the local legislature, the probable income of the King, the relative merits of the Catholic and Protestant faiths, and the difficulty experienced by men of genius (such as themselves) in getting remunerative work, by which they probably meant large salaries for doing nothing.

If downtown has a central heart, then it beats somewhere about the Parade. In the vicinity and the square itself, several stone busts stare out onto the surrounding city life. Where guns guarded the former fortress first built on the site in 1694, an array of statues now watch over bougainvillaea and park life. Queen Victoria's centrepiece figure has been ousted by Sir Alexander Bustamante, the fiery first prime minister of independent Jamaica. His lifelong rival and cousin, Norman Manley, stands proud with a leading abolitionist, Edward Johnson. Only one earlier statue survived the ravages of the 1907 earthquake, that of Sir Charles Metcalfe, who governed the island between 1839 and 1842. The secret of survival lay in his bulk, or more precisely in the weighty pedestal that was designed to secure the monument of Admiral Rodney during its temporary relocation from Spanish Town in 1873. Thanks to this plinth, the elderly governor remains staring resolutely up King Street. Seldom visited by affluent residents of the city, whose shopping, business and bureaucratic needs are largely dealt with uptown, the surrounding streets are jam-packed with the everyday bustle of Kingstonians, and a diversity of buildings that chart the city's history.

Duke Street

Stepping east of the Parade, Duke Street retains its traditional link with the legal profession. The seat of Jamaican legislature can be found at Gordon House, on the corner of Beeston Street. A nondescript brick and concrete building erected by 1960, it was named after the inspirational National Hero, George William Gordon, who steadfastly challenged the colonial government and was hanged for his part in the Morant Bay Rebellion of 1865. The House of Representatives and Senate share the same space, but were formerly berthed in the visually and historically more exciting Headquarters House, one block down the road at 79 Duke Street. This house was built by Thomas Hibbert as the outcome of an infamous wager between four Assembly members in 1755, who challenged each other to create the most luxurious house in town, and, the winner vainly hoped, to provide a suitable home for the woman they all wished to wed. Only Hibbert's home still exists, and none of the Assemblymen came close to their intended goal of marriage. Now housing the Jamaican National Trust, Hibbert's folly now stands as a beguiling glimpse of Kingston's architectural past.

Duke Street is one of the few downtown thoroughfares not to have been completely deserted for uptown offices. Brian Meeks, writing during the strife-torn 1970s when Cold War conflict rubbed icy shoulders with Jamaican partisan politics, composed a few lines for Duke Street's office dwellers:

down Duke St.'s
closed bound-
aries crew cut
accountant
ticks off a
number/closes
the doors
on a stars and
stripes file.

Any Kingstonian street stroll will reveal the extremities of a city with more than its share of social differences. The well-heeled professional classes populate, during office hours, the same spaces as the destitute. Outside the Duke Street insurance office in which Anthony Winkler used to work, a beggar regularly greeted him: "Because of hideous bone deformities, he could neither sit nor stand upright, but was perpetually twisted with his head drooped between his knees and his mouth dripping inches off the ground. When I walked past he would hoist a wordless supplicating hand above the rubble of flesh and bone like a snake head sniffing for fresh meat." Thirteen years later, like many downtown workers, he had moved to an uptown location, perched on a wheeled platform by a shopping mall.

Institute of Jamaica

One block across, East Street houses the headquarters of the Institute of Jamaica. The Institute was established in 1879 by the former governor, Sir Anthony Musgrave, to encourage literature, science and the arts following the deliberate strategy of separating slaves, and later the working classes, from labour-distracting education. It is something of a cultural multiplex, with a series of divisions catering for the full range of cultural activities and influences. Towards the sea front on Ocean Boulevard, the National Gallery and the African-Caribbean Institute of Jamaica, associated with the unique Memory Bank of oral histories, are precious satellites of the central location. East Street houses the reading rooms of the National Library of Jamaica, centres for learning, and the Natural History museum. The latter, like many of its cousins from earlier days, clings on to displays of dusty rocks and stuffed corpses, and a few bored or morbid visitors. Clearly an aficionado of taxidermy, Patrick Leigh Fermor paid a visit during the 1940s and was entranced by all aspects of the venerable institution: "I found it hard to stay away from the Institute of Jamaica. It possesses the best library in the West Indies, far better, even, than that of the priests of St. Louis de Gonzague in Haiti... Stuffed animals and birds and cases of botanical geological specimens fill another part of the building, and the walls of the basement are covered with portraits of island dignitaries."

The library stands out for the depth of its collection, with books dating back to sixteenth century and copies of the main newspaper, *The Daily Gleaner*, from 1834. It attracts a wonderful range of clients, from professional researchers, to passionate local historians, school pupils and print-addicted browsers.

Faith in the City

Churches, chapels and shrines feature large in Kingston's landscape, as they do island-wide. The abundance of faith-based places provides for a broad spectrum of beliefs, which Jamaica's turbulent history has frequently put to the test. Travellers often remark on the population's piety and the popularity of Sunday services. Zenga Longmore, visiting from England, was taken to church by her Jamaican relatives:

> *Everyone goes to church on Sunday, and the ones who don't are bowed down with guilt and excuses. Only the 'quashie dem' don't go ('quashie' being the hoi polloi, the lumpen, and 'dem' being the plural; plurals and tenses are few and far between in Jamaicanese).*
>
> *The service to which Delson's family took me was packed to the hilt. There were no seats available, and most of the congregation stood outside in the street, white dresses and feathered hats glistening in the sunshine...*
>
> *A woman preacher shrieked and screamed about the many guises of Satan. Amens rent the air.*

The various faiths still hold much sway; evangelical churches, in particular, continue to make a visible and audible impact on the Sunday scene, and social censorship remains a strong focus of gossip. The role of community priests may have waned, but de Lisser's tale of a young woman who leaves the country to work in the capital rings true for many. In *Jane's Career*, he recounts the words of wisdom offered by Daddy Buckram, the chief elder in the village, to the novel's namesake:

> *"Jane," he continued impressively after a pause, "Kingston is a very big an' wicked city, an' a young girl like you, who the Lord has blessed wid a good figure an' a face, must be careful not to keep bad company. Satan goeth about like a roaring lion in Kingston, seeking who he may devour."*

If Satan lurks among the alleys of downtown Kingston, the plethora of Christian places of worship alone might do much to divert devilish ways. Daddy Buckram strongly advised the young Jane to follow a Christian path, which for many people over several centuries began at the Kingston Parish Church, dominating the southern side of the Parade and standing opposite the ornate and similarly aged Ward Theatre. While actors and audiences today delight in the theatre's popular bawdy "roots" plays, the congregation of the parish church adheres to more formal performances of hymn and prayer.

The tranquil interior of the church reveals its remarkable history through plinths, plaques and tombstones. Rich merchants, high-ranking civil and military agents of the colonial regime line the chancel. Three mural monuments by John Bacon, a leading sculptor of the Royal Academy, were commissioned by the families of John Wolmer, a most influential goldsmith and municipal patron during the eighteenth century, Mr. and Mrs. Malcolm Laing, and Mrs. Ann Neufville.

The original church was largely destroyed during the 1907 earthquake, but its location and the building itself retain the atmosphere of a former era. Anthony Trollope gives a glimpse of the former edifice during the 1850s. Although not to his liking, it is easy to imagine the dull mix of colonial and clerical influences during that period.

Very little excitement is to be found in the Church-of-England Kingston parish church. The church itself, with its rickety pews, and creaking doors, and wretched seats made purposely so as to render genuflexion impossible, and the sleepy, droning, somnolent service are exactly what was so common in England twenty years since; but which are common no longer, thanks to certain much-abused clerical gentlemen.

The most notable grave harks back to seafaring days at the turn of the seventeenth century. Buried beneath an imposing black marble tombstone is Admiral John Benbow, who died from his wounds in 1702 after heroically harrying the French fleet of Admiral du Casse. Severely outgunned, Benbow outmanoeuvred the legendary French admiral, despite a gun-shattered leg and the ignoble desertion of four of his captains who wished not to take on such a battle.

Of more recent appearance, but equally devastated by the 1907 earthquake and subsequent fire, the Coke Memorial Hall on the eastern side of the Parade has provided one of the many opposition

voices to the established Anglican Church over the last two centuries. Rebuilt in its original style, the crenellations and ornate, red-brick façade contrast beautifully with the whitewashed tower and structure of the neighbouring parish church. The Hall was built in 1840 and was named after Dr. Thomas Coke, the founder of Methodist missions in the West Indies. Coke travelled throughout the region and many chapels record his visits. The Methodist Church directly challenged many of the colony's established practices, including slavery, which led to its temporary closure by the Jamaican Assembly not long after meetings began.

A host of churches and faiths provide a litany of prayers and spiritual paths for Kingstonians. The Anglican, Roman Catholic, Methodist, Presbyterian, Baptist and Moravian movements established during colonial times have been supplemented by a large number of more recent evangelical denominations and vie with popular beliefs that evolved during slavery. The Tabernacle Baptist Church, Seventh-Day Adventists, Church of God, Church of the Brethren, Salvation Army, Christian Scientists, Jehovah's Witnesses, Society of Friends, Mission of God, Bible Students, Church of Deliverance, Church of Latter Day Saints… just a few of the venues whose services meet spiritual needs about town. Sunday morning sidewalks are dotted with faithful attendants, Bibled and en route to their chosen church. Patrick Leigh Fermor remarked on the range of rituals on offer during the 1950s.

Places of worship abound. The Church of England, the Catholics and the Jews represent the main religious currents, but a hundred Protestant sects flourish in the back streets of the capital, developing, from orthodox Anglicanism, through the Methodist Connection, the Quakers, the Seventh Day Adventists, the Good Tidings and the Salvation Army into

the odder revivalist cults of the Shakers and the Holy Rollers and the
queer excesses of the Pocomaniacs.

African Echoes

Zion Revival and Pocomania are just two of the syncretic religious beliefs to have developed from the tortuous crossover of slavery and colonialism, fusing Christian fundamentals with African-origin deities. The former emphasizes reading and interpretation of the scriptures, while the latter is more focused on ritual dancing, healing and collective possession by the spirits. Many authors have found inspiration here, both negative and positive, visual and spiritual, for their writings on Kingston. Philip Sherlock's poem "Pocomania" drums up the movement, passion and conviction of followers, grouped in dance and spiritual tenure:

Black of night and white of gown
White of altar black of trees
'Swing de circle wide again
Fall and cry me sister now
Let de spirit come again
Fling away de flesh an' bone
Let de Spirit have a home.'
Grunting low and in the dark
White of gown and circling dance
Gone to-day and all control
Here the dead are in control
Power of the past returns
Africa among the trees
Asia with her mysteries.

Patrick Leigh Fermor, as might be guessed from his concern for "queer excesses", displays limited sympathy during his visit to a revival meeting in Trench Town. He recounts how faith gripped a congregation, entranced by the leading priest, or Shepherd:

I counted thirty-four at one moment, all prostrate. Their flailing feet
raised a cloud of dust. The barking and howling had sunk to a chorus

of moans and gasps and sobs as the vessels of possession squirmed and
writhed, or, with arms outstretched, rolled over and over. The throes of
incarnation were reminiscent of a net-load of fish which has just been
hauled out of the water and emptied on the sea-shore. The Shepherd
remained upright in this squirming tangle of humanity, leaping and
whirling and clanging his bell and summoning, in stentorian apostro-
phe, the last of the lingering celestial from the clouds.

Orlando Patterson's detailed description of a Revivalist meeting in
his novel *The Children of Sisyphus* (1964) catches more of the faith's
location and essence, commenting on its underpinning resistance to
white colonialism:

In the space between the cluster of little huts and the church was a tall
white pole with painted black rings at intervals of about a yard from each
other. Tied to the top of the pole was a red flag at one of which was a black
cross patched on upside-down with some other material and at the top
end was painted in white 'REVIVAL ZION BAPTIST OF GOD',
which was the name of the church. Immediately below the flag was a
wooden sign on which was scrawled in an irregular mixture of common
and capital letters, commas and full stops, 'THE WAGES OF SIN IS
DEATH'. Between the 'S' and the 'I' of the word 'SIN', however, another
hand had scrawled in black paint the letter 'K' and, as Dinah was to
learn later, this was the source of profound mystery among the church
members.

Dinah, the protagonist in this forceful tale of downtown Kingston,
then steps forward confidently on her new journey into the ethereal
space of the church.

She went inside. The scent of their bodies and clothes swept upon her.
Perfumes, cananga water, perspiration, leaves and flowers and herbs all
combined to give a strange, exotic, ambivalent stench. It was sickening,
it was sweet, it was nauseating. But in this very nausea, in the effect of
total revulsion it had on her, there was a syrupy, molasses-like nostalgia.
The soft beating of the drums, the hum of their voices, the herbs, the

stench, swirled in the depths of her. Senses overwhelmed, palate cloyed,
in an instant she was purged.
  … And the labouring began. The tickle trickled to the brown stream.
The river came down. Came gushing down. Down the veins of their
flesh that swelled with heat. It was such an agony. Such a sweet, gurgling,
rushing agony. It twisted the flesh that wrapped their necks. It wrenched
their shoulders, every muscle writhed. Torment. The river knows no
bank. Everything goes down before it. Trees, houses, cows and rich man's
castles, donkeys and American motor cars. It was Gabriel, mighty rhap-
sodic Gabriel. She held on to her sister. For joy, for pain. But Gabriel
would not let go and she fell to the ground in ecstasy.

Forms of spiritualism have been the backbone of popular Jamaican religion for centuries. Myal and kumina are two well-practised faiths that sprung up from the fusion of popular beliefs involving European Christendom and devotion to the spiritual worlds of enslaved African labourers on the colonial plantations. At these ceremonies, drums beat biting rhythms, while a priestess might sprinkle rum, offer tobacco or ganja to the spirits and leads members into a glimpse of the spirit realm, an earthly cosmos in which people and spirits interact and influence one another. Believers' human frames may become enveloped and ridden by the spirits of other people, animals or deities. Erna Brodber's novel *Myal* (1999) describes this public transcendence in sensitive, and at times subtly humorous, ways: "Anyone who had never seen Miss Agatha Paisley in the spirit before would think it a coconut tree in a private hurricane that was coming down the road."

Forms of worship have developed through the centuries, from illicit gatherings in the barracks of the slave-labour plantations, often disguised by a thin veil of more "acceptable" Christian adoration in the eyes of the European planters, to regular meetings amidst the din of community life in the modern city's yards. H. J. Buchner, who attended a ceremony as an invited observer during the nineteenth century, described a myal gathering in full flow:

As soon as darkness set in, they assembled in crowds in open pastures,
frequently under large cotton trees, which they worshipped, and counted
holy; after sacrificing some fowls, the leader began an extempore song, in

a wild strain, which was answered in chorus; the dance followed, grew wilder and wilder, until they were in a state of excitement bordering on madness.

Obeah, akin in several respects to Haitian vodu or Cuban santería, incorporates a range of activities and beliefs and remains a potent force within Jamaican society. In her controversial monograph about the "search for Jamaican identity", written at the time of independence, Katrin Norris outlined the great cultural difference between the popular and elite classes. The former, she argued, relied heavily on popular spiritual frameworks, most notably in the regular counsel of the obeah sage: "The direct descendant of the African witch-doctor is the Jamaican obeah-man. Every village has at least one 'go-good' or 'four-eye' man or woman. He [sic] is consulted in times of ill-health, bad fortune in business, crossed love or other troubles, and is expected to help his client and bring retribution to his enemies." Spiritual journeys lead to both good and bad outcomes, sources of evil for some and of help for others. While Zenga Longmore appears sceptical, the influence of obeah remains potent today:

Obeah is the bane of Jamaican life. It creates a suspicious world where your neighbour is blamed for the smallest accident. Strangely enough, the only obeah people I met were good Obeah Fathers and Mothers. They were small, hunched people with eyes and intense mannerisms. Soon I came to the conclusion that hardly anyone actually put the obeah on, but many made and spent money taking it off.

The city's alleys and yards are places of religious intensity, where spirits and Kingstonians cross paths in a myriad of daily performances and experiences. While myal or obeah ceremonies are often private events, people passing through town may readily share the religious fervour and passion of public performances in the church and chapels A foretaste can be viewed every Thursday evening on CVMTV, during one of the many evangelical shows, when the ebullient Bishop L. M. Allison leaps into a dancing, shaking, and sweating Gospel hour. The Rev. Herro V. Blair provides the real thing at the Faith Cathedral Deliverance Centre on Waltham Park Road, communicating with the

Holy Ghost and the swaying, praying and faithfully paying congregation. The buzz of the devout translates through tongues, while newcomers are warmly welcomed and helpfully pushed to the front to meet the Reverend in full flow.

Kingston's many spiritual tastes are captured by the plethora of radio stations, providing chat shows, politics, top tunes, oldies and, of course, the gospel. Since 1993, the multi-denominational Love FM has fused the tastes of Roman Catholic, Pentecostal and Seventh Day Adventist groups to pound the public with 24-hour good news and advice. Beyond music and gospel, the radio station announces services, gives counselling, and offers details of church-run dental and health clinics, scholarships, thrift shops, shelters and musical events.

Missionaries, Scots and Jews
Old and new Kingston meet in this world of worship and social support. Roman Catholicism is headquartered on North Street, just beyond the Parade, in the modern, bright concrete Holy Trinity Cathedral. By its side, the Jesuit school of St. George's College has educated a series of successful alumni. One such former pupil who continues to have a dramatic influence on the downtown faithful is the charismatic Father Richard Ho Lung. Following years of service devoted to Kingston's sufferers as a Jesuit priest, he established the Missionaries of the Poor in 1980. Father Ho Lung, whose work and dedication has been described as a Caribbean version of Mother Teresa's in Calcutta, established centres on High Holborn, Laws, Hanover and Tower Streets in East Kingston to help the destitute, disabled and those suffering from HIV-related illnesses. As part of a spiritual and material mission to help the less fortunate, Father Ho Lung directs his self-tutored musical talents into fund-raising annual productions and tours. His compositions have gained an eclectic following, with one song hitting the heights of the Jamaican charts.

A few blocks west of the Missionaries' work, the Scots' Kirk on Mark Lane presents a different visual and aural experience. The St. Andrew Singers were for many years one of the most popular choirs in the city, but perhaps the most noted feature of this chapel is its octagonal Georgian brick structure and the grand gallery supported by Corinthian pillars. Funded by Scottish merchants on the island, the

Kirk was built between 1813 and 1819. Its Presbyterian roots are now part of the United Church of Jamaica and Grand Cayman, but it is a clear reminder of the strong Scottish influence on the island's colonial history. Edward Long wrote of this in the eighteenth century:

> *Jamaica, indeed, is greatly indebted to North-Britain, as very near one third of the inhabitants are either natives of that country, or descendants from those who were. Many have come… every year, less in quest of fame than of fortunes; and such is their industry and address, that few of them have been disappointed.*

Long, counting the prevalence of Campbells and Argyles, alleged in generally pejorative terms that their "sounder constitutions" meant that the "natives of Scotland and Ireland thrive here much better than the European English." Lady Maria Nugent also remarked on the number of industrious Scots in her journal. In 1801, she guessed optimistically that "almost all the agents, attorneys, merchants, and shopkeepers" were from that country. The trials and tribulations of Dr. Colin Maclarty and his attempts to gain a medical partnership in Kingston, which was seen as far more profitable and of higher status that the plantation practices during the 1780s, are recorded among others by Alan Karras in *Sojourners in the Sun* (1992). Karras mined a rich array of eighteenth-century letters and accounts to chart the tales of migrants, or sojourners as he terms them, who trained professionally as doctors or lawyers in Scotland then sought to earn their fortunes hastily in the American colonies. The personal papers of Alexander Johnston, for example, contain a wealth of details concerning his pursuit of riches in the 1760s, which took him from the wind-lashed north-east coast of Scotland, via Edinburgh, to spend the next twenty-four years as a physician in Jamaica.

Edward Long's *History of Jamaica* (1774) is one of the main contemporary texts to record the earlier days of life in Kingston. For this it is invaluable, but its breadth of knowledge also includes an alarming rhetoric of racism, perhaps not surprising in a book written at the height of slavery in Britain's most prosperous plantation colony. Long describes in detail the various faith groups and peoples of the city at the time, relating that "the Jews were very early settled in this island, attracted no less by the quantity of gold and silver brought into circulation here, than the mild disposition of the government towards them." He surmises, "I think they owe their good health, and longevity, as well as their fertility, to a very sparing use of strong liquors, their early rising, their indulgence on garlic and fish, Mosaic Laws, sugar, chocolate and fast." By the mid-nineteenth century, the Jewish community constituted a third of the white population and Jewish merchants were concentrated in the western part of Kingston, with later business interests moving east to lower King Street, East Queen Street, Hanover, Duke and East Streets.

The Sephardim, forming the Iberian Jewish community, built a synagogue on the corner of Princess Street and Water Lane in 1750, which Long described as "a handsome, spacious building". The Ashkenazi Jews of British and German descent, on the other hand, built their synagogue on Orange Street in 1789. The earthquake of 1907 destroyed these original buildings, but the impressive gleaming white synagogue that remains today is located on the corner of Duke and Charles Streets. It was built in 1912 and is one of only a few

synagogues in the Western Hemisphere to have a purpose-built sand floor to commemorate the forced secrecy of Judaism. The two separate Jewish congregations were joined in 1921 as the United Congregation of Israelites.

During his Kingston travels, Patrick Leigh Fermor was clearly astounded by the city's range of religious buildings and intrigued by their histories.

> *I could return to the bosky shelter of the South Camp Road by a round-about route past the Good Tidings Chapel, the Synagogue, the Chinese Club and the Catholic Cathedral, which is a reinforced-concrete version of St. Sophia. The Synagogue, though nothing much to look at, is alone of its species in the whole world, for the fire of 1882 destroyed both the Sephardic Synagogue of the Spaniards and Portuguese—who, impelled by the Inquisition, arrived here in the same fashion as in the other Caribees—and the English-German Synagogue of the Ashkenazim. The two communities, driven together by adversity, pooled their funds and built a synagogue in which they now both worship... Only here, among the coconut palms and the mangoes, does a Henriquez or a de Cordova bow down in worship beside an Eisenstein or a Weintraub Rothschild and Sidonia unite.*

Nineteenth-century immigration heralded the arrival of several important groups, who have contributed significantly to the city's progress. Portuguese migrants arrived as servants or labourers and later occupied trade, professional and government positions as they climbed the social ranks. Chinese settlers started as estate labourers in the mid-nineteenth century, although many arrived during the first decade of the twentieth century, and soon dominated the retail trade. In 1930, claims Colin Clarke, there were around four hundred Chinese grocery stores on the island, with Kingston's Chinatown situated principally on West, Orange, and Princess Streets. Racial discrimination in terms of physical and legalistic abuse was consistently hurled at Chinese communities, partly due to the visible success of their enterprises. Immigration laws restricted Chinese immigration until as late as 1947. The Chinese Benevolent Society, established in 1891 at 131 Barry Street to protect the Jamaican Chinese population, still actively maintains an important vitality through educational, social and cultural associations.

A third group to make its mark was the East Indians who disembarked as indentured workers, after colonial agents were sent to Madras and Calcutta to lure labourers to the West Indies. Between 1845 and 1916, 38,000 people arrived from India, on contracts which nominally paid for a return passage after a fixed term of work, usually in the cane fields. Finally, Syrians of Palestinian or Lebanese origin migrated to Kingston at the start of the last century, often starting out as itinerant merchants. The grandfather of former Prime Minister Edward Seaga founded a successful dry goods store on West Queen Street at the turn of the nineteenth century. Issa, Hanna, Shoucair and Joseph were but a few other immigrant family names also soon established as respected retail outlets on Orange, King and Harbour Streets. Club Alaif, located in Vineyard Town, just south of Merrion Road in East Kingston, was the historical social centre for the Syrian population whose growing wealth and physical appearance, like that of the Portuguese descendants, made them more "acceptable" to the discriminating white elite. Like the former Club India off Old Hope Road, membership waned as access very slowly opened up to the established colonial clubs, whose previous restrictions of "whites only" gradually became as politically and socially untenable as they were repulsive.

Emancipation Days

The ultimate and most vile form of discrimination, that of slavery, disappeared from Kingston's landscape less than two centuries ago. The religious groups, as active then as they are now, were firmly divided in their perception of how slavery, the colonial government and society should be moulded. Many of the non-conformist churches focused their efforts squarely with the slaves' material interests and pushed for abolition.

News of the French Revolution and subsequent slave-led rebellion in Haiti shivered down the spines of slave-owners and spurred ripples of revolt in Jamaica during the late eighteenth and early nineteenth centuries. Public opinion in Britain rumbled to and forth, stimulated by abolitionists such as Granville Sharp and William Wilberforce. The former highlighted the evils undertaken by the notorious Liverpool slave ship *The Zong*, while the latter directed the case for the abolition of slavery to Parliament. The slave trade was abolished in 1808, but slavery as an institution still remained intact within the British Empire. Parliament passed acts aimed at easing the brutality of slavery, forbidding whipping in the field, or the flogging of women, but the Jamaican Assembly, the voice of the plantocracy, and many within the Anglican Church refused to pay heed to these changes.

During Christmas 1831, slaves in the west of the island initiated a strike, believing that the Jamaican planters were withholding their freedom granted by the British Parliament. Sam Sharpe, a Baptist preacher, had relayed news of the anti-slavery movement and led the protest, which soon developed into the largest slave insurrection in the island's history and one of the most violent. Hung in 1832, Sharpe has since been nominated a National Hero for leading the rebellion that ultimately forced the British government to act in favour of abolition.

Following the Emancipation Act in 1833, the end of slavery was declared officially in Jamaica the following year on 1 August. Since freedom was to some extent portrayed as "a gift" from the British rulers, freed slaves allegedly chanted on the streets:

Queen Victoria gi wi free,
Tiday fus a Augus, Tenk Massa.

Full freedom on the island, however, was yet to come. The Act allowed for a period of "apprenticeship" to accustom the landowners and workers to new conditions of wage labour. The apprentices had to work without pay for forty hours per week in exchange for lodging, food, clothing, medical assistance and the use of vegetable gardens ("provision grounds") to ease the transfer. Not surprisingly, this system had little success. In many cases, the condition of workers' lives worsened as the planters sought to maximize their exploitation of the labour force. The Proclamation of Freedom four years later brought forward universal liberty. On that first full free morning demonstrations and celebrations occurred across the island. In the then capital of Spanish Town, a hearse containing shackles and chains that had enslaved workers was driven through the streets and ceremoniously burned.

Rev. William Knibb, posthumously awarded an Order of Merit, described the celebrations in front of him as Governor Sir Lionel Smith read the Proclamation of Freedom to a crowd of around 8,000 packed into the main square of Spanish Town: "The hour is at hand, the Monster is dying... the winds of freedom appeared to have been set loose, the very building shook at the strange yet sacred joy." Andrew Salkey's poem, "Because of 1833", looks beyond the immediate gains of freedom and addresses the tortuous times of apprenticeship and the ongoing dispossession from the land:

Free is when you' yard
only grow f'you own rich mineral,
f'you own sugar cane an' banana,
an' f'you own dandelion tea,
an' when the groun' spread out an' is f'you own.

With the battle against slavery won, Kingstonians were still governed by an Assembly that seemed more intent of pleasing the wealthy landowners than addressing the needs of the rural and urban majority. A defining moment in Jamaican and British colonial history occurred in 1865 when Paul Bogle, a farmer and Baptist priest, led a group of 400 dissenters to the courthouse at the south-eastern town of Morant Bay to protest against a magistrate's decision. The local militia was rapidly assembled and the Riot Act read from the steps of the courthouse. In the ensuing violence, the courthouse was burned down and fifteen people killed. The response of Governor Eyre, fearing island-wide rebellion, was to send forces to quell the disturbance, which extended the following day to several estates. Composed at the time, but recorded by Walter Jekyll in 1907, "War Down a Monkland" sang of the military response from the surrounding barracks:

Soldiers from Newcastle
Come down a Monkland
With gun an sword

Fe kill sinner oh!
War, war, war oh!
War oh! heavy war oh!

The ensuing violence left 493 people dead, over six hundred flogged and a thousand houses burnt. Paul Bogle and George W. Gordon, a legislator who supported the cause, were arrested and hanged. The latter had spoken out against the Jamaican Assembly and colonial government: "A ruler who does not assuage the sword with justice becomes distasteful, and instead of having the love and respect of the people, he becomes despised and hated." Karl Marx later added, "The Jamaican story is characteristic of the beastliness of the 'true Englishman'."

"Because of 1865", the third of Andrew Salkey's poetic chronology, summarizes the career of General Eyre, who, remembered in Australia in several name places, is vilified by many Jamaicans for his actions:

Eyre who did give him blessed name
to one Australian lake
one Australian peninsula
an' a Jamaican genocide

Such cruelty caused much consternation in Britain; nevertheless a defence fund for Eyre, who was recalled to London but acquitted of blame, gained the vocal support of Thomas Carlyle, John Ruskin, Lord Alfred Tennyson, Charles Kingsley and Charles Dickens. The Jamaican Assembly was dissolved in favour of Crown Colony status, leaving the island under direct rule from London until limited self-government in Kingston was reinstated in 1944.

Market Places
One of the institutions that developed under slavery, but which endures and is still celebrated today is that of the Sunday market. The Consolidated Slave Laws of 1792 set out certain regulations concerning slavery, one stating that slaves should be released from work on Sundays to tend to their provision grounds. Markets developed on these days, where slaves traded their produce and crafts. Victoria Market once

stood by the wharves at the bottom of King Street, the frenetic atmosphere of trading mixed up with the awkward ramblings of newly arrived visitors as they set foot on shore. The main Sunday market in Kingston was on West Queen Street and formed the basis of what was, until recently, the celebrated, enclosed chaos of Jubilee Market, which spilled westward from the Parade. Built over a century ago and originally known as Solas Market, this famous iron-girded covered market was gutted by fire in April 2003.

The sprawling Coronation Market, south of Spanish Town Road near the graveyard of the disused railway station, survives as the mainstay of downtown market life. It was named after the succession of George VI to the British crown, but popularly nicknamed Duppy Market since it occupies the site of an old cemetery. Lorna Goodison tuned into these associations when she wrote "Was it Legba She Met Outside the Coronation Market?" (2000). The poem follows the meanderings of a medicine man in the market and slowly reveals his spiritual identity as fellow spirits quietly assemble around him amid the clutter of the market:

> *Under the arch of the Coronation Market*
> *she watches the crooked man approach.*
> *He is dromedary with a double hump,*
> *one of muscle and cartilage, one a crocus bag sack*
> *swollen with the rank weeds and fragrant leaves*
> *of his travelling bush doctor's business.*

While the burnt-out site of the Jubilee used to present a bewildering array of fruits, clothing, batteries, hardware and shoes in the dark recesses of the covered den, this latter market spreads like a frazzled blanket under the streaming sun. Redemption Market, formerly on Princess and West Queen Streets, witnessed both the pleasure of successful bargain-hunters and the pain of those whose possessions had just been lost. Here goods seized by the town bailiffs were displayed, to be bought back by the erstwhile owners or sold afresh. Nearby were the "grass-yards" where hay was fed to the draft animals before their return trek to the country. Amid the fodder, horses and oxen, the precious commodity of charcoal was also sold from their carts. Chigger Foot Market on the corner of Princess and Heyward Streets was yet another point of sale for the masses.

In the eighteenth century, Long described the abundance of fruit and vegetables in Kingston's markets: "In short, the most luxurious epicure cannot fail of meeting here with sufficient in quantity, variety and excellence, for the gratification of his appetite the whole year round." By the end of the next century, Kingston was the booming commercial centre of the island and celebrated with the International Exhibition of 1891. Given the mercantile success of the town, it seems strange that John Bigelow, editor of the *New York Evening Post*, failed to sense the penny drop:

Though Kingston is the principal Port of the Island, it has but little of the air of a commercial city. One looks and listens in vain for the noise of carts and the bustle of city men; no one seems to be in a hurry; but few are doing anything, while the mass of the population are lounging about in idleness and rags.

Mikey Smith more sensitively summed up the to and fro, the noise and vibrancy of city trading in his poem "I an I Alone":

'Shoppin bag! Shoppin bag! Five cent fi one!'
'Green pepper! Thyme! Skellion! Pimento!'
'Remember de Sabbath day to keep it holy!
Six days thou shalt labour,
But on the seventh day thou shalt rest.'
'Hey, Mam! How much fi dah piece a yam deh?
No, no dat; dat! Yes, dat!'
'Three dollars a poun, nice genkleman.'

Today's downtown street markets throb with the majority of the city's shoppers who have neither the desire nor resources to scour the air-conditioned aisles of uptown supermarkets. These are hustling sales pitches, where the jousting between seller and buyer, both needing a good price to survive or to save enough for the next contest, makes shopping a serious business. Informal street selling is as much a part of today's economic reality as it was for colonial Kingston.

The boutiques and supermarkets of New Kingston are a world away, although the majority of the lasting emporiums started their business life downtown. King Street housed the first stores, lined up along a busy crawl of roadside vendors and browsers. Of these shops, Nathan's was the biggest. The store's balcony, which caught the afternoon breezes, was a popular spot for those who could afford it to meet and momentarily escape the heat of the pavement. Now much of the shopping has migrated to uptown superstores and malls, and Sundays are fully given up to the consumer bug, replacing the Sunday markets where self-grown produce once used to be sold and bartered. Mona Macmillan recalled Sundays in town during the mid-twentieth century, which seem far removed from the crowded malls and streets of today, although the iced delights of "Skyjuice" are still very much in demand:

Kingston is traffic-less on a Sunday and the children have the streets as a playground. Ice-sellers pushing two-wheeled carts with a red rag on the handle as badge of their trade (a red strip tied to a pole is shown outside shops where ice is sold), are the only active people. Hymn singing echoes rather forlornly through the empty streets..."

Modern air-conditioned malls, such as the Island Life Centre on St. Lucia Avenue, provide their own consumer buzz in the midst of the high-rise financial buildings bounded by Trafalgar Road, Half Way Tree Road and Old Hope Road. It is unlikely, however, that today's shoppers feel the same way as the heroine of de Lisser's novel, *Jane's Career.* Jane Burrell arrives in Kingston fresh from the countryside and is immediately overwhelmed by its retail splendour compared to her rural origins. Her friend had told her of "the glories of shopping on a Saturday night in Kingston, which alone, according to the experienced young women, made life in the city well worth living." Arriving in Kingston, her dreams seem soon to be met. When she walks along a street of shops, gazing at "what appeared to her to be a great avenue of light, admiration reached to ecstasy, and for the first time she felt glad she had come to town." The commercial bustle and incessant movement of Kingston dazzled Jane as much as the bright city lights:

The little Syrian shops filled to overflowing with showy goods intended to capture the fancy of servant-girls and women from the country; the groceries and salt provision shops, containing all manner of what to the working classes of Kingston are the most delicious delicacies; the crowds of vendors and higglers, each one calling out his and her wares and inviting the passer-by to stop and purchase; the electric cars, all lighted up now and moving swiftly on their lines with a constant clanging of warning gongs; the hubbub, the incessant movement of hundreds of people, the sound of religious singing, which pierced its way through all the other noises; and then the market itself, that market to which Jane's mother had come occasionally to sell her goods, and which to Jane's wondering eyes looked as though it contained all the food that could be grown in a whole year in all the villages that she had ever seen—all this filled her with unspeakable delight.

Trams and Traffic

Tramcars rolled into Kingston in 1876, with electric lighting introduced not long after. Little remains of their presence, save for their literary echoes. Louise Bennett describes a usual ride in "Rough Riding Tram":

> *Me dis a-roll an toss, me head a-spin,*
> *Me basket drop!*
> *Jane draw de 'tring an ring de bell,*
> *An meck de mad-man stop!*

The electric tram was phased out during the late 1940s in favour of buses, but is affectionately remembered for its relative reliability. Bennett, who must be among the most prolific producer of odes to the tram, makes fun of the noises issuing from the new buses, nicknamed "chi-chis" due to the sound of the compressed air-operated doors:

> *Cho, New-Bus big an pretty,*
> *An New-Bus shine an new,*
> *New-Bus drive sweet, wid nice sof' seat,*
> *But New-Bus got de flu!*

Today's traffic snarls more forcefully and much faster than before. Shoppers battling by the Parade or traversing Coronation Market must contend with passing cars and crawling buses. Laurie Gunst describes a hectic morning on East Queen Street:

The street was roaring with market day traffic, and the new Japanese minibuses everyone called 'quarter millions' were farting a black pall of diesel smoke through the harsh sunlight. The rumshops, barber shops, tailoring establishments, and cookstands were all doing fast business, and the street vibrated with Saturday morning energy.

In contrast to the energy of the large markets, the Crafts Market on Pechon Street and Port Royal Street by the waterfront operates a more sedate style of turnover. Positioned a good score of miles away from the nearest tourist encampment, this concentration of craft-based commerce is more visited by locals buying presents for friends or their own homes. Not far from here and skirting Coronation Market, Spanish Town Road corrals the northerly lower-income townships of Trench, Whitfield and Denham Towns. The existence of a toxic tanning industry since the eighteenth century traditionally repelled wealthy residents, leaving this part of town to the poor. The relentless procession of vehicles along the road cuts a clear line north-west from the Parade. Gunst describes its path as "a speedway that goes by the city's industrial terraces and the sprawling shantytown called Riverton City. The first shanties had gone up around a garbage dump, and now the area was a home to thousands; the children of Riverton City formed their own posses to fight off the john-crow buzzards that competed with them for food."

Few residents living uptown, whose predecessors shunned this part of the city, bother to venture around these parts. Spanish Town Road has come to symbolize more a civil battlefield in the minds of many than an out-of-town highway.

Orange Street

Lorna Goodison, in "In City Gardens Grow No Roses as We Know Them", frames the separate lives of the wealthy and the poor by telling the story of servants who transplant earth from their uptown places of work to their barren yards downtown. She describes the scarce foliage of Orange Street, formerly an affluent business and residential sector, whose only connection with the wealthy classes now lies in those who provide domestic labour and the garden soil that they bring back:

> *Outside the street ran hard*
> *a still dark river of asphalt.*
> *At the core of the many-celled tenement*
> *lay the central brick-paved courtyard*
> *severe square of unyielding red soil*
> *for the only tree in one hundred and seventeen*
> *Orange Street.*

Orange Street troubles form the focus for Mikey Smith's famous dub poem "Me Cyaan Believe It", in which a fire lays waste to doubly distressed lives:

> *Deh a yard de odder night*
> *when me hear 'Fire! Fire!'*
> *'Fire, to plate claat!'*
> *Who dead? You dead!*
> *Who dead? Me dead!*
> *Who dead? Harry dead!*
> *Who dead? Eleven dead!*
> *Woeeeeeeee*
> *Orange Street fire*
> *deh pon me head*
> *an me cyaan believe it*
> *me sey me cyaan believe it*

Life After Cross Roads

Heading uptown, the have and have-nots grow further apart. Some see Cross Roads not merely as a road junction, but a social intersection after which the minority rich become the residential majority. Iron grilles girdle homesteads, but the hedged roads seem friendlier to the moneyed few. Long driveways and fierce dogs keep unknown visitors at bay.

Slipe Road, South Camp Road and Mountain View Avenue are the main arteries that feed the new business heart of town. Laurie Gunst describes one such route up north, through the spiced smoke of roadside jerk-chicken stalls:

The Windward Road turned from an industrial strip into a Kingston thoroughfare at the corner of Mountain View Avenue, where a cluster of rumshops had their wooden doors open to the sidewalk and night-long domino games were in full swing. Through the car window came the familiar click and slap of plastic-ivory pieces being slid and hammered onto the board tables, and the shouts, curses, and laughter of the players.

Lorna Goodison's "Bun Down Cross Roads" adds to the humour with her comical tale of Bun Down, a "bad word merchant" who is arrested but pays above the given fine "to curse until I have reached this sum."

Bun Down could concoct in ripe and fruity tones
unique and extravagant combinations
of forty shilling words and never repeat
a particular formation once, in the distance
between King Street and Cross Roads

Sabina Park and the National Stadium

One of the few zones where the polarized extremes of Kingston society come closer are the sporting Meccas of Sabina Park and the National Stadium on South Camp Road and Mountain View Avenue respectively. The former is the renowned home of the national sport, cricket, fuelling passions that grip the sound waves belted forth from radios and televisions at test match times. Office workers grow headphoned ears, afternoon appointments dry up as people migrate to watch the evening overs, and dancehall is muscled out of bus and taxi speakers by the crack of leather on willow and the background roar of an appreciative—or vexed—full house. In the ground itself, Red Stripe and rum vapour inflame the hot air, the George Headley Stand squeezes to overload and the boisterous, booming mound displays tourists and middle-class Jamaicans at play in public.

In recent years, Jamaica's football team, the Reggae Boyz, has inspired a similar ardour across town at the National Stadium. Qualification for the World Cup in 1998 boosted local leagues and set up soccer as a new sensation, long after Bob Marley had led the way as a devoted practitioner. During home international games the stadium's bleachers are coated gold and green. The Reggae Tiger mascot, garnished in a green acrylic sauna suit with a delirious smiling head, troops around the evening dusk scene, barracked by fans as the floodlights glaze the grass pitch behind. Peanuts, prawns and bottles are hurled around the stands. Amid the dusty heat, boom boxes rattle the air before the teams emerge and the battle true commences.

The National Stadium was also once the site of a famous and battering staged fight, when Smokin' Joe Frazier took on Big George Foreman in January, 1973 to defend his Heavyweight Championship of the World. Around 36,000 Jamaicans turned up to see Foreman's whirlwind punches knock a stubbornly resistant Frazier to the floor. The latter's recent accession to the heavyweight crown, following Muhammed Ali's disqualification for refusing to join the US military draft, had not endeared him to the Kingstonian crowd. Foreman, the underdog, received a tumultuous welcome and left the island with the champion's belt. Local promoter Lucien Chen did his utmost to woo big capital to town and transform Kingston into a premiere big fight venue in the Caribbean, but it was not to be.

While wealthier uptown residents occasionally venture down to the sports arenas or theatres, Kingston remains a city split in two, socially and spatially. Aptly capturing the downtown's confidence and spirit, Andrew Salkey's "Saturday in Kingston" relates a woman's evening stroll, looking for the next opportunity and the next means to make sense of the city:

> *a downtown girl*
> *rolled her hips,*
> *sprung on marble-ball feet,*
> *and grinned*
> *and began selecting*
> *her Saturday night friend;*
> *there was a gradually increased speed*

in her twist of neck
and flick of finger-tip;
there was a trick of rhythm in her view of the world,
a doubt-excluding bounce
in her step;
the sidewalk
slipped away unnoticed,
under her vaseline smooth
patent-leather shoes,
as sidewalks should
under a downtown girl.

CHAPTER THREE

Uptown

"It's chaos, of course, but it's a fascinating one... But after all the city is the people; the small artisans as well as the workers. And the hedges of the bungalow gardens even farther north aren't old and thick enough and sufficiently obfuscated with cobweb traditions to keep out the spirit of life with much success."

Kenneth Pringle, *Waters of the West*

"No credit. Mr. Trust is dead."

Shop sign, Hope Road

Barely four miles, but a great gulf, separate uptown and downtown Kingston. Oxford Road neatly severs Cross Roads from New Kingston, invisibly slicing apart the city's social spheres. It is perhaps not hard to picture the different lives of the wealthier and the poorer, but the drive uptown from Harbour Street via Slipe, Half Way Tree and Constant Spring Roads to the neat neighbourhoods of Arcadia Gardens, Aylsham and Cherry Gardens conjures up images of difference beyond even the most lucid of imaginations.

The wealthier areas have stretched northwards along Liguanea Plain, to nestle within the foothills of the Blue Mountains, or to wind their way up to Stony Hill. Vanessa Spence describes one of the prosperous but precarious hillside dwellings, caught between startling vistas and precipitous banks, in *The Roads Are Down* (1993).

Carla lived very inconveniently on the other side of town, in Red Hills. She had one of these huge five-bedroom concrete houses perched on a slope so sheer that the contractors had had to put in a three-hundred-foot retaining wall which cost more than the house. All her neighbours were

*similarly blessed, and after earth tremor, they could be seen anxiously
inspecting their property from the road for habitat-threatening cracks.*

The introduction of trams in 1876, the newly flowing arteries of
water supply, and the earthquake, which devastated much of
downtown in 1907, spurred on the outward growth of the city.
Previously, urban affluence had tended to reside in the eastern half of
the town, away from the poorer western neighbourhoods and the
hubbub of the port. In 1923 the parishes of Kingston and urban St.
Andrew were joined into the Kingston Corporate Area to assist the
booming capital's management. Former estates sold during the first half
of the twentieth century created space for the concrete suburbs to grow,
and Kingston edged towards a city of a million people.

The boundaries and styles of uptown and downtown have shifted
over time. The eponymous heroine of Herbert de Lisser's *Jane's Career:
A Story of Jamaica* develops an understanding of the city's distinct
areas:

> *She roughly divided the city into two districts, uptown and downtown,
> and she fixed the boundary between them to her satisfaction. All that part
> of Kingston south of Heywood Street, where she lived, was the downtown
> section; there it was that large stores and business offices of the city were
> situated, where the motor-cars were most often seen and where hand-
> somely attired ladies went shopping, and, to the west, the railway termi-
> nus, which she passed on one occasion when taking a belt-line car-ride.
> Above Heywood Street: there the suburbs began and Jane had now come
> to know most of them by name.*

De Lisser's account clearly marks the changing areas of Kingston in the
early twentieth century, as the wealthy downtown folk moved to
uptown residences, away from an increasingly impoverished
downtown.

> *Manchester Square and Kingston Gardens she regarded as the residen-
> tial quarters of wealthy people, though they are really suburbs inhabited
> by the middle classes of the city's population. Smith's Village, Hannah's
> Town, Allman Town, and other 'Towns' which need not be mentioned,*

contained a mixed description of houses occupied mainly by persons of the lower middle classes and by servants: of the eastern side of the city Jane knew next to nothing... nor was she aware that to the west, and not very far from where she lived, were long streets filled with buildings in all stages of decay; houses gaunt and weather beaten, revealed in all their ruin and decrepitude by the blinding sunlight that poured down from the bright blue sky twelve hours and more a day.

The railway has long since ground to a halt and the suburbs have marched well beyond Heyward Street. Even by the 1890s the first suburban growth was streaming out along Half Way Tree, Hope, Old Hope, and Constant Spring Roads. Three decades later, visiting writer Kenneth Pringle attempted to map the chaos of Kingston, a chaos that enthralled him. He chose Victoria Park, more commonly called the Parade, as his focal and social point of separation:

Upper Kingston is marked off from Lower Kingston by Victoria Park, with its cannae and its giant banyan-trees under which sit and lie the unemployed. North of the park the clubs offer cricket and whisky and football and billiards to the middle class, and, in the opinion of parson, schoolmasters, bank boys, and sporting young ladies, keep the flag of civilisation flying. Upper Kingston would like to consider itself the head of Lower Kingston the body. It is true that a genuine intelligentsia does there exist. But in general the attempt to detach the head from the body, where it is attempted among the prosperous, results in a marked subsidence of energy from both. There are some very off ghosts living round about the Hope Road.

More concisely he added, "Roughly speaking, the posher you are the farther you live from Kingston. The élite have houses way up on Stony Hill, or in the remoter areas of Constant Spring and Halfway Tree. Then as you come down to Cross Roads you find the bungalows of clerical workers and the smaller professional gentry." By the 1960s, the city was well and truly divided, a source of comment and concern. In a lighter tone, Barbara Gloudon, writing as long-time columnist "Stella" in the *Star* and *Daily News*, clarified the vocabulary of the city's imagined and real split:

One room is an apartment downtown. Studio apartment is the same thing, only uptown. Downtown house with nuff different-different people in it tenement yard. Uptown is apartment house. Downtown, you have back verandah. Uptown you better call it patio. Downtown, room with cooking facilities is just that. Uptown a flat. In the wrong neighbourhood, a big old house is a big old house. Uptown is executive residence.

Whether the city's differences are visible or verbal, one of the most divisive forces is that of fear, separating and dividing people into their imagined citadels of safety. Mr. Trust may not be dead quite yet, but his operations are circumscribed in areas where strangers are unwelcome or suspect. Anything or anyone outside the norm, in an uptown suburb or downtown neighbourhood, elicits cause for concern or outright anxiety. Mutabaruka's "Sit dung pon de wall" tells the story, both ironic and sad, of a homeless person who every day watches a suited-commuter nervously pass him by:

A sit dung pon de wall
a watch im a watch mi
is lang lang time a sit dung ya
a watch im a watch mi
im pance match im shirt
nat even im shoes look like it tuch dirt
nu shoes pon mi foot
me head well dre'd
rock stone still mi bed

When the street dweller changes his usual position one day, this unnerves the passer-by, who takes fright and runs into the path of an oncoming car: "so im start to run/an a car lick im dung."

New Kingston
Uptown today revolves around New Kingston and the main drag of Knutsford Boulevard, lined at the southern end by luxury hotels and the exclusive Liguanea Club, then stretching north through high-rise offices, banks, embassies, air-conditioned restaurants, and shops. At

night the avenue transforms into a more edgy place, as the Asylum club and surrounding bars belch out dancehall music and pumped-up punters.

On Oxford Road, just along from the visa queues that edge along the United States' Embassy frontage and the grey block of the National Housing Trust headquarters, Emancipation Park, opened on 1 August 2002, offers an open space, decorated by bandstand, fountains and a jogging track. Donated over twenty years ago to the Jamaican government by the gentlemen of the Liguanea Club as a green site, the park is most famous for a $4.5-million sculpture, "Redemption Song", by Laura Facey Cooper. Depicting a ten-foot naked couple of slaves looking skywards, the sculpture was widely appreciated, and criticized, by those who saw their physical attributes as somewhat exaggerated. The "over-endowed" male figure is matched by an overtly buxom female, drawing admiring glances and prurient interest from passers-by. On a more starchy note, the majestic décor and traditional profile of the Liguanea Club quietly continues as a remnant of times past, scarcely brushed by surrounding change.

Satellites to the concrete and steel Mecca of Knutsford Boulevard, the outlying shopping nodes of Constant Spring Road, the New Kingston Shopping Centre on Dominica Drive and the Sovereign Centre on Hope Road provide a cool sanctuary for the shopping classes. Downtown residents venture north to these consumer havens, but the prices and armed guards can be a deterrent. Walls of fear shelter the generally more affluent lifestyles of uptown, but similar imagined and real exclusionary spaces are charted on the mental maps of all Kingstonians. Pringle spared no contempt with his criticism of the social divide:

Respectable Kingstonians consider that even agriculture is a base pursuit,
and they wedge their children in the already chronically overcrowded
clerical and professional careers... They send them to schools where they
are taught to despise the people and the devil and the flesh. But they
know that they go to school to learn make-believe... to succeed and boss
and bully and climb as high as they can on other people's backs. And espe-
cially they learn to dream of a house with a tennis-court, right away
from the rabble, with an iron gate and an estralia hedge in the selecter
portions of St. Andrews.

Within the private schools of uptown, richer pupils are soon
conditioned to live out the joke that they are more likely to undertake
a family shopping visit to Miami, than head downtown. Many uptown
residents have not visited King Street or roundabouts for three decades
or more, even when it constitutes an air-conditioned auto trek of only
four or five miles. When asked about their lack of southerly motion,
the response will engender either a broad expression of foreboding or a
rhetorical, but why?

Olive Senior wryly and caustically parodies "The Lady", Mistress
Marshall of 12 Daimler Close, Kingston Heights, the stereotypical
elderly uptowner, whose fading vision fills with fear and annoyance:

Mistress Marshall calls Eunice/ bring tea and the
papers/ no one dead no one born/ that she knows of/
but she turns to page eight/ and it's just as she feared/
for the columnists say the p.m. is failing/ the
county is falling/ the party is foundering/ the
people are restless/ and the prophets of doom are
predicting a crash/ you see what I mean Mistress
Marshall doesn't know/ why her husband so worthless/
to stay in this place/ every night the black people/
just waiting to break in/ to rob and kill and worse/...

Some traces of "downtown" are to be found amid uptown quarters, as
pockets of poverty stubbornly hang on in the northern section of town.
Less prosperous residents of Hermitage, Grant's Pen, Standpipe Lane
and Birdsucker Lane live cheek by jowl with more affluent locals, but

usually behind corrugated-iron yards, working as domestic staff, gardeners or guards for their neighbours. Occasional spatial proximity seldom leads to social closeness. Perry Henzell makes this clear in his Kingston-based political novel *The Power Game* (1997): "The rich lived in the hills, but the poor were trapped in the shanty towns that filled the flat land between the mountains and the harbour and for many their dream was so different from the reality of life in the city as they found it, that they had to choose between killing the dream and risking death to keep it alive."

Roads Leading North

Uptown residents seldom walk, unless trussed up in Nike trainers, huffing around the Mona Reservoir at dawn or dusk, within car alarm-shot of their neatly stabled motors. Street walking is rare for visitors, but uptown wanderers will soon meet the guinep and paper sellers, sponge-ready windscreen wipers and casual hustlers who have "seen you before, brudda." Slipe, South Camp and Marescaux Roads lead directly north to New Kingston from downtown and make engaging excursions as street scenes and houses change with each step. The hike north today differs markedly from Edward Long's eighteenth-century perambulation.

> *The road, leading from the bridge towards Kingston, is for about a mile extremely romantic: on one side is a range of steep, rocky mountain, which scarcely admits of room sufficient for carriages to pass at the foot of it; on the other side is a branch of the Salt River, fed here and there with small rivulets oozing from the bottom of the mountain.*

During July, Marescaux Road is lined by luxurious mauve, then yellow, lignum vitae. Sandwiched between the busier, pulsating traffic arteries of Slipe and South Camp Roads, this avenue seems quieter and calmer, despite the steady stream of cars. Two famous educational establishments on the west side of the road add a certain solemnity to the drive. Mico Teachers' College, an enormously impressive wooden colonial building, dating from the early 1900s, is one of the oldest teacher training colleges in the world. The Lady Mico Charity established it in 1834 as a primary school to educate emancipated slaves, who had been deliberately kept from schooling under slavery. While several such colleges were instituted in the Caribbean, only the Kingston institution remains. The original funds for its foundation came from an unusual source. In 1670 a nephew of Lady Mico steadfastly refused a £1,000 bequest, rather than face marriage to one of her six nieces. The untouched dowry was thus invested, a portion being set aside to ransom Christian captives from the then active Barbary pirates. As piracy waned, the considerable collected assets were used to create the Mico Colleges.

Just south of Mico College, an equally famous and older academic institution, Wolmer's School, was founded in 1729 with the endowment of a Kingston goldsmith. The present school grounds were the site of a remarkable feat of national publicity and nineteenth-century endeavour. A vast wooden palace, with Moorish turrets, was purpose-built for the Great Exhibition of 1891, a Jamaican version of Britain's Crystal Palace extravaganza four decades previously. The grand design of ornamental fountains, landscaped gardens and pavilions provided an impressive display of regional cultural and economic success, but failed to recoup the initial financial outlay of £30,000. Nevertheless, it marked "the most extraordinary commercial event in the history of the Gulf of Mexico and the West Indies."

Further north, to the east of South Camp Road, lies Up Park Camp, home to the island's military since the 1780s. This bastion retains a significant location bordering uptown and downtown. When troubles flare in the latter as living prices rise or politicians and their hoods squabble, the armoured jeeps roll out of the barracks to quell, or some would argue fan, the fires of discontent. The southern entrance to the base is called Duppy Gate after the chilling appearance of a deceased colonial officer, who still inspects the machine-gun-toting guards at night.

Half Way Tree

Slipe Road connects with Half Way Tree Road at Cross Roads, a hectic interchange of cars, buses, shoppers, watchers and workers. Half Way Tree Road exits the skirmish to head northwest and arrives at Half Way Tree, the current site of the red-brick St. Andrews Parish Church, with its remarkably dusty but fascinating graveyard. A chapel has been located here since 1666, although the foundations were re-laid after the 1692 earthquake. The interior of the church lies a world away from the noise of Hagley Park and Eastwood Park Roads. Rachel Manley vividly recounts a family funeral and surrounds at the church:

> *The church was packed. The small mutterings of ushers trying to get people squeezed in to fit, and the hum of the fans overhead, were more immediate than the traffic sounds of Half-Way-Tree, which reminded one that, just outside, commerce, traffic, ill-tempered motorists, whistling peanut-vending bicycles, filthy-lunged country buses coming to town, men at the side of the road spitting and hoisting their crotches as though to confirm that they were still really men even if they were unemployed or simply vagrant by disposition—all this was still going on. Life, the inescapable road, would still be out there when this gathering of heart-broken and curious and polite mourners returned to the afternoon.*

Half Way Tree, a thundering traffic intersection marked by a looming clock tower built as a memorial to King Edward VII in 1813, was formerly the main junction between cattle ranches and sugar estates to north of the town. It was the principal settlement of St. Andrew Parish and was surrounded by nineteen sugar estates by the end of the eighteenth century. The township was named after a cotton tree that shaded a market and inn until the 1870s. Former fields surrounding the settlement became the first outlying suburbs where the wealthy retired to savour the healthier air of the Liguanea Plains at their leisure. Edward Long wrote at the time:

> *The village of Half-way tree is situated a little more than two miles North from Kingston, at the intersection of the three roads which lead to Spanish Town, to St. Mary, and St. George. This village enjoys, with a good air, the most agreeable views. Behind are the Majestic Blue Mountains, rising above one another in gradation, till they seem to touch the clouds: on each side, lively fields of canes, intermixed with elegant villas and pastures: in front, the harbours of Kingston and Port Royal, crowded with shipping, some at anchor, others plying in various directions: beyond these the Healthshire hills in St. Catherine, gradually*

declining towards Old Harbour: and lastly, the horizon closing on the beautiful azure of the ocean.

The "golden triangle", framed by Hope, Half Way Tree and Old Hope Roads, conceals a wonderful array of beautiful homes, glimpsed from the street through gaps in thick hedges or down winding drives. Rachel Manley describes her former family home, Drumblair, the unassuming yet elegant domestic headquarters for two generations of Jamaica's most distinguished political clan.

> *There was nothing spectacular about the old wooden two-story house set far back from the road. It was not even in a fashionable area, but rather poised precariously on the journey between the city and its ghettos, and the lofty slopes of its suburbs. It has often been described as elegant, but it was too visceral and self-willed a place to be so, for elegance is a product of control. The gate, a plain iron grille hinged to a cracking square cement post, always hung open lazily, despite the thick 'Chinese hat' hedge on either side guarding the house from view. The companion post carried the inscription of the name in frank block capitals on a marble inset. The initial slope of the circular driveway was steep enough that even a car needed a burst of new energy to make its way up. And there, at the top of the encircled front lawn, stood the house. It appeared not to take itself very seriously. It was large, but not in the sense of having many rooms—more in the way that you look at a puppy's paws and say, 'These are large paws; this will be a big dog.' It was just meant to be a large house. It looked out at the world from under a shady sombrero of shingles. At its waist, a similar frill of roofing adorned it like a fat ballerina's tutu. A veranda enclosed by a criss-cross wooden railing circled the ground floor like the dash of a hasty signature... Drumblair.*

Such grand houses fit snugly in Jamaica's distant past, yet wrestle more uneasily with today's increasingly divided society, replicating the ill-structured inequalities of colonial days. Michelle Cliff, in the short story *Columba*, describes Charlotte, "a woman of property" and her house during the 1920s. Behind the shutters of some households, certain scenes may be not too dissimilar today.

Her small house was a cliché of colonialism, graced with calendars adver-
tising the coronation of ERII, the marriage of Princess Margaret Rose,
the visit of Alice, Princess Royal. Bamboo and wicker furniture was
sparsely scattered across the dark mahogany floors—settee there, table
here—giving the place the air of a hotel lobby, the sort of hotel carved
from the shell of a great house, before Hilton and Sheraton made land-
fall. Tortoise-shell lampshades. Ashtrays made from coconut husks.
Starched linen runners sporting the embroideries of craftswomen.

Further north, the former Constant Spring Hotel rivalled
downtown's Myrtle Bank Hotel for opulence. Built in preparation for
the Great Exhibition of 1891, the new hotel made full use of the new
electric tram car, and was famed for being the first of the capital's
buildings to have electricity and indoor plumbing. Adorned with its
own post office, one hundred lavish rooms, French chef and a golf
course set in vast grounds, the hotel failed to live up to its promise and
was transformed into the Immaculate Conception School during the
1940s by Franciscan nuns. Occasionally, less grand villas stand idle in
vaguely unkempt grounds, the modern signs of overly expensive
upkeep or the outcome of familial migration overseas.

The landscape is now one of low-density bungalows, modern and
ageing villas, shopping malls and offices; a mix of nouveau and colonial
lines, angles and gates. Gated domestic garrisons have been
progressively fortified over the years as gunshots have echoed more
regularly or sounded more clearly in the still of the night.

Michael Thelwell aptly captured the subtle meanness of uptown
streets in *The Harder They Come* (1980), inspired by the blockbuster
Jamaican film of the same title. Ivan, the down-at-heel hero newly
arrived from the country, is confronted for the first time by the cold
shoulder of affluence and the vicious snarl of guard dogs. In one of the
film's most evocative moments, Ivan traipses through uptown territory
in search of work. Jimmy Cliff's soundtrack anthem "Many Rivers to
Cross" sums up the hopeful despair of the city's dispossessed,
emphasized by the unwelcoming dogs:

The houses are large and cool looking, set well back behind spacious
lawns dotted with miniature fruit trees, flowering shrubs, and beds of

flowers. From the road it is hard to see into these homes, their privacy ensured by tall hedges and fences. The ornate iron gates are all locked. Most have forbidding signs warning of bad dogs. The signs are not fake as he quickly finds out when he approaches the gates. Great well-fed beasts, barking and slavering, rush out, snarling and baring their teeth at him...

King's House: Independence Day

The most secluded and well guarded of all uptown residences is that of King's House, residence of the queen's representative, the governor-general. Initially part of Somerset Pen, and later the home of the Lord Bishop of Jamaica, the thirty acres of parkland hide the house from mainstream view. Located at the junction of Hope and East King's House Road, the existing building dates from 1909. A concrete exterior conceals stately interior treasures, notably the heavily impressive portraits of King George III and Queen Charlotte by Sir Joshua Reynolds. James Froude described the original elegance of King's House soon after Kingston was established as the country's capital in 1872, and before it fell victim to the disastrous earthquake of 1907.

All the large houses in Jamaica—and this was one of the largest of them—are like those of Barbadoes, with the type more completely developed, generally square, built of stone, standing on blocks, hollow underneath for circulation, of air, and approached by a broad flight of steps. On the three sides which the sun touches, deep verandahs or balconies are thrown out on the first and second floors, closed in front by green blinds, which can be shut either completely or partially, so that at a distance they look like a house of cards or great green boxes, made pretty by the trees which shelter them or the creepers which climb over them. Behind the blinds run long airy darkened galleries, and into these the sitting rooms open, which are of course still darker with a subdued green light, in which, till you are used to it, you can hardly read. The floors are black, smooth and polished, with loose mats for carpets. All the arrangements are made to shut out heat and light.

Of waning political importance in a country that seems set to opt for republican status and drop the anachronism of the British monarchy, King's House is ironically guaranteed an annual front-page media spot on the first Monday in August when the declaration of independence is honoured. Celebrations formerly took place at the National Stadium, but were relocated to this secluded residence. Dry speeches are animated by a parade and dancing on the lawns. School children perform folk dances, often with a fusion of contemporary dancehall, which is not always appreciated by assorted dignitaries and purists. A radio commentator for RJR evidently fell into the latter group, remarking on the enthusiasm of young performers from St. Thomas: "This dance is far more of a free for all than the last, and I'm afraid there's a lot of wining, but it is not that offensive." If "wining", a suggestive hip and crotch gyration, raised eyebrows, the pageantry, pomp, and circumstance quite enthralled the same presenter who marvelled at the "wonderful precision and order of the military" and seemed surprised at "female fire officers swinging their arms as vigorously as the rest." All seemed to be going well, until she was forced to lament the rowdy behaviour of a dancer touching his "scrotal area".

The quadrille or *bruckins*, a traditional dance associated with emancipation celebrations, are often performed. *The Sunday Gleaner* reported the moves thus: "Bruckins is a graceful dance, involving an upright stance. The body moves forward by a marching step, the length of which is extended by thrusting the pelvis. There is also a horizontal semi-circular open and close step, which is unique to the Jamaican dance. These steps are accompanied by a rowing motion of the arms." With similar clarity, the annual speeches of the governor-general and prime minister inevitably urge Jamaica's citizens forward along the path of prosperity.

Beyond the walled grounds of King's House, the rest of the population busily celebrate the national holiday with more flair at clubs, bars, or on the beach. Louise Bennett's poem gustily heralds independence in 1962, despite pessimists declaring that "E'ting gone to hell now".

> *Independance wid a vengeance!*
> *Independance raisin Cain!*
> *Jamaica start grow beard, ah hope*
> *We chin can stan de strain!*

The rather more visible Jamaica House, the office of the prime minister, is fenced within the King's House compound. Built in the early 1960s, the one-storey building had an unusual opening party. At the first official function held in August 1964, thousands of uninvited guests made a nuisance of themselves on the lawn. The island's invited dignitaries were attacked by resident ants that slowly bit their way through the guest list, until fidgeting and scratching unravelled the occasion's formality. Almost a century earlier during colonial times, Froude described the style of similar elite social gatherings with characteristic condescension:

> *There were lawn parties and evening parties, when all that was best in the island was collected; the old Jamaican aristocracy, army and navy officers, civilians, eminent lawyers, a few men among them of high intelligence. The tone was old-fashioned and courteous, with little, perhaps too little, of the go-a-headism of younger colonies, but not the less agreeable on that account.*

Of still greater antiquity, the prime minister's official residence of Vale Royal at Lady Musgrave and Montrose Roads is a most beautiful building, constructed in 1694 and bought by the government in 1928. Typical of a merchant's residence of the period, the design incorporates a lookout tower from which to keep note of ships in the harbour.

Devon House: Old Style, New Tourism

Vying with Vale Royal for uptown architectural honours, but winning easily in terms of accessibility, Devon House and its shaded grounds at the junction of Hope and Waterloo Roads are a deservedly popular attraction. The distinguished mansion was built in 1881 by George Stiebel, a Jamaican wheelwright who made his fortune in the Venezuelan gold fields. Not only Jamaica's first black millionaire, he was also the first black custos or magistrate of St. Andrew Parish, and as such his appointment was a significant social and political step, although universal adult suffrage did not arrive until 1944. Slipping slowly towards decay, the building was restored by the government in 1967 and initially used to house the National Gallery, until the collection was relocated downtown.

While most visitors are content to sample the outdoor treats of locally made ice-cream and cakes or pose for wedding photos near the fountain and gardens, the antique interior holds enticing fragments of the past, with muffled colonial airs and lacquered grace. Boutique tourism by day is transformed into a luxurious nightlife of food and drink in the courtyard. While independence celebrations are housed at the governor-general's place, Devon House puts on a show for Emancipation Day. Roots plays, a maypole routine, and heritage classics form the bulk of the performance menu, while a booming sound system seals the entertainment package.

Hope Road
Beyond the fence of Devon House and the walls of adjacent residences, Hope Road growls day and night as the major east-west through flow for uptown traffic. Rainy weather typically floods this route, as torrents tumble down from the hills en route to the murky waters of the bay. Vanessa Spence atmospherically recounts the rainy season travel woes in her novel *The Roads Are Down* (1993):

Every morning and evening it would rain for a couple of hours. The roads in Kingston would be virtually impassable after half an hour of rain. It had always been that way. Some of the roads were built in the beds of dry rivers, and where a river has once gone, it will always try to go again. In Kingston, in the rainy season, the rivers could go exploring.

The drains were choked full of rubbish and the gullies could not carry the water away fast enough. Cars broke down in the middle of Hope Road and in the side streets of the main roads old cars were abandoned for days. It was a common sight to see people clambering on top of their vehicles after they had hazarded a particularly deep stretch of water, and their cars flooded while they were fighting with the gears.

The afternoon downpours might not suit motorists, but they can provide a welcome benefit for the struggling Hope Botanical Gardens, a wonderful collection of plants, full of flowers but down on funds. Major Richard Hope, an English officer who took part in the 1655 conquest of Jamaica, gave his name to the area after being granted a substantial estate that extended from the Blue Mountains to the sea. Stone aqueducts, still standing today near the Gardens and on the university campus at Mona Heights, transported water from the Hope River to the sugar mills and serviced Kingston's water needs in the eighteenth century. The public gardens were designed during the 1870s on a large expanse of the Hope Estate bought by the Jamaican government. Typically enthusiastic for the aesthetics of tropical flora and fauna, Kenneth Pringle introduces the Gardens' delights:

The public gardens of any country are the concentrated and richest expression of its possibilities, and Hope Gardens in St. Andrews with its twenty acres of magical exuberance is the heightened evocation of Jamaica... On lawns set with beds of canna and zinnea strut the peacocks gorgeous as the minions of kings. Under the arbours of brick-red and magenta bougainvillea chatter in their cages paradisal green parrots with crimson gorgets: all the coloured doves of the valleys and the highwoods croon where on the ground below the ivory and scented flowers of frangipani shower like stars among the beaches of petals. Hanging-gardens of orchids overlook a sunken walk, where a fountain plays among the formal perfection of double pink and blue water-lilies in a basin which reflects the sculptured foliage of a palm. The walls of this walk overflow with scarlet hibiscus, bubbles of wine in the sunlight, from whose open throats hang yellow tongues.

From a similar period, Charles Hyatt, author of the *When Me Was a Boy* stories for radio, reminisces about growing up in Jamaica during the 1930s. At the time anywhere above Cross Roads was considered out of town, and Hope Pastures really were green meadows, spiked by mango trees and tall grasses.

An my most favourite place of all was Hope Gardens. Firs' of all the Tramcar ride to Hope Gardens was excitement in itself. The ride along an it pass through some place that a downtown schoolboy doan get to see very often. Then when yuh reach it! Boy! From the gate right up to the main park is like a different world. I use to t'ink myself that that mus be how the Garden of Eden did stay. When you look pon the bloomin' flowers bed then and the water lily in the big long fountain; an the fish! Now that was my favourite part, the Aquarium. From shark to turtle. Big fish, likkle fish, pretty fish, ugly fish.

Hope Gardens have consistently been threatened by developers, eager to concrete over the lawns and flower-beds for a one-off harvest of houses. The curators have nevertheless valiantly defended their manicured turf, palms, cacti, bougainvillea, bandstand, lake and a poet's corner against the bulldozers and the money behind them.

Similarly challenged, but less visibly successful, is the unfortunately named Hope Zoo, a sad depot for a declining collection of animal desperadoes. A Hollywood version of events would conclude with the dramatic liberation of the fated inmates, but no such finale appears on the current script. The few visitors touring the cages marvel more at the hopelessness of the crumbling zoo, rather than at the wonders of the stranded animal kingdom. Zenga Longmore, visiting with her young relative, is left similarly bemused, but strangely elated.

> *The first cage we looked at had a large sign reading "Indian Coney"...*
> *But the Indian coney appeared to be suffering from an advanced state of*
> *stage fright. The next cage had no sign—and no animals. The rest of the*
> *cages followed suit.*
> *"Is why we nah guess then what seem so hobvious now? De zoo have no*
> *hanimals!"*

Papine and Mona

The decrepitude of the zoo is thankfully juxtaposed with Papine's freshness at the eastern extremity of Hope Road. Buses, bikes, cars, shoppers and higglers fill the main square, side streets, indoor and open-air markets. Overlooking the noisy scene, the Roof Top Lounge café provides a vantage point to the mountains beyond or upon the fuss below. This small suburban locale, interestingly, has attracted several compositions on the theme of madness or otherness. Roger McTair's "Ganja Lady" evokes individual emptiness and communal chaos:

> *At Papine her justborn child curled to her breast,*
> *sons playing in dirt and grass*
> *the square shimmers, trucks, cars, carts roll past,*
> *the child sucks content, the ganja lady stares*
> *her hair unkempt, the world oblivious.*

Abdur-Rahman Slade Hopkinson similarly connects with "The Madwoman of Papine", again picturing personal confusion in a public place:

Four years ago,
in this knot of a village north of the university,
she was in residence
where a triangle of grass gathered the mountain road,
looped it once, and tossed it to Kingston,
where grampus buses, cycling students,
duppies of dust and ululations in light
vortexed around her.

The small suburb of Papine lies a few minutes north of the extended campus of the University of the West Indies. The buses roar or chug up from town, bringing a variety of voyagers. Claude McKay's poem "Papine Corner" (1912) captures the atmosphere of this junction, which hovers between frenetic activity and the flirtatious bustle of a busy square:

When you want to meet a frien',
  Ride up to Papine,
Where dere's people to no en',
  Old, young, fat an' lean:
When you want nice gals fe court,
  An' to feel jus' booze',
Go'p to Papine as a sport
  Dress' in ge'man clo'es.

Students and shoppers pack down for the ride. Shared cabs or "robots" stream around the central ring road of the university depositing staff and students, while bus-bound passengers traverse the open grasslands on their way to class, or catch lifts back to Papine and town.

Established in 1948 on the former grounds on the Mona sugar estate, the university has been instrumental in formulating significant political, economic and cultural foundations for independent Jamaica. Part of a Caribbean-wide network, UWI is well respected as "a place for light and learning". Dotted around campus, ruins of the old sugar mill and remnants of an aqueduct contrast the university's present-day importance as a keystone for future generations, while the past lingers in the framework of a reassembled limestone sugar warehouse from Trelawny, which now constitutes the university chapel. Beautifully striking murals by the Belgian artist Claude Rahir cover the external walls of the Assembly Hall and the Caribbean Institute of Mass Communications. UWI is a place to look, roam and read beneath the shade of the mango trees. The library holds an extensive collection of Caribbean materials, catalogued online and accessed via a network, which on occasion distributes a beaming message of "Smile, have a productive day," before closing down for the duration.

The neighbouring University of Technology lies on the north side of Hope Road, and has developed an impressive Sculpture Park, linking art and technology in a stunning outdoor exhibition. The School of Hospitality next door manages Lillians, one of the neighbourhood's leading restaurants and deservedly busy. Parcelled between the universities and Hope Road, Mona Heights is the model of modernist suburbia. In *The Children of Sisyphus* (1964), Orlando Patterson describes the calm and cool of a typical Mona residence through the experiences of the downtown protagonist Dinah.

> *The house was a large, 'L'-shaped green and white structure with a flat roof. It was situated a little way in from the road on one of the little gradients at the foot of the hill. Most of the front of the yard was taken up with a pear-shaped swimming pool. In the hot morning sun the water gleamed a fresh, blue-green radiance, with every now and then little ripples trickling over it as a cool mountain breeze fluttered by. The lawns around the swimming pool were velvet-green, the leaves of the grass being broad and growing thick together gave the appearance almost of being a carpet. On the strip of the lawn around the pool were the low, evenly placed almond trees, all like green umbrellas with spots of gold where the leaves had changed colour, casting their shade on the western side of the pool, a little of it falling on the path that led from the road to the house.*

The security felt by Dinah contrasts with the implicit fear felt by many uptown residents, walled and grilled by their real and perceived fear of raiders. Anthony Winkler describes his brother's home in *Going Home to Teach* (1995), strategically locked and bolted to keep out murderous thieves:

My brother's house is 'grilled,' like all the houses in this neighbourhood, and he must lock it up. There are cast-iron burglar bars across the windows; there are iron gates inside the front door. The bedroom area of the house where we will sleep is sealed off from the living room and kitchen by a wrought-iron gate. My brother locks it carefully.

Security concerns have changed Kingstonian lifestyles dramatically, as Winkler continues:

When I was a child practically every home in middle-class Kingston wore an open veranda around its front like a bib, and it was to this cool spot that people retired at the end of the day to drink and chat in night breezes. Now the verandas of many were enclosed behind wrought-iron cages and Kingstonians took their nightly airing and drinks behind padlocked gates. Night brushed over the city like a menacing shadow, and in the darkness you heard sirens occasionally baying in the distance.

August Town

Padlocked gates, grilles and armed guards are the garden ornaments of uptown Kingston today. Fear and confusion have bred further anxieties and mistrust, a cycle that seems endemic in the city. Not far from the protected gardens of Mona and College Common, August Town remains an unusual pocket of deprivation, neighboured by the communities of Angola and Hermitage. All three are seen by many as transplanted segments of a dangerous downtown. Over a century ago, the former settlement was home to the Bedwardites, a clan of white-robed believers who followed the messianic visions of Alexander Bedward, self-proclaimed messiah and leader of the Jamaica Native Baptist Church. His foresight that black power would transcend white colonialism, the perceived threat of the day, was sufficient for his spiritual madness to be confirmed and he was incarcerated in Bellevue Hospital, dying in 1930. Bob Stewart, who taught for many years at the University of the West Indies, recalls a different but equally challenging message from August Town. He took note of the music which in recent times echoed from the village during the evenings, "a peace" amid the city's political violence and turmoil, in "August Town":

The valley that night
was a chalice of music
dissolving the malice
of day heat.

CHAPTER FOUR

The Ghetto

"The mean, derelict smell of human waste mingled with the more aris-tocratic stink of the factory chimneys. Towards the right of the highway several meagre cows strayed in a dry, scorching common. And on the left were the shacks: dreadful, nasty little structures—a cluster of cardboard, barrel sides, old cod-fish boxes, flattened tar drums and timber scraps. A few, more luxurious, consisted of the carcasses of old cars."
Orlando Patterson, *The Children of Sisyphus* (1964)

"...and I stand robed, royal in the kingdom of the poor."
Lorna Goodison, "October in the Kingdom of the Poor" (2000)

Visiting writers often complained of the state of the Jamaican colony during the nineteenth century, likening the demise of the plantations and the spoiling economy to a festering canker or critical illness in a once robust body. Anthony Trollope, ever bemoaning Jamaica's declining contributions to the British imperial coffers, quipped: "It is one of the few sores on our huge and healthy carcass; and the sore has been running now so long, that we have almost given over asking whether it be curable." At the turn of the eighteenth century, the memoirs of William Hickey record his concern for the well-being of the island colony, "considered as one of the most unhealthy in the West Indies, or in the world."

Modern Jamaica stands as a free state, and anxieties have focused inward, none more sharply than on Kingston's so-called ghetto, an unfathomable mix of poverty, loyalty, violence, and political vendetta. Contemporary commentators have diagnosed the country's pressing ills not only in the lingering malaise of a fragile economy, but more specifically in the shooting pains of turf war and gang patronage within a divided downtown.

The troubled summer of 2001 reflected Kingston at its best and worst: an effervescent cricket series at Sabina Park, carnival capers and tourism on the up. And then the rumble of neighbourhood tensions, competing power blocs and shoot-to-kill policing opened up raw, open conflict. A curfew was imposed on parts of East and West Kingston, as armed police and military jeeps scoured tense streets in an effort to control the inexorable rise of political and territorial violence. Parts of downtown Kingston have earned their fearsome reputation as garrison communities, where walls of loyalty and respect to local politicians or power brokers have effectively sectioned the city.

But these moments of extreme fear and occasional shoot-outs between cops and dealers, neighbourhood "dons" and their opponents, are not the stuff of everyday life for everyone all the time. The downtown communities are troubled on a more frequent basis by poverty and joined more regularly by the common daily grind of survival.

First views on arriving in town via East Kingston give a fleeting glimpse of ghetto life. Anthony Winkler, driving from the airport, reports his initial and fearful sights of poverty on returning to Kingston in *Going Home to Teach*. "Then we are on Windward Road, and nosing through into the first of Kingston's thousand slums. We drive through quickly, ignoring the noises and clamour, not looking at the rows of dirty shops, the ramshackle hovels, the throngs of people who slouch and lean and sag and eye us as we pass. The stench trails after us and lingers in the open car."

Similar scenes shock Zenga Longmore when she arrives in Kingston for the first time:

Shacks made of corrugated iron and wood, lay higgledy-piggledy by the roadside, with people standing outside them, stock still, arms folded, waiting for nothing. Women dressed in ragged dresses sat on doorsteps staring ahead of them with shuttered faces, their hair tied tightly around bright yellow curlers. Men wandered slowly in and out of the shanty houses, wearing torn-off shorts, and oil-stained tee-shirts. Some of them were leaning against the box-like buildings and staring into space.

Connotations of the ghetto suggest lives of segregation and marginality, living on the edge of a society that separates itself into clear social trajectories. Diane Austin-Broos observes that lower Kingston was increasingly called "ghetto" during the 1970s, as those who could afford the move evacuated to the malls and safer zones of uptown: "The violence that erupted in downtown Kingston and eventually spread from the western sections to the east, curving around to the Wareika Hills and encapsulating slums becoming 'a ghetto', laid waste the booming service centre and the employment it had provided." Conflict between neighbourhoods of differing political persuasions pushed not only lives but the city itself into peril. Poet Dennis Scott offers a foreboding picture of the present in "Apocalypse Dub":

Then you closed the window
and turned up the radio, the DJ said greetings
to all you lovely people.
But the children coughed like guns.

Kingston shows many contradictory faces in its downtown areas, which make headlines with sporadic acts of war, yet often reveal surprising riches within pockets of poverty. Lorna Goodison celebrates the beauty of the city and success of the poor in adapting, despite the lingering effects of colonial dependency in "October in the Kingdom of the Poor":

a taffeta rain-streaked lavender purple sky
like the wide skirts of queen elizabeth's dress,
sprinkled with stars silver and spaced.

Ghetto Lives

Kingston's ghetto is in reality a fragmented network of mainly downtown neighbourhoods, united in poverty but divided by political and gang factions. The city as a whole is a concrete and corrugated iron patchwork of towns, former landholdings or estates that were developed as tenement yards or settled as shanty towns as the plantation economy and strictures of a slave-based society waned. The city's lower income area grew as former slaves, and then field workers or their offspring, left the large rural estates and small villages to rebuild new urban lives in Kingston.

A typically detailed account is by Herbert de Lisser, the renowned editor of *The Daily Gleaner*, whose influential and highly descriptive novel tells of a young woman who leaves the countryside and arrives in Kingston to work for an affluent household downtown. *Jane's Career* highlights many of the social tensions apparent in Kingstonian society at the start of the twentieth century, as the capital grew rapidly. Jane Burrell, the heroine, eventually flees the callous treatment of Mrs. Mason, initially sharing a room in a tenement yard, while facing the reality of urban life outside the homes of the wealthy.

> *The moonlight streamed down upon the yard, throwing into relief every part of it, the ramshackle range of rooms, the little superior two-roomed cottage on the other side of yard, the odds and ends of things scattered all about. The poverty of the place stood confessed, and Jane, seated on a box by the threshold of her friend's room had before her eyes the material evidence of the sort of life which most of class must live.*

Since the Second World War the city has expanded into suburbia as rural migrants have flowed into town. Many new residents, however, moved first to the downtown areas, adding to the densely packed yards of the former estate lands. In *Countryman Karl Black* (1981), Neville Farki tells the tale of Karl as he leaves life in rural Jamaica to find work in the capital, eventually in August Town, an uptown part of "downtown": "Kingston is a town of many towns—Allman Town, Whitefield Town, Trench Town, Jones Town, Rae Town are just a few. August Town in many ways resembles most if not all of those towns. It has its stores, shops, rum bars, supermarkets, big houses and its fair share of slums. Its people, like those of other towns, are largely working people. They provide their share of labour for the factories from Spanish Town Road to Rockfort, the business places from Papine to Parade, the public places from Mona to Three Miles and the residential homes from Beverly Hills to Constant Spring."

The "ghetto" is clearly comprised of many parts, but still chillingly emphasizes the social split between the have-much have-less sectors of Kingstonian society. Ruth Glass, in her ominously entitled collection of essays, *Clichés of Urban Doom* (1989), contrasts the visible divisions, grouping the "ghetto" populace on the edge of a social abyss. Her original article was published in *The Listener* in 1962, only a few months before the colony of Jamaica gained independence and the full challenge of moulding together a grossly unequal society was to be faced full on:

> *Nowhere can this contrast be more clearly seen than in Kingston, where almost a quarter of the island's population now live... It has been a dual growth, motivated by prosperity and by destitution; both in a sense parasitic, as both have occurred without a firm economic basis for urbanization. The top groups have climbed up to new suburbs strung along the ranges of the hills. Down below, the dreadful shack dumps of Western Kingston have become darker, denser, larger—through the continuous influx of rural people, unable to subsist in the country, looking for a foothold at the fringes of the urban economy. Brand-new gleaming roads and houses, furniture, refrigerators, large cars—that is the picture of Mona Heights and of similar suburbs to which a minority have retreated. In and around Kingston Pen, where the masses exist in a state of appalling unrelieved neglect, the sights, the smells, the sounds, even the forces of heat and rain, are those of a different world. Here there are flimsy, miserable huts, thrown together, made of refuse – paper, cardboard, packing cases, bits of sticks and part of discarded motor-car bodies. Here there are open drains; no latrines; no sewage disposal. There is constant water famine; barely one stand-pipe for hundreds of people; it is a maze of sodden dirt tracks through a jungle of habitations, unfit for living creatures of any kind.*
>
> *...But in Kingston the jungles are exceptional both in extent and degree of abandonment they expose.*

Orlando Patterson delved deeper into these urban neighbourhoods during the 1960s, recounting the lives of Dinah and others in *The Children of Sisyphus*. Here we observe the physical squalor and moral emptiness involved in the struggle through poverty and the daily ordeal of survival.

The tough, silent meagre little dogs; the uproar and clammy tang of the nearby market, stale, freakish smells of lamb and fish and meat. The clanging of the pans, the pots and mugs and grey aluminium dishes being sold in the stalls on the pavement which they now passed. All was instilled in the dreary consciousness of the garbage-men, marking the tenacious trail of the mute, relentless asses. Seeming to pass, yet for ever present. As fierce as the blazing heat of the morning sun. As cruel and indifferent as the vacant, black faces of the babies clinging to the naked breasts of their pregnant mothers whose swollen bellies continue to cast moving shadows of gloom on the murky streaks of the gutter by the pavement below them. As meaningless as the garbage stacked up behind them.

The rawness of life in the Kingston ghetto is similarly and starkly brought to the fore by Christine Craig's short story, "The Colony" (1992). Peter, a new, young arrival from the countryside observes with a mixture of horror and indifference the new urban world around him.

Peter lay in bed, arms crossed behind his head, staring out past the scraggly garden to a crowded street. A thin boy in ragged clothes hurled his pushcart in between a car and a bus, narrowly missing a collision between all three. The bus driver hurled a stream of invective at him. The man in the car mopped his brow nervously and the boy sped away laughing. Three men sat outside a bar noisily playing dominoes occasionally aiming a kick at a couple of mangy dogs who were sniffing around in the gutter for non-existent scraps. A woman with a large, pregnant belly was embroiled in a heated argument with a man, he punched her in the face and a few passers-by paused, drew closer, watching with a cold curiosity to see the outcome of the fight.

Just north-west of the Parade, beyond Orange Street, Jones Town forms a dense mesh of busy streets and compact yards, enclosed family and communal barracks of brick, tin and card. Patterson describes in bleak and desperate terms such a yard, fenced by cacti:

There was a strange silence in the place. Even the noises that the hungry made, the whimpering of the old women, the knock of the dominoes on the raw wooden tables in the little arid openings that the men made as

*they gambled, even the sounds that the children made as they played
without laughter, they all added to the silence rather than detracted from
it. There was always a hush, always a pressing, eerie, squalid hush forced
down by the bludgeoning cacti, by the little arid, dusty patches, by the
complexity of the narrow, crooked pathways which lost themselves in an
unending maze.*

Roger Mais and the Dungle

Similar in expressive detail and passionate intensity to Patterson's
narration of downtown poverty, Roger Mais' remarkable trilogy of
novels, *The Hills Were Joyful Together* (1953), *Brother Man* (1954) and
Black Lightning (1955) bring to life the Kingston of an earlier era. The
second novel, *Brother Man*, tells the story of a shoemaker and
Rastafarian, John Power, who faces the uncertainties of survival in a
low-income neighbourhood. The physical urban scene in which
Brother Man lives is richly portrayed, as is the messianic role that Mais
gives to his protagonist, conjuring up a potential saviour from the
slum.

Mais (1905-55), an active supporter of the left-of-centre People's
National Party (PNP), intended that his writing would "give the world
a true picture of the real Jamaica and the dreadful condition of the
working classes." The "yard", argues the West Indian academic
Kenneth Ramchand, is a microcosm of Kingston life in the inner-city
neighbourhoods. The prison chaplain in Mais' first novel, *The Hills
Were Joyful Together*, is the voice for authorial social commentary that
introduces a strong and challenging element of environmental
determinism: you are where you live; you are trapped in this world
until the next. The priest, hurrying to destroy a wasp's nest, speaks
starkly of a life without redemption: "What happens to people when
their lives are constricted and dwarfed and girdled with poverty...
things like that and that and that come out of it... moral deformity,
degradation, disease... there I go again, talking the way I shouldn't...
heaven help us, for all are guilty before heaven... God forgive us all, for
all of us stand, with these, in need of forgiveness."

The Dungle was a former rubbish tip, where the poorest of
Kingston lived and scraped over other people's refuse to find daily
rations. Novels about the ghetto tend to emphasize not only the harsh

realities, but also the communal aspects of shared poverty. In *Brother Man*, Mais employs a Chorus of People for his additional commentary, in prose and a gaggle of voices, sounding the visuals of the downtown neighbourhood in which the novel is set:

> *The tongues in the lane clack-clack almost continuously, going up and down the full scale of human emotions, human folly, ignorance, suffering, viciousness, magnanimity, weakness, greatness, littleness, insufficiency, frailty, strength. They clack on street corners, where the ice-shop hangs out a triangular red flag, under the shadow of overhanging buildings that lean precariously, teetering across the dingy chasm of the narrow lane.*
>
> *Over washtubs in the noisome yards where the drip-drip of the eternally leaking stand-pipe makes waste in the sun-cracked green-slimed concrete cistern, and under the ackee tree or the custard-apple tree or the Spanish-guava tree or the Seville orange tree behind the lean-to pit-latrine in the yard, they clack-clack eternally telling their own hunger and haltness and lameness and nightness and negation, like flies buzzing an open remitting sore, tasting again, renewing, and giving again, the wounds they have taken out of the world.*

The urban environment that authors such as Patterson and Mais recount is threatening but vital. Their downtown narratives are those about people getting by, thriving, or failing under duress; the vitality of the ghetto is represented as one on the edge, well beyond that which most visitors to the city will ever experience. Within the home, there is tension and unease. Papacita and Girlie in Mais' *Brother Man* exist in a fraught sphere of well-advised mistrust and their relationship ultimately ends in a savage domestic stabbing. Cordelia, hurtling through insanity, suffocates her child then hangs herself in her room. Familial and even friendly relations are never far from misunderstanding or breakdown.

It is against this unsettling social landscape that Mais constructs the messianic figure of Brother Man, who is juxtaposed to the character of Bra' Ambo as Life or Goodness is to Evil; the healer and the destroyer. The novel is heavy with melodrama and overworked, at times farcical, but the imagery clearly suggests that the mysterious and violent side of life downtown is never far away, even for those living uptown.

The Rastafarian Brother Man is rejected by the neighbourhood in which he lives as an outcast: "Within a matter of days he found himself without a friend in the world... The people whose sick he had healed carefully avoided him in the street; the people he had helped in their hour of need openly jeered at him." Mais points to a Kingston that is unbelieving, unforgiving and perhaps condemned, beyond resurrection. Anti-Rastafarian sentiment turns upon Brother Man and eventually results in him being severely beaten by the mob. He leads his few followers from the ghetto to the main drag downtown, King Street, before heading to the old racecourse, now the National Heroes Park to preach against evil.

Mais was writing in the 1950s, before the Ras Tafari faith received world-wide recognition through the lyrics of reggae flowing from the ghetto. The same residents of the Dungle, Back-o-Wall, Trench Town or Tivoli Gardens would more likely cite politics, drugs and gun culture as the evils of today.

Trench Town

Beyond or perhaps because of the overwhelming pressures of poverty and urban malaise that confront many downtown dwellers, ghetto lives have been the seedbed for a rich and vibrant music and arts scene, which has gripped both Kingstonians and international audiences. Later chapters explore the music and performance venues in more detail, but Trench Town, the stamping ground of a young Bob Marley, more than any other downtown district has clearly marked its place on the world cultural map.

Bob Marley penned several tributes to the people and place surrounding his early musical forays. "Trench Town Rock" celebrates the neighbourhood's buzz, while some of his most famous lyrics open "No Woman, No Cry" with "I remember when we used to sit in the tenement yard in Trench Town." "Trench Town" states simply the pride and resistance brewing in the neighbourhood: "Pay tribute to Trench Town."

Trench Town, east of Jones Town and just north of May Pen cemetery, developed as a fledgling low-income settlement during the 1920s. The area was set aside to house returned troops from the Second

World War and was later registered as one of the four main squatter camps in the city by the Central Housing Authority in 1951. Following the hurricane of that year, the camps gave way to a housing scheme to cater more formally for the city's growing population. Between 1921 and 1943 the population of the Kingston Metropolitan Area doubled from around 60,000 to 120,000 residents. Social and economic pressures multiplied as the urban labour and housing markets were unable to cope with the increased number of city dwellers, many of whom had recently migrated from rural areas.

Trench Town was once the site of valuable real estate, housing middle-class families on a former sugar plantation owned by the Lindos, one of the twenty-one families who allegedly controlled most of Jamaica's economy during the nineteenth century. Some argue that the neighbourhood derived its name from a large trench that ran through the former squatter camps. Others remember Mr. Trench as a builder on the housing project who became the new settlement's namesake. One- and two-storey concrete units were constructed during the 1950s and 1960s, now forming the shells for most of today's homes. Central courtyards with communal access to water and cooking facilities mark the typical Trench Town yard. As the area developed, so did the popular arts scene. Driving along the now dusty and dilapidated Central Street, it is hard, but fascinating, to imagine that Louis Armstrong once performed in the gutted remains of the Ambassador Theatre.

In *The Traveller's Tree* (1950) Patrick Leigh Fermor refers to a Trench Town before the main housing projects were started and well before the political and gang violence since the 1970s made the neighbourhood synonymous with the rough part of town. The visiting English writer found a sort of beauty in the nocturnal neighbourhood.

Trench Town is a labyrinth of slender alley-ways. Warm and sinuous troughs of dust uncoil between tall hedges of candelabra cactus. In the blaze of the moonshine it looks secret and mysterious and astonishingly beautiful. Gaps in the bristling palisades revealed huts of timber and palm-leaf and dusty courtyards: cool and silvery expanses with here and there a donkey or a couple of goats—portentous figures in that brilliant light—munching above the dark pools of their own shadows.

Valerie Bloom's more recent dub poem, "Trench Town shock (a soh dem sey)", reflects more accurately the current perception of the neighbourhood today, fuelled by recurrent stories in the Jamaican press of gang- and turf-based troubles:

Dem try fi aim afta im foot
But im head get een di way,
Di bullit go 'traight through im brain,
At leas' a soh dem sey.
Dry yuh yeye, mah, mi know i'hat,
But I happen ebery day,
Knife-man always attack armed police
At leas' a soh dem sey.

The harshness of life in a low-income district fills much of the musical and literary commentary from and about Trench Town. Chris Salewicz's wonderfully rich narrative of his Kingston travels and interviews as a journalist stresses the cultural and political importance of Trench Town. In *Rude Boy: Once Upon a Time in Jamaica* (2000) Salewicz explores the "ghetto's" explosive past.

Trench Town is seen as barometer for the rest of Jamaica, says Tappa Zukie a deejay and resident of the Rema half of Trench Town: 'Trench Town is a microcosm of what's going on in Jamaica. 'Wha' 'appen in Jamaica,' says Tapper, 'begin in Trench Town. All Jamaica check Trench Town. When we start war, all Jamaica fight.'... It was not until 1967 that the reality of a near-anarchic state, one in which both police and party hitmen were taking on the roles of overmighty medieval English barons, presented itself in specific terms. That year the police were sent to Marcus Garvey Drive to clear out the shantytowns. The shantytown dwellers responded by lobbing Molotov cocktails, an incident recorded in Desmond Dekker's huge international hit '007'.

The urban renewal of the 1950s and 1960s not only built a new cityscape, but also provided rich grounds for political patronage. By swearing allegiance to local politicians, or being forcefully co-opted by their street-soldiering party loyalists, whole neighbourhoods exploited the largesse of the main political interests, namely the Jamaica Labour Party (JLP) and the PNP. Perhaps most infamously, the low-income settlement of Back-o-Wall was razed in the late 1960s to be replaced by Tivoli Gardens, just south of Trench Town. The resulting modern concrete houses and apartments were bequeathed to the government's supporters, ensuring a JLP garrison of loyalty ever since. Likewise, the PNP garnered neighbourhood strongholds, wooing community leaders, the dons or bosses of Kingston's ganglands. Direct political power play, trading material favours and providing "bodyguards" with firearms, lay at the base of a decaying urban democracy. In this manner, downtown neighbourhoods became hotspots of political allegiance, marshalled by local powerbrokers.

Politics and Turf

Since the 1970s, particularly around election time, downtown districts have been territorially marked by political loyalties and, more recently, by dons with paramilitary retinues and absolute turf control.

Laurie Gunst's provocative book, *Born Fi' Dead: A Journey Through the Jamaican Posse Underworld*, focuses on these ideological and criminal connections and the dramatic lives of those involved. Describing residents as the "sufferers", she spent several years living with people in Southside, an area east of South Camp Road and traversed by Victoria Avenue leading into Windward Road.

Southside, and the aptly named adjacent Tel Aviv, like Tivoli Gardens, have been the scenes of violent shoot-outs in recent years, as political henchman, and then the runners for the local dons and dealers have fought over territory and people's lives. Amid these scenes of terror, however, lie clear spaces of hope. A walk around Stephen Lane reveals a quite different Southside. Pat Stanigar, a leading Jamaican architect, has designed a number of colourful and creative offices, and runs his business in the midst of occasionally turbulent times.

Gunst, who clearly felt deeply for the lives of the sufferers, came to experience something of the matrix of poverty and conflict in which they find themselves. Uzi, named after his weapon of choice, is a central figure in her account of the Renkers gang, which ran the roost during the 1990s. On the crumbling, bullet-pocked concrete walls of Southside, the war-torn ghetto where the Renkers posse was born, Uzi's name was scrawled in green, the colour of the Jamaica Labour Party. Brian Meeks' poem "The coup-clock clicks" abruptly describes the extreme violence that sometimes defines Kingstonians' perceptions of downtown neighbourhoods:

Jones town
cries out for water.
the rat a tat
staccato
automatic death
carves out its
place
in history.
children fall
at barricades,
crumpled faces
age
before their
time.

Force and violence in its various forms are arguably inherent aspects of urban society, developed through social tensions and economic conflict. Kingston, emerging from the violent legacy of Port Royal's pirating and the tensions engendered by slavery, has retained its fair shared of troubles. Political and increasingly drug-related gang savagery has taken a toll not only on the day-to-day running of downtown, but on the fear invested in the sufferers and those living outside. Richer Kingstonians have largely rejected downtown communities, many fearing to travel downtown for shopping or business trips, or even out of curiosity. Some residents of New Kingston have not ventured south of North Street for over thirty years, barely four miles from their caged patios.

Ghetto Lines

While talk of "the ghetto" persists in a variety of circles, in many respects it is misleading. Residents of West and East Kingston have clearly faced troubled times, not of their own making, but fomented by the power brokers around them who are carving out turf for political or economic motives. In practical terms, however, a "ghetto" has been created at times of severe stress, when troops have been called out on the streets of Trench Town, Tivoli Gardens or Hannah Town. Curfews have been infrequently enacted and no-go zones forcibly established, ostensibly to quell the riots, but some argue also to provide a clear line from which to defend the luckier uptown dwellers, those largely caught on the more gentle side of political dispute. Oku Onuora's poem "Echo" highlights the fearful normality of growing up in distressed surroundings:

i a tell yu is nu fun
curfew
baton lick
tear gas
gun shat
jail
no bail
dats de lot i haffi bear
fi i de ghetto youth

In July 2001, the Jamaica Defence Force (JDF) called out all National Reserves, the Third Battalion, the Jamaica Regiment and all members of the JDF not on leave to patrol the streets of Kingston. A government spokesperson reluctantly acknowledged that this was the largest domestic military mobilization since the 1976 state of emergency, when political conflict between the warring JLP and PNP garrisons brought downtown to a bloody standstill. Amid claims of police brutality and open hostilities between state, political and community partisans, a subsequent weekend witnessed 25 deaths and 30 injuries in West Kingston.

Despite claims of political, police or business antagonisms, there is often no pattern to the street violence. Unrelated, frequently petty, incidents have sparked gunshots. In Admiral Town, a gunfight started when a man slapped the mother of the neighbourhood don. In Park Lane, street shootings followed the theft of a video camera. Current murder tolls amount to over one thousand per year, an all-time high and second only in *per capita* terms to war-torn Colombia in the region. Sometimes the attacks on public locations reach surreal or bizarre proportions. A police command post on Spanish Town Road, near Coronation Market, was attacked with sticks of dynamite lobbed from passing vehicles, while to the north, newly constructed wards at the Kingston Public Hospital are riddled with bullet holes. Laurie Gunst expands on why the "nightly barrage of gunfire peppered the streets around the hospital":

The hospital was dangerously close to the border between the JLP's West Kingston stronghold and the PNP's Concrete Jungle garrison. Gunmen had recently murdered a hospital porter and torched two of the wards, then killed a policeman and his girlfriend. She was in labour at the time, and he was trying to get her to Jubilee (the childbirth clinic).

Much of the fury stems from long-standing rivalries between politicians and neighbourhood dons. JLP areas such as Rose Town, Tivoli Gardens and Denham Town have stood and fought firm against the neighbouring PNP strongholds of Hannah Town, Arnett Gardens, Whitfield Town and Wilton Gardens, commonly called Rema. Fighting at one point forced the closure of May Pen Cemetery south of

Spanish Town Road as funeral processions became targets. A shocking news story, but not uniquely so, appeared in *The Gleaner* on 7 August 1998: "Tavan Thompson, 9, and his four-year old brother, Rajay, were sitting on the sidewalk near the McIntyre Villa Housing Scheme, eating mangoes when they were killed by gunmen."

A report by Julian Henriques that appeared in 1980, at the height of election time, referred to Hannah Town in West Kingston as a "war zone", as the PNP battled against the JLP: "There, two sets of men, both equally deprived, fight to the kill for a political party that holds out nothing for them. As one Hannah Town youth put it to me: 'Every day the cup fill [with violence] so it soon run over.'" Henriques asked pupils at the local school how the troubles affected them.

> *The children tell me that they were sometimes afraid to come to school and often had to wait for the gunshots to finish before they could leave the house. Then they always had to walk a particular route and avoid certain streets. If you walk on the right of the street, they told me, then it meant "You Peanut" (that is a PNP supporter). If you walked on the left, it meant, "You Jelly" or a JLP man. "What happens if you walk down the middle?" I asked. "Then you informer," came the instant chorus.*

Olive Senior's poem "Childhood" relates the experience of growing up in a society where harsh violence seeps through the events and emotions of youth in both urban and rural surrounds. She laments the role which brutality plays in the day-to-day life of Jamaica:

> *Rivers flow red and swollen with the clay*
> *of upstream mountains where the*
> *rains fall. Mockingbirds call*
> *in the woods from the roseapple tree*
> *echo the cry of crazy-lost children*
> *and the bird-filled hills fear still*
> *sudden death. By slingshot.*

For sure, Jamaica grew from a cruel concoction of slavery and imperial mercantilism, but perhaps, as Anthony Winkler suggests, Kingston in recent times has fast forwarded to a noticeably more ferocious future: "Thieves had stalked the Jamaican night for as long as I could remember. In the old days they carried stones, clubs, knives and machetes, and the householder armed with a pistol and a faithful dog had the advantage. But in these troubled times the thieves walked the night with guns and a murderous fire in their eyes."

Gun Court

The government responded to lethal weaponry in the 1970s with more arms and a Gun Court on South Camp Road to isolate those arrested for gun crime. Chris Salewicz visited the razor-wired block of the Gun Court, as ominous-looking as it is notorious.

> *The Gun Court had a reputation that was fearsome. To all intents and purposes, the place was a concentration camp, and certainly it had been built to look like one: gun towers, barbed-wire perimeters, visibly armed guards, a harsh, militaristic feel immediately apparent to all who drove past its location on South Camp Road. The Gun Court was a product of Michael Manley's Emergency Powers Act of 1975. Into it was dumped, for indefinite detention or execution after a summary trial, anyone in Jamaica found with any part of a gun.*

Politicians from all parties have made efforts, rhetorical for the main part, to end the spates of gun violence in Kingston's downtown. Perhaps the Gun Court reflects a more sinister reality, expressed in words by a young boy in the country, recently returned from the capital in Christine Craig's short story, "In the Hills":

> *He spoke for awhile then of his hot, bitter existence in the city. No job, no money for him. When the big ones spoke it had sounded so simple. Stay with me, learn to hate, learn to kill and you will have a job, you will have a house and you will be free.*

Hatred, or group fear, leads to mob violence. On 27 March 2000, *The Gleaner* reported: "A 24 year-old man who reportedly went on a robbery spree in the Barbican area of St. Andrew yesterday morning was set up on by an angry mob who disarmed him and beat him to death." Expectation, as well as revenge, can fuel alarming collective reaction.

Following the electoral violence that seized downtown Kingston during 1980, Lorna Goodison charts the failings of the "green-clad muse", the dollar-driven drugs economy entwined with the channels of political patronage and dependency in "Jamaica 1980":

For all over this edenism
hangs the smell of necromancy
and each man eats his brother's flesh
Lord, so much of the cannibal left
in the jungle of my people's tongues.

We've sacrificed babies
And burnt our mothers
as payment to some viridian-eyed God dread
who works in cocaine under hungry men's heads.

The signs of decaying social fabric are there to be seen. During the same election year, at a school in Hannah Town, a young pupil was heard to say, "Teacher, I like you." "Thank you, that's a nice thing to say," replied the teacher. Then the child followed up by saying, "Teacher, would you like me to get you a gun?" St. Anne's secondary school is located on the sniper alley borderline between the JLP-loyal Denham Town and PNP Hannah Town. School attendance dropped from 2,000 to 500 during the late 1990s, and about 2,000 people left the school district due to the troubles. Politicians and social workers feared that violence had become fully ingrained as a way of life for too many Kingstonians.

Don Robotham's recent research on youth unemployment and violence in downtown Kingston records: "And you see when a man idle? Anything happen when a man idle, you know! You see when a man hungry? A man go tief! And when a man tief, you know and a next man see him tief, him a go want do him things. And the next man sees him..." And so the circle curves more viciously. A radio relays the reggae refrain, "A hungry man is an angry man," while "Popcorn", the community leader in Tivoli Gardens upholds the innocence of local residents. The police, he argues, have "troubled an anthill and everyone know what happen when you trouble an anthill."

Future Hopes: Trench Town Culture Yard

The above news stories, readily plucked from the pages of *The Gleaner*, highlight the terrain of fear and physical violence that has shaped some parts of downtown Kingston for much of the last thirty years. But among these hard-hitting tales, are many brighter instances of a rejuvenating downtown. The former home of Bob Marley in Trench Town at 6, 8 and 10 Lower First Street has been transformed into a Culture Yard, creating a cultural and entrepreneurial space for local residents. Clichés notwithstanding, it is impossible not to visit and talk with those involved in the project and find yourself sitting in a landscape of hope.

The Trench Town Culture Yard and Village, managed as a community-based project, celebrates Bob Marley's and Trench Town's rich musical legacy. For many years, Marley's former home was visited informally by his fans and tourists. Now, the yard has been opened up, rooms restored, the Wailers' van parked nearby and evocative possessions of Bob and the band returned to their original rooms. Every week or so, informal concerts by local and leading national musicians are performed in the yard, revelling in a revived musical arena.

Mikey Smith, a local community leader and chair of the Trench Town initiative, knew Bob Marley well and helped to establish the project in 1995, following troubles between Matthew's Lane and Tivoli Gardens. The energetic Kingston architect, Chris Stone, oversaw the renovation of the yard, which was formally opened in February 2000 on the 55th anniversary of Marley's birth. At the opening ceremony, Rita Marley reminisced over their years in the tenement yard and the lack of privacy for a young couple, pointing to the kitchen, the place where they first made love. Later that same month, Prince Charles visited the Culture Yard and was presented with a tam, a woollen Rasta hat lined with artificial locks, by Rita Marley. He promptly sported the headgear back to front. As Stonemam, the yard's Rasta sage, commented on the prince's brief visit to this centre of New Jerusalem, it was an occasion when "King meets

King—we try to teach him." It was also, he added, as Bob the Prophet intended.

For many, the Culture Yard is a spiritual place, focusing an emotional attachment to Bob Marley on hopes for a revived community presence in the neighbourhood and beyond. In practical terms, the project is a direct attempt to open up access to "the ghetto", to create a space of music and cultural celebration in an environment scarred by violence. Few lines more fittingly highlight the rationale for the Culture Yard than Bob Marley's "Trench Town Rock": "you're grooving in Kingston 12…"

"You ever have bad dreams that keep you awake at night?"
Downtown Kingston can undoubtedly be a rough place to live, not least to visit. City life can be alienating for the excluded and marginalized. Jean Binta Breeze's classic dub poem "Riddym Ravings" tells the story of a madwoman, a homeless rural migrant now trapped in Kingston, abused and left to roam the streets, with the continual sound of a radio playing in her head:

> *Eh eh*
> *No feel no way*
> *Town is a place dat a really kean stay*
> *Dem kudda – ribbit mi han*
> *Eh ribbit mi toe*
> *Mi waan go a country go look mango.*

Her plight, pregnant and left to wash in a street standpipe until one day she is sent to Bellevue Hospital, exemplifies life at the margins for many in Kingston.

In Roger Mais' novel, Minette asks Brother Man about his fears and nightmares. He replies, "Bad dreams? Sometimes. We all get them. But they go. And other dreams, and visions, come in their place." Projects such as the Culture Yard and the optimism of an alternative path suggested through the architecture of Southside's Pat Stanigar or Chris Stone in Trench Town encourage a transition that is slowly changing Kingston's ghetto, and as importantly, those living beyond the fences of the yards. Safe zones downtown are encouraged by participation. Trench Town residents are briefed that visitors will be around the neighbourhood, retracing the footsteps of Bob. "Don't hassle the tourist" was a famous, if controversial and patronizing, campaign initiated by the Jamaica Tourist Board to ease the hard sell on unsuspecting and gullible visitors to the North coast beach resorts. Such enthusiasm, and the need to engage with tourist dollars, is not new in Jamaica's service-dependent economy. In the 1950s, Mona Macmillan wrote from her perspective as a temporary resident in Kingston: "Visitors who come as obvious tourists will get plenty of attention from porters, taxi-drivers, beggars and touts of all sorts—some apt to be vociferous and overwhelming." She added, with some pride, that she herself was never "troubled" on any on her promenades through the city.

While Kingston's downtown is more renowned for its turbulent headlines, the increasing openness of the streets is slowly breaking down the well-grounded fear that strangers and danger are one and the same.

I wandered back to the noise and bustle of the narrow lanes and crowded streets of slums. It was Saturday and there was a Saturday night air about the slums. The people were colourful and gay. Not even poverty seemed able to subdue them. And their lilting voices made the English language sound strangely exotic and charged with a new vitality absent from it when mere Englishmen spoke it.

When Peter Abrahams penned the above thoughts in *Jamaica: An Island Mosaic* (1957), he tended towards the romantic, but more recent writings also show that there is much to celebrate at the expanding margins of Kingston's cultural and social scenes. C.G.O. King suggests that "Behind Jamaican literature lies a unifying spirit of shared experience." The next chapter follows the literary and personal careers of famous Kingstonians who have helped to shape the city's collective present.

CHAPTER FIVE

Heroines and Heroes:
The City's Nation-Builders

"Why
did you damage
the statue
of the National Hero?

—Because I have plenty damage
inside me.
You want to see
My scar?"

Olive Senior, "City Poem" (1985)

National Heroes Park

Dust-blown and dry at the northern tip of East Street, National Heroes Park houses the tombs and monuments celebrating Jamaica's select seven. The Order of National Hero was created in 1965 to celebrate the founding figures of the new state, "symbols of transformation" who participated in the enlightened struggle for freedom, according to Kamau Braithwaite, one of the region's great literary figures. Among those elected so far have been Nanny of the Maroons, inspirational woman leader of the runaway slave revolt during the seventeenth century; Samuel Sharpe, who instigated the 1831 slave rebellion that hastened abolition; George William Gordon and Paul Bogle, both campaigners for universal human rights; and Marcus Garvey, Sir William Alexander Bustamante and Norman Washington Manley, whose actions and ideas during the twentieth century helped to shape the country of today. Controversial, charismatic, outspoken and visionary, key moments of these three latter lives were lived within the capital's streets.

The courageous deeds of the nation's finest are further celebrated each year in mid-October on National Heroes' Day by a ceremony held at the park, once the site of the island's leading race course. Tucked into the southern curve which now winds into the home straight of a vast barren brown-grassed space to the north, the heroes' enclosure stables a range of eminent worthies. Memorials to these dignitaries are corralled alongside the shrines to the Heroes themselves. Beside the tombs of Sir Alexander Bustamante, Norman Washington Manley and Marcus Garvey, whose remains were flown from England in 1964 with full state honours, lie those of former Prime Ministers Michael Manley and Donald Sangster. Accompanying them, a nearby bronze statue records the visit of the great South American liberator, Simón Bolívar. As a result of his revolutionary activities on the Spanish mainland, he was exiled in Kingston for seven months in 1815, living at a boarding house on the corner of Princess and Tower Streets. It was here that he wrote the "Jamaica Letter" in which outlined his vision of a united and independent mainland American republic. Three months later, he survived an assassination attempt and was forced to flee the island, but his flight marked the beginning of a heroic struggle for liberation in the Americas.

Garvey and the Racist Legacy

A more recent American freedom fighter, Martin Luther King Jr, declared his admiration for one of Jamaica's great protagonists, Marcus Mosiah Garvey. During a visit to the University of West Indies campus at Mona in 1965, Dr. King told an exhilarated, red-gowned and capped audience crammed into the Assembly Hall to face the challenges of the hour as Garvey had done before them. They must act upon Garvey's heroism, he argued, and strive for black liberation. The following day amidst the fierce heat of June, he laid a wreath at the Heroes' Park grave, praising his courage and dignity. Garvey's legacy for African Americans in the United States, he announced, was "a sense of personhood, a sense of manhood, a sense of somebodiness."

What had this Jamaican, born in the rural parish of St. Anne, achieved to earn such praise from one of the greatest political activists of the twentieth century? Marcus Garvey sparked the first flickering flames of black activism in modern times, from which Martin Luther King fuelled the fires of the civil rights movements during the 1960s. Although born in Jamaica, Garvey's greatest successes were achieved in the United States. He preached against colonial and social oppression, and established the United Negro Improvement Association in 1914 to champion black interests. African ancestry in the Americas, he argued, was not a stigma to be suffered, but a source of pride and dignity. It was a platform for radical political mobilization. Garvey was energetic, controversial, talented, persuasive, progressive, Jamaican and black—a national hero.

As a child and adult, Marcus Garvey experienced the full force of the colonial and racist context into which he was born. He left school at fourteen, but also left behind a playmate from a neighbouring white household: "Her parents thought the time had come to separate us and draw the colour line. They sent her and another sister to Edinburgh, Scotland, and told her that she was never to write or to try to get in touch with me, for I was a 'nigger'. It was then that I found out that there was some difference in humanity, and that there were different races, each having its own separate and distinct social life."

This was Jamaica at the turn of the twentieth century, but the curse of racism lingers in perhaps more subtle forms. Ruth Glass reported in the 1960s, during the time of Luther King's prominence, forty years after Garvey's first intervention: "In Jamaica, points of time no more than 200 or 100 years ago seem like yesterday." She added, "It is when you go into the slum camps of Kingston (and few outsiders from the comfortable areas of Kingston ever do)—it is then that you are directly confronted by colonial history: you are in the presence of the aftermath of slavery."

Garvey and many others before and after have devoted their lives to the removal of this legacy. Race or colour differences map much of Kingston's social terrain. In the 1950s, Peter Abrahams described Jamaica as a rush of people in a continuum of "colours":

Cars, lorries, carts and human voices rent the air. People hurried in all directions; women in lovely cotton prints, men in the regulation white shirt, tie and sleeves buttoned up at the wrists... And everywhere, in the streets, on the side-walks, in big and shops, were the people of Kingston: black and brown and white and yellow and every other shade and grade of colour.

Forty years later, Anthony Winkler's ruminations amid the arrival chaos of the Norman Manley International Airport similarly focused on a kaleidoscope of colours:

The faces in the room are black, brown, swarthy, some glinting with the yellow glow of the Oriental, some an indescribable stew of races… Long dead Englishmen peer out of coal black dark faces; former slaves smoulder under the yellowish skins of mulattoes; an East Indian ancestor lies mummified inside the body of the half-Chinese lady resignedly waiting her turn to battle customs. 'Out of Many, One People,' is the Jamaican motto.

It is all here in the airport. Three hundred years of colonialism: a people who were brought here as slaves or came as plunderers…

Aesthetics—celebrated, loved, loathed—were the visual marker of Garvey's incipient message that race mattered, as a source of active pride rather than passive shame. Una Marson's poem relates wryly the "Kinky Hair Blues", highlighting the commonly heard grievance of hair colour and type:

I like me black face
And me kinky black hair.
I like me black face
And me kinky black hair.
But nobody loves dem,
I jes don't tink it's fair.

A lingering bias for "straight hair" still holds among many Jamaicans. Fernando Henriques describes the efforts undertaken by some islanders during the 1950s to "whiten" up. He comments, with some contemporary pertinence, that "one's place in the scheme of things in Jamaica is thus largely determined by how you look in relation to the European." Skin lightening with the use of chemicals was a precise art form in the city's salons: "Hairdressers in Jamaica also help women to achieve a fairer complexion. They use a pack made up of peroxide, clay, and fuller's earth, which is worked into a paste and coated on the face. It is left on for about a quarter of an hour. The effect is supposed to be that of a light smooth skin."

Times have moved on, but skin bleaching still occurs today. Creams containing the harsh chemical hydroquinone bleach outer layers of skin, and are often bought and applied liberally. The alternative popular scrub is the home-made potion of toilet bleach and toothpaste. Once bleached, an additional Kingston special is the "fowl pill", popped by women to plump themselves into a state of fashionable curvature, which is then poured into skin-tight "battyriders". These hormone tablets, bought at livestock stores, are more commonly fed to market-bound chickens, where the side effects of halitosis, nausea and diarrhoea perhaps cause less of a stir.

Corpulence and clarity of complexion are much sought-after in the dancehall, although Buju Banton received a shower of criticism for the lyrics of his hit song, "Love mi Browning", which praised the beauty of his light-skinned lover. Such is the confusion that still reigns with regard to race, colour and complexion. Little has changed since the 1950s when Peter Abrahams commented that "There are hangovers of the old colour attitude among some whites. And there are some coloureds who have no time for blacks save as inferiors." The minority population of white Jamaicans still benefit from the legacy of wealth and past colonial privilege, although many left the island during the political violence of the 1970s. The majority of the population, however, remains poor. Ruth Glass, during her brief but biting review of Jamaican society, clarified her vision of the country's historical lineage of uneven wealth: "In Jamaica, prosperity still has a light skin, however varied in shade; poverty—almost always—has a black one."

Whiteness has long marked the boundaries of assumed polite society along Kingston's social faultlines. Edward Long, firmly distanced from the masses and accepted within polite eighteenth-century society, was moved to comment on the self-indulgent figures of the island-born elite: "The native white men, or Creoles, of Jamaica are in general tall and well-shaped; and some of them are rather inclined to corpulence." Roaming among the decadent dinner circles of high society, he connected climate and fidelity and fielded a barrage of assumptions: "With a strong natural propensity to the other sex, they are not always the most chaste and faithful of husbands." He concluded, "They are too much addicted to expensive living, costly entertainments, dress and equipage."

Two centuries later, Patrick Leigh Fermor embarked upon a similar foray into other people's lives, swallowing the stories of Jamaican sailors in a dockside rum shop. The vile nature of Jamaica's colour-bar during the 1940s was deceptive yet apparent at once:

> 'But the black man, he stays right where he is. Right here.' He lit his pipe. 'We're always going somewhere. But we never get there.' There was a sound of assent from others at the table. 'That's right, boss. We're all equal but we ain't equal.' I was surprised by this general agreement, though it confirmed feelings that had first occurred to me in Barbados: that our middle course between the French and American extremes—that is, colour bar that is non-existent in law but in social practice violently alive—leaves the coloured race stranded in a limbo of uncertainty whose invisible frontiers materialize when touched, and only then, into walls of adamant. Being invisible, it is often impossible, without collision, to gauge their distance.

The invisible ceiling reveals itself amidst Kingston's social strata in *The Children of Sisyphus*, when a newly-won school scholarship is viewed as a conspiratorial irrelevance by Rachael, an elderly neighbour who has long-suffered the "colour-bar" and views education with suspicion:

> 'Higher dem studies? Den is wha' yu an' yu pickney business wid dat fur? That is backra business. Wha' de rass yu goin' sen' yu pickney fe higher her studies fo'? Is bust yu wan fe bus' de pickney brain? Education no mek fo' neager people, yu know.'
>
> 'Jus' move off! Yu see me pickney look like dem other little dry-head, black pickney dem 'bout de place. Yu no' see she 'ave backra blood in a her. Is her father she get de brains from. Me black an' stupid, but her sailor father give her all de brains she need.'

Race Matters

"No honest person familiar with Jamaican life could deny for a minute that the bogey of blood looms over every chair." Kenneth Pringle lamented the contours of 1930s racism in *Waters of the West*, but the issues linger. Black and white stories are criss-crossed with the ambiguities of colour. Many visiting and resident white authors made often lecherous asides within patronizing or derogatory statements on the population's racial mix. The Glaswegian writer Michael Scott expressed his tastes anonymously in *Tom Cringle's Log* (1833), describing the John Canoe parade on Christmas Day during the early nineteenth century: "But the beautiful part of the exhibition was the Set Girls. They danced along the streets, in bands from fifteen to thirteen. There were brown sets, and black sets, and sets of all intermediate gradations of colour... I had never seen more beautiful creatures that there were amongst the brown sets—clear olive complexions, and fine faces, elegant carriages, splendid figures—full, plump and magnificent."

A century later, Zora Neale Hurston would write in *Voodoo Gods* (1939) that "Jamaica is the land where the rooster lays an egg. Jamaica is two per cent white and the other ninety-eight per cent all degrees of mixture between white and black." She highlighted the semantics of "lightening up" among parts of the population who preferred to connect themselves to a European rather than African heritage:

> *The joke about being white on the census records and coloured otherwise has its curious angles. The English seem to feel that 'If it makes a few of you happy and better colonials to be officially white, very well. You are white on the census rolls.' The Englishman keeps on being very polite and cordial to the legal whites in public, but ignores them utterly in private and social life.*

Hurston's comments on the "frantic stampede whiteward to escape from Jamaica's black mass" ring true in the pages of *Wide Sargasso Sea* (1966), a novel by Jean Rhys who captures the fear of Jamaican whites finding themselves among free and hostile former slave workers. The changing circumstances of an emancipated labour force threatened the decadent comfort of the white elite. The novel extrapolates the life of

Mrs. Rochester, the unsettled first wife in Charlotte Brontë's *Jane Eyre*, who arrives in Jamaica from a smaller Caribbean island. Menace and psychological insecurity underpin the narrative. The bubbling discontent and contempt for the white elite is expressed by Esau, himself the offspring of a shamelessly callous planter and his enslaved mother: "The heart know its own bitterness but to keep it lock up all the time, that is hard."

Revolt among the ranks of the enslaved underclass was a constant fear for the white colonial elite of Kingston. In 1807 Governor Coote issued secret instructions to raise additional militia to "prevent insurrection or insubordination among the negroes, whose minds already elated by the abolition of the Slave Trade which few of them rightly understand, will be full prepared and disposed for any mischief during the relaxed discipline of the Christmas Holydays."

Hurston completed her comments on racialized fears with the sadly comic tale of a visiting dignitary from the United States, who was unaware of or perhaps deliberately provoked the sense of racial sensitivity in Jamaica society:

> *I was told that John Hope, the late president of Atlanta University, precipitated a panic in Kingston on his visit there in 1935, a few months before his death. He was quite white in appearance, and when he landed and visited the Rockefeller Institute in Kingston and was honoured by them, the 'census white' Jamaicans assumed that he was of pure white blood. A great banquet was given for him at the Myrtle Bank Hotel, which is the last word in swank in Jamaica. All went well until John Hope was called to respond to a toast. He began his reply with: 'We negroes...' Several people nearly collapsed. John Hope was whiter than any of the mulattoes there who had had themselves ruled white. So that if a man as white as that called himself a negro, what about them? Consternation struck the banquet like a blight.*

It was this unease, the negation of an African past and present which Garvey sought to enlighten and empower. His rhetoric ranged from gentle reflection to fire and brimstone attacks on racialized inequalities. One of Garvey's earlier verses, "Keep Cool", published in 1927 in his newspaper *The Negro World*, adopted a restrained, "we-

shall-overcome" calmness to the divisive impact of racism in Jamaica
and beyond:

> *Throw your troubles far away,*
> *Smile a little ever day,*
> *And the sun will start to shine,*
> *Making life so true and fine.*
> *Do not let a little care*
> *Fill your life with grief and fear:*
> *Just be calm, be brave and true,*
> *Keep your head and you'll get through.*

But time for passive resistance sped by. Building on the Jamaican
legacies of forceful resistance and revolt, Garvey laid the ideological
basis for future black power movements and civil rights activists.

Revolts, Revolution and Garveyism

The Maroons or runaway slaves had led a series of revolts and wars
during the previous centuries, but it was Garvey who brought the
political fight for equality to the streets of Kingston during the
twentieth. Born in St. Ann's Bay on the north coast in 1887, he headed
to the capital city as a teenager and found work as a printer. Immersing
himself in words via work and self-tuition, he was a proud and
independent thinker. Friends recalled his constant study and devotion
to learning, always carrying about himself a pocket dictionary which he
studied whenever possible, finding quiet corners of the Parade or the
printing press workshop in which to read. Viewed by many as a prophet,
the "Black Moses" was far from being a retiring bookworm. He spoke
out at political meetings, picking up the torch lit by earlier activists like
Robert Love or the black revivalists such as Alexander Bedward, and
soon collected a committed following. A far cry from his earlier verse,
"Centenary's Day" forcefully bears out his call for black liberation:

> *Our father bore the stinging lash*
> *Of centuries of slavery's crime;*
> *But we are here without abash,*
> *For we shall win in God's good time.*

To Afric's shore we're bound again,
In freedom's glory won at large;
In thoughts we claim just a bargain,
To sail in liberty's fair barge.

On the streets and in the halls of Kingston he tested the waters of the revolutionary tide: "Rise, you people, for you are God's children and you are the equal of any people in the world—one aim, one God, one destiny." This was to become the rallying cry for the United Negro Improvement Association (UNIA), which he launched in 1914 after touring Central America and Europe. He championed the Back to Africa movement, an implicit tenet of the subsequent Ras Tafari movement: "For God's sake, you men and women who have been keeping yourself away from the people of your own African race, cease the ignorance; unite, arise, take on the toga of race pride." Garvey confronted racial discrimination and the colonial establishment in the same blow. His rhetoric of race shattered the political silence for black representation and equality, bringing him into direct conflict with Kingston's brown middle class. By asking the popular masses to reject the present and seek a future built on a black past, Garvey's call was muted in Jamaica. "I was openly hated," he penned on reflection, "and persecuted by some of these coloured men of the island who did not want to be classified as Negroes."

In 1916 Garvey took his message to the United States. It was here that the seeds of his political discontent and campaigning took roots. He launched his own shipping company, the Black Star Line, as part of UNIA, to provide the seafaring vessels for the return to Africa and to "write the name of race across the commercial history of the world." Hundreds of people lined Kingston's harbour front as the flagship, the *Yarmouth*, sailed in on her maiden voyage. Cries, cheers and excitement buzzed among the crowded downtown streets as hundreds saluted the parade of the ship's crew and officers. The reception was much cooler among the lighter elite, guardians of the commercial and political status quo. Herbert de Lisser, precise commentator on the city's events as editor of *The Daily Gleaner*, guardedly mused that "a new spirit has passed over the lower classes, which has nothing to commend it except its ignorance."

This fresh ardour was for African redemption, representation and liberation. A dangerous cocktail was mixed, which the US authorities feared to taste on home ground. Following a trial on charges of mail fraud, Garvey was sentenced to prison and eventually deported back to Kingston in 1927. Again the crowds greeted him, but the peak of his personal political success had already passed, even if support was still considerable. Hundreds of UNIA chapters now existed around the world. The *Negro World, New Jamaican* and *Black Man* newspapers were published voices for the cause. Edelweiss Park, a social centre for black advancement, political evangelism and spiritual upliftment at Cross Roads in Kingston, was established by Garvey and his followers. He helped to lay the foundations for Jamaica's first organized political party, the People's Political Party. Elected office for Garvey himself, however, proved elusive. Bankruptcy, ill health and a conviction for contempt of court forced his passage to England in 1935. Here he died five years later, largely forgotten on Kingston's streets and among the political class, but his legacy lasted. Twenty-four years later, his dying wish not to be left in a "land of strangers" was finally fulfilled when his remains were brought home to rest as a National Hero, only a stone's throw away from the premises of the printers who first brought him to the city.

Troubled Thirties, Liberated Sixties

While Garvey lived out the remainder of his years in the cold climate of London, the heat of civil unrest agitated the masses of Kingston. Wildly unjust class and colonial strictures were pushed to snapping point by the Jamaican riots of 1938. Global economic downturn in the 1930s heightened the inequalities of Kingston life, and brought the people out on the streets in anger and frustration:

> *it was impossible,*
> *at that time,*
> *to count the accusing fists*
> *and the fires;*
> *but the flames promised to crack*
> *and shatter the colonial looking-glass,*
> *and spike the approaching,*

indifferent independence,
the late emancipation,
something like broken glory,
a dragging freedom,
a received liberation:
somebody else's ironic gift;…

Andrew Salkey's poem "Upheaval 1938" captures the blaze of rioting that brought Kingston to a temporary halt. While Garvey had stoked the fire for race-based protest, political kindling for the next quarter of a century was passed to the hands of two extraordinary cousins, Sir William Alexander Bustamante and Norman Washington Manley. Fighting at first side by side, these two politicians fought over and forged Jamaican statehood. They were both nation builders and National Heroes. As Thomas Wright (Morris Cargill's pseudonym) versified in *The Daily Gleaner* during 1962 upon the declaration of independence:

God bless Sir Alexander
And God bless Manley too
The finest founding fathers to be had.
But we have the usual trouble
That with us is nothing new
We really don't know which one is our Dad.

Despite the turbulent times of the 1930s, the crown colony system still determined Jamaica's path during the 1940s and 1950s. Holding the political reins, colonial ideology and mores proved resilient and difficult to break down. Michelle Cliff recreates a young girl's memory on the eve of independence in her short story "Contagious Melancholia" (1998): "As we enter the house the wireless is tuned to the Queen's message, coming to us live from what my father calls the Untidy Kingdom. He believes this puts them in their place, as when he refers to our neighbour to the north as the Untidy Snakes of America."

Kingston was a capital city, but without independent power. Debt, high unemployment and a dependent economy shackled Jamaicans to external overlords, while the corrosive colour-ranked class legacy lived on. Andrew Salkey's "Saturday in Kingston" pauses from the weekend revelries to review the state of the nation and its exploited workforce:

I looked at the regiment
of rum bottles,
at the vivid labels,
and saw two cane-cutters
carrying bundles
on most of them,
and heard:
"Massa, we workin',
we still workin' 'ard for you!"
I thought of black shoulders
under cutting lashes
instead of black faces
grinning on rum bottles.

It is from this background that Bustamante and Manley emerged, shaking tailcoats, ballot boxes and the political landscape.

Political Theatre: the Manleys and Busta

Norman Washington Manley (1893-1969) headed Jamaica's most notable clan of the last century. He was a barrister by profession; his wife Edna fashioned the contemporary Jamaican art scene, while one of his sons, Michael, followed in his footsteps as a political and national leader. His granddaughter Rachel is a respected Jamaican author and poet. Piecing together the lives of the Manleys echoes the evolution of Kingston. Their stories are lived within and around the capital. The history of the clan, and in particular the city-based political battles between Norman Manley and Alexander Bustamante (1884-1977), shaped the Kingston and the country of today.

The vital organ of Manley's political career was the party that he launched in 1938, the People's National Party (PNP). A few months after civil unrest had scarred the city's streets, Manley packed the Ward Theatre with the announcement of this new socialist-inspired political force. Crowds streamed out onto the Parade and a new political era began. Beside him on the stage, his distant cousin and future political rival Bustamante glowered and conjured with the audience. While Manley's rhetoric was cool and seemingly remote, Bustamante's voice leapt at the congregation. What Bustamante lacked in political tact and precision, he howled with energy and bravado. Manley himself recounts Bustamante's firepower in his unfinished autobiography. During the street confrontations in May of that year, Bustamante had clambered upon the statue of Queen Victoria in the Parade. A dramatic confrontation ensued as the police descended upon the workers gathered in the square to hear out their champion. As the law enforcers raised their weapons, the towering figure of Bustamante, topped by a mop of windblown hair, ripped open his shirt and challenged the police to fire: "You cowards. Shoot me, but leave these unfortunate hungry people alone." The police and crowds dispersed without harm.

Bustamante's rabble-rousing antics were clearly fit for the stage of the magnificent Ward Theatre, and Norman Manley's assured, yet poised, style of politics was far removed from the hustle and bustle of his robust cousin. While the first outing of the PNP was Manley's showpiece, his future opponent would return with his own party, the Jamaican Labour Party (JLP), on the eve of the first full elections in the country's history. In 1944, a third party, the Jamaican Democratic Party (JDP), held a rally in the Ward Theatre, which was full with an expectant audience of well-to-do supporters. As the genteel meeting and oratory processed, a towering figure rose from the back stalls and pushed his way to the front. The speaker flustered to a halt. Bustamante had risen from the ranks, proceeded to centre stage and exited the theatre amidst an astonished silence. Without words, but with the silent stamp of his disdain, Bustamante had condemned the JDP to the political cheap seats. He advanced from there to win the first general election.

The Ward Theatre, despite its connection with momentous political passages, did provide some moments of light-hearted and mischievous personal pantomime for the Manleys. Rachel recounts the tale of the visit with her grandfather, whom she called Pardi. On this occasion, he was already a distinguished figure in politics and a national leader. "When we went to the pantomime at the big Ward Theatre in Kingston, he joined me in the little alcove beside the special box where he usually sat, and we aimed peanuts at the shining bald pates underneath, ducking back into our seats if we scored a hit. More than once, we missed and our missiles lodged in a lady's hairdo."

Bustamante's style was summed up at the time by Peter Abrahams: "He has in turn, been waiter, salesman, dietician, moneylender, police inspector and traffic manager for a New York tramway company... In 1944, grown into a magnetic, flamboyant political personality, he offered the poor of his country Utopia; and they preferred it to the hard work Manley promised." While he was clearly a respected mover, shaker and diplomat, Bustamante was also something of a dandy. Born William Alexander Clarke in 1884, he rebranded himself as a Bustamante, drawing on an assumed Spanish flair and a twist of the grandee. The early days of his travelling and fantastical adventures remain shrouded in an alluring mix of the possible and improbable. His *Who's Who* entry highlighted his adoption as a teenager by a Spanish sailor, a few years of high jinks on the seas, fighting a war in Morocco, medical expertise in a New York hospital and tours of exploration through Central America. O. Phelps adds dryly, "The sole authority on much of Bustamante's personal history is Bustamante himself. The common view regarding this source is that while always interesting— in fact, often dramatic—it is highly unreliable." It is clear, however, that at the age of fifty-four as the respectable owner of a modest loan company, he whipped up a non-stop strike-organizing, riot-appeasing and commotion-leading political whirlwind that carried him to the premiership. It was rumoured that a strict diet of brandy and carrot juice fuelled this towering physique and unquenchable political fire.

Following a series of impassioned letters to *The Daily Gleaner* from "Bustamante", the early mystique of his political career was launched with the self-penned and simple reply to numerous questions about the writer's identity: "Bustamante is a lonely fighter." Kingstonians, eager for dramatic heroes, palpably clustered to his rising image as an activist and his literally towering frame and shock of unruly hair. Eccentric behaviour added to the crafted allure and his popular draw. The Jamaican sociologist Fernando Henriques recounts one of many performances that enlivened Kingston's downtown:

The Corporation or Parish Council of Kingston, of which Mr Busta-mante was a prominent member, had been having a stormy meeting.

According to the Daily Gleaner of May 13ᵗʰ (1947) this is what followed: During these verbal clashes thousands of ex-service men and others were marching... calling for the PM to show himself outside the Corporate Building—As he made his appearance the crowd milled around him, while policemen surrounded him, and his supporters stood firm to prevent any jostling. Someone reported to the Labour chief that his car had been damaged, that the tyres had been cut, the glass in one of the headlights broken, and air let out of the wheels. Mr Bustamante's face reddened. He made a sudden movement with both hands towards his hip, yelling as he did so: "Keep back, keep back. The rest of you keep back. Keep back I say." As he brought his right hand up there was a revolver in it. The left hand fumbled for a while in the hip pocket, but ultimately emerged and there was second revolver in it. Mr Bustamante went into a crouch and waved the revolvers about in front of him, shouting at the people to keep back, while someone in the crowd echoed: "Keep back. The man mad, he's going to shoot"... At that moment the revolver in Mr Bustamante's left hand was discharged, the revolver being pointed downwards towards the pavement... and a stampede was on. In that moment Mr Bustamante and his supporters entered a taxi and drove away. Shortly after he left quiet was restored... The confusion over, an onlooker commented: "The Chief must be losing his power. He was very slow on the draw."'

Matching tailored suit, socks, handkerchief and pomaded locks put a distinctive style onto the outspoken and rebellious tearaway of Kingston's mid-twentieth century political scene. In direct contrast to his eccentricities, his political viewpoints traversed the boundaries of radicalism and conservatism. As the years wore on, he almost became the staunchest supporter of the "old days", while the Oxford-educated barrister Manley substituted fiery words with a firm determination to build a new, independent nation from the rubble of colonialism. Patrick Leigh Fermor wrestled with this ambiguity, ending his visit to the island with little advance on an explanation:

What seems very surprising is that Mr Bustamante, the pistol-packing, hard-living and humorous ex-rabble-raising demagogue, whose every word and gesture have an engaging histrionic phoneyness, should be the leader of the more moderate party; while Mr Manley—darker, equally aristocratic in appearance, but whose reserve and poise and purity of speech remind one constantly that he is a Rhodes scholar and a K.C.— should be the leader of the extreme left P.N.P.; as far left, he told us, as it is possible to be, short of revolution and public violence; but (he dropped his low voice still lower to lend emphasis to what he was about to say) entirely unconnected with the Communist Party.

On a quite different stage, Manley's diligence at the Bar was matched by his appetite for political victory. He described the vigour of his legal engagements and rhetoric in terms of "an absolutely egotistic determination to win every case… a total will to win, so that you stop at nothing but deal with maximum concentration, maximum personal observation, maximum study, maximum everything, and the reward was winning."

The locus of this urge for veracity was 21 Duke Street, the office from where Manley conducted his legal affairs. The time shared between political and legal duties was a constant source of concern during his early years, but ultimately they often overlapped as he led legal campaigns for workers' rights, or famously, secured the release from prison of his cousin during the labour disturbances of 1938. In a poignant moment in his diaries, Manley records the feeling of hurt as Bustamante leapt from his cell to address the crowds on the wharf, proclaiming his own invincibility as the people's leader, while failing to mention the many hours of negotiation by which Manley had secured his release. He and his wife were left behind as the crowds swept Bustamante away: "I'll never forget as long as I live, the echoes of our feet on the boards as we walked through this deserted place. And this was my first experience of the sort of man that I was going to have to work with."

The clip-clop and clatter of Manley's buggy, drawn by the mare Firefly, sounded daily up and down the chamber-lined Duke Street. This main strip for the legal profession was also home to a centre of trade union operations, as Bustamante installed his office within shouting distance of Manley's quarters. Firstly, he rented small offices at Numbers 1A and 30, before advancing the headquarters of the

Bustamante Industrial Trade Union to permanent residency on Duke Street. Further along the same street, the corner of North Street proved to be the first meeting point with Bustamante's other great passion in life, his wife "Miss G", later to be "Lady B". Gladys Longbridge was crossing the road with friends, hurrying to the Moravian Church of the Redeemer for Sunday service. A "strange-looking" man, she recalled, with "bushy hair and his hands in his pockets" addressed them: "Little girls, where are you going?" The next encounter, according to Jackie Ranston's detailed account of Bustamante's life, was at Arlington House, a hotel on East Queen Street where Miss G was working as a cashier. The Arlington was a place where the important and influential wined and dined. Again she was recognized and soon employed by Bustamante as his secretary. They remained colleagues and partners for life.

While Bustamante was building up his union empire, his cousin retained modest chambers and devoted his construction energies to the Manley household. The initial Kingston home for Manley, his wife Edna and their first son Douglas was the first floor of an apartment on Hope Road, later to become part of the Andrews Memorial Hospital. True domesticity for the Manley clan, however, found its place at Drumblair, a former merchant's house and pen residence near King's House. A healthy distance from legal affairs downtown, Drumblair, as well as providing sanctuary and space for the family, also became a pivotal meeting point for the forging of the new Jamaican nation. Here, Norman and Edna entertained politicians, union leaders, artists and writers. These were the fresh voices and views for the country.

The fledgling state's new shape and the spirit of independence became entwined in this home, which now no longer stands; a product of suburban redevelopment. The dynamic mix of Norman and Edna's legal, political and artistic flair was all around and apparent in Rachel Manley's sensitive memoir, *Drumblair* (1996). She tells of her life as a young girl with grandparents, Pardi and Mardi:

> *The papers delivered to Pardi on Her Majesty's service were strewn over one side of a bruised but elegant oak table. Whether by nature or by sloth, Mardi could never understand the intricate structure or concept of legislation. She had a profound belief in the natural order of life, and little*

interest in just how it came about. The universe spilled through her quite unconsciously. Order was the rising of the morning sky, and the magical nymph-light of the moon between the trees at night. Order was the yin and yang of the rain and the wind, of woman and man. Order was the inevitable arabesque of the years and the lifelong journey of the soul through the skins of time, selving and unselving, being or only watching, watching or only being. Order was her Piscean world of dreams under the sea, tides which interpret but never define us.

Happily joined in marriage, the country's leading artistic and political talents worked to shape the nation. As early as the 1930s, Zora Neale Hurston could write of Edna's sculptures and use of "native" inspiration that "the *West Indian Review,* which is the voice of thinking Jamaica, has found her." Of her husband, she similarly wrote, "Jamaica has its Norman W. Manley, that brilliant young barrister who looks like Pitt in yellow skin, and who can do as much with a jury as Darrow or Marshall ever did."

High Octane Leaders

While many would more readily envisage his son as a tearaway speedster on Kingston's thoroughfares, it was the father Norman who raced along the narrow streets and open country roads, once Firefly and the buggy had been put out to pasture. The intensity of the grand statesman's legal precision, was matched by the fiery passion which he hurled behind the wheel of a car—even the black Mercedes Benz, given to him as a present by the PNP on his 75th birthday. His friend Philip Sherlock remembers the reply of thanks: "I know the Mercedes is a fast car. When I was young I loved fast horses, and I loved a woman—still love her—with a fast and lively mind and wit and habit of coming to fast decisions—yes or no." Legends of legal sagacity and swiftness surround Manley's career, but he also had occasional encounters at speed with law enforcement officers. But this did not prevent him from screeching through and claiming an (unofficial) speed record for travelling between Kingston and Montego Bay.

Bustamante kept most of his alacrity and dazzle for the political and public stage. His pleasure was the solid response of the masses, styling himself as a man of the streets, the "Chief". After the early years wandering, Bustamante's colourful life had returned to Cross Roads in Kingston, where he ran a milk business. Manley recalls seeing him a few times, scouring the streets with a milk van. Before too long, the streets would be crowded as thousands herded to see him and to hear his bellowing rhetoric and bullish gestures. In direct contrast to Norman Manley's more stately, restrained style, Patrick Leigh Fermor describes the booming Bustamante as "the former riot leader and *enfant terrible* of the island", whose public performances unleashed a "unstaunchable flow of bravura, humour, invective and peroration."

Manley and Bustamante were firmly involved with the growth of unionism on the island. For a while, they *were* unionism in Jamaica, but operated in quite different styles, as a visiting British politician, Bill Brown, discovered in the late 1940s:

> *I have been a Trade Union official all my adult life. But I unhesitatingly yield the palm to 'Busta'. The constitution of his Union is flawless! 'Busta' is the life-president. 'Busta' appoints and dismisses the principal officers. 'Busta' accepts into membership and expels therefrom. 'Busta' calls disputes on and calls 'em off. The constitution provides no strike pay for the first two weeks of a strike. So 'Busta' calls them off just before the two weeks are up! It is all most admirably arranged.*

In trying to distinguish between the politics of the two parties and their leaders, who were both from broadly socialist origins, he continues:

> *...the PNP is socialist and opposed to capitalism, while Bustamante's Party prefers to 'milk the capitalists' rather than to destroy them... The white population, while feeling no enthusiasm for 'Busta', regard him as, on the whole, the lesser of two evils. 'Busta' blackmails them; Manley would (politically, of course) murder them.*

Patrick Leigh Fermor refers to the politicians' strategies for harnessing mob reaction for tactical leverage:

> *Riots, often begun by entirely different parties and sometimes for the most trivial reasons, are fairly frequent events in the streets of Kingston. The town, while we were there, was still in convalescence from a recent*

outbreak. Frequent glimpses of Mr Bustamante and Mr Manley, the first cousins and bitter political enemies whose factions are as firmly embattled against each other as those of the Capulets and the Montagues in Verona, are constant reminders of this split.

As always, Bustamante could be relied on to step one extravagant stride further. On the occasion of the West Indian Royal Commission visiting Kingston in the aftermath of the 1938 riots, Bustamante organized crowds to dress up in rags and to flaunt abject poverty in the face of the commissioners in order to force home the country's plight and labour misery.

Bustamante was undoubtedly one the Jamaica's most flamboyant and effective characters in modern times. John Hearne's first novel, *Voices Under the Window* (1955), describes a political protagonist who cuts a style not unlike Bustamante. He was the boss, cajoling voters for their patronage, but mucking in as one of the workers. In Hearne's fictional account, a crowd of unemployed men are waiting outside the House of Representatives for the Minister of Labour in "a way they had been waiting for a number of years: waiting and looking for jobs they were promised at election time; waiting for food, for clothes, for a little money to feed the children their women had once a year":

When he came and was stepping out of the clean car on to the dusty sidewalk they moved forward to him. They asked him about the work his party had promised at election time. 'Plenty of work soon, boys,' he had told them, 'just be patient. Plenty of work soon. Lord, boys,' he had said, 'you don't think I've forgotten you!' Then he had gone inside the House, a black man like themselves but one with great powers of expression in words. He could say nothing and make it sound like a roll of drums. And at public meetings when he was speaking into the great, eye-shining spread of faces he could cry like a bereaved woman, the tears pouring down his broken, vein-ridged face as it showed alive and passionate in the yellow light from the huge kerosene flares on the platform.

Busta was best at blood-and-guts bombast, playing to the crowd's emotions rather than intellect. Rachel Manley assesses her distant cousin's powerfully blunt prowess, compared with that of her grandfather:

> *As many voters could neither read nor write, symbols were used to distinguish the parties on the ballot. The JLP used a bell, and the PNP had used the profile of a head. Pardi thought it symbolized everything in which the party believed and for which it fought. But Busta had easily finessed that high-minded concept with the clamour and distraction of ringing his bell. Even the comrades' silent fist raised in salute of solidarity in struggle was no match for the turmoil the noisy bell created; although innocent of the more radical post-war political connections of the clenched fist and the term 'comrade', Busta soon linked both PNP features to their wider, more sinister modern association with communism.*

Norman Manley, she suggests, was erudite, but lacked the people's touch. Her grandmother Edna agreed: "She felt that Busta was what we are, broken and flawed by history; that like Busta we had survived by evolving flamboyant, cunning and opportunistic."

Michael's New Politics

Norman and Edna had two sons, Douglas and Michael. The latter followed his father to lead the nation, with the nepotistic weight that often accompanies such transitions, but without the frustration of having never been leader of an independent Jamaica. While Norman Manley had battled for most of his career to gain statehood for Jamaica, it was his rival, Bustamante who became the first prime minister in 1962. Perhaps this was the bitterest blow of Manley's career, but he lived to see his son become prime minister in 1972. His granddaughter, Rachel, outlines her own father's feelings on such a lineage of power:

> *Michael was often asked how it felt to be in the shadow of such a father, and he said that the question always surprised him. He found the world the way it was, with his father and mother and a big brother who, whether at home or away, were facts of his life. Whatever shadow they cast, it was a shade of his life, a depth of existence that he never questioned*

any more than the clarity of air or the ponderous heads of mountains lean-
ing over Kingston's shoulders...

Still his father's presence had indeed filled his sky. He could remem-
ber as a boy of ten first going into Jamaica College, his father's Alma
Mater. He was in the hall on the first day of term, and there on the
walls above him loomed long wooden plaques engraved with the names
of the school's heroes... cricket, track and field, rifle shooting, football.
The Rhodes Scholars. Those who had gone on to distinguish themselves
with military medals in the Great War. On each was his father's name,
over and over.

While Norman led the PNP during the 1950s and 1960s, his son
had adeptly chartered the twisted contours of Jamaican political
intrigue and favour. He had mastered the game of "politricks", as many
dismissively call it. Laurie Gunst describes the time she saw him in
downtown Kingston, electioneering in 1972:

I watched him from the seashell-pink roof of a bank in the square as he
brandished the sceptre everyone called the 'Rod of Correction.' The rod
was said to have been given to Manley by Ethiopia's Haile Selassie when
young Manley visited East Africa in 1970, and by the time of his first
victory election it had become the PNP's most powerful symbol of author-
ity and righteousness. The crowd went wild when Manley raised it high.
His followers were calling him Joshua by then, the prophet who would
lead them into the Promised Land.

'Lick them, Joshua!' the crowd roared as if with one voice. 'Lick them
with the Rod of Correction.'

The English writer Quentin Crewe journeyed through the Caribbean
during the 1980s, "touching the happy isles" and also recording the
charismatic spell of Michael Manley, "a man of such superlative charm
that one person said to me, 'I never dare to go and see Michael, I know
he will persuade me to believe something I know isn't true.'"

Michael raised the fervour and heckles of the electorate, but few
leaders have since led in such style. Yet his persuasion and
showmanship, however successful, was not appreciated by all. His
model of democratic socialism sailed a dangerous path in a world split

between superpowers of East and West. His admiration for Fidel Castro, the United States' arch-enemy, and the metaphorical statement that he would gladly "walk to the top of the mountain" with Cuba's leader, torpedoed the country's finances. Michael had marched alongside workers through the streets of Kingston with the zeal of his father. As the journalist John Maxwell wrote, he "totally committed himself to a struggle which most of us knew could not be won, but which he realized in the depths of his soul was necessary to fight: win, lose or draw." On the international stage, however, the Manley stride covered less ground.

As Jamaica became more and more isolated from international funding and access to credit during the 1970s, the mounting opposition to Manley's Third Way shifted popular politics to the right. Kingston endured its own terrible cold war, as the two main parties scratched, ripped and shot each other apart. Thousands of Jamaicans fled the island during the 1970s as the economy faltered and the country staggered along a political precipice. Anthony Winkler relives those times while the political dream seemed to run dry: "We continued suffering by jawbone. It went like this: Mr Manley would wake up one morning with an urge and decide to give a speech about it. Everyone would sit up and take notice and wonder what the speech meant and what the devil the government was up to now. And more people would become sufficiently agitated to spark anew another rush for visas."

Manley finally lost power to the JLP's Edward Seaga in 1980, after an election in which an estimated 800 Jamaicans, mostly in West Kingston, were killed in political violence. Seaga's market-oriented policies may have won favour with the Reagan Administration, but the island's economy continued to suffer under inflation and government cutbacks. Seaga stayed in power until 1989, but that year a chastened and "moderate" Michael Manley won elections. Gone now was the firebrand rhetoric, replaced by talk of reconciliation and compromise. After three years Manley, stricken by cancer, handed over the premiership to Percival J. Patterson, ushering in a decade of PNP dominance in which the party won a record four consecutive terms in office.

Political Passions

Kingston's heroes, Garvey, Manley and Busta, carved their success and fame in the salons and on the streets of twentieth-century Kingston. Perhaps part of their achievements already existed in the urban fabric of a nation torn by historical change, social upheaval and political passions. Earl McKenzie's novel, *A Boy Named Ossie* (1991), highlights the extent of "politricks" in the Jamaican political animal farm. Ossie hears his father laughing outside their home and walks to the verandah:

> *There was a pig in the yard with a 'Vote PNP' placard hanging around its neck. The pig belonged to Mass Enos, their bearded neighbour, who was a People's National Party (PNP) supporter. Mass Enos knew that his pig came to their yard after breakfast each morning to see what it could get, so he had decided to use the animal to promote his political preference.*

Returning to the National Heroes Park, the politics and ardour that made these heroes great is scarcely reflected in the drab, brown expanse of a summer-scorched dustbowl. Plans are afoot to refashion the park, but as it stands now, earlier visits and times may have done the heroes more justice. Norman Manley was often seen at the former racecourse, kitted out for grand events such as the Knutsford Park Silver Jubilee Race Meeting, hollering for Edna's co-owned horse, Roysterer; quite a contrast from his inner will to transform radically the visage and underbelly of a British Caribbean colony. In 1938 Bustamante was also at the racecourse, addressing an impassioned crowd of two thousand Kingstonians who were ready to tear up the suffocating roots of colonial rule and follow his call for change: "I will make history for Jamaica... my action will break the neck of cowardice in this country." Many years later, Manley would be back at the racecourse chanting a different tune and shaking a broom on the election night of 1955. His party's slogan was "Time for Change" and on this occasion he too was a championing a new era, ready to sweep out lingering colonial cobwebs.

Garvey, Manley and Bustamante were beguiling orators and wordsmiths, able to capture a crowd's passion not only with their rhetorical prowess, but with an enthused and clear commitment to what they believed was right in the world, and what they held at heart to be true for Kingston. Their successors, especially in the political arena, had tough acts to follow.

Since the 1980s, politicians have had to share their city territories with financially more powerful community and gang leaders, frequently fuelled by profits from the international drug trade and crime. The dons—not all of whom, it must be said, are hooked on rapid, illicit profiteering—hold as much weight today as the heroes of the past. The new years of the second millennium were led by some of the old party retainers, but by and large, fresh political leadership waits in the wings. Whether the next chiefs come from just around the block or via Miami's schools and malls remains to be seen.

CHAPTER SIX

City Soundscapes

"Jamaica's an island surrounded by sea
(It has that in common with Cuba)
Its national tunes, to a certain degree,
Are founded on Boop-boop-a-duba."

Noël Coward, "Jamaica" (1984)

"Down Temple Lane,
the drums were beating brass
in the shattered drinkers' heads;
the drums blared like sudden eyes,
eyes that bulged,
brilliant eyes, like suneyes,
dancing, eardrum-thumping eyes,
lunatic, ganja eyes,
bongo eyes;
head, hips and hands
smashed Caliban!"

Andrew Salkey, "Saturday in Kingston" (1973)

The iconic business end of Kingstonian music is firmly rooted at 220 Marcus Garvey Drive, an unlikely neighbour to the export factories and oil refinery of Newport West amid the industrial landscape of the western harbour. But it is here, at the Tuff Gong studios that Jamaican stars, past and present, have recorded tunes, usually as far removed from the frivolity of Coward's ditties as they are close to the energies of Salkey's Saturday night in the city. Founded by Bob Marley in 1965, Tuff Gong International has set the style for Kingston's commercial music industry in recent years. Chris Blackwell's Island Records first brought Bob Marley and the Wailers to international attention, but contemporary home-grown production remains rooted in downtown Kingston.

The city itself has become the subject of international song. UB40's "Kingston Town" lyrically romanced the capital's scenes to a world-wide audience in the 1980s, at a time when the streets were more resonant of gang gunfire than starry-eyed reggae lullaby:

> *There's magic in Kingston Town*
> *Oh Kingston Town, the place I long to be*
> *If I had the whole world I would give it away just to see the girls at play.*

The following pages outline the places behind Kingston's extraordinary impact on the world music scene. With a population standing at barely a million, the city's musicians continue to create new musical trends and successes out of all proportion to its size, projecting local dancehall or ragga to global audiences and luring international artists to downtown recording studios. Major music conglomerates from outside Jamaica have failed to dominate the city's local labels—the creative and financial backing of new sounds remains firmly from the block.

Catch-a-Fire Starters
From amid the jam-packed racks of the Clocktower Music Record shop at the heart of Half Way Tree and the early dancehall days of the Pinnis Club, Chris Blackwell emerged as an unlikely mover and shaker of the early Jamaican music scene. Leaving schoolboy days at Harrow well behind in England, Blackwell, a white Jamaican, set up his first recording label in 1958. During the same year, recording at the same studio on Bell Road, the future prime minister of the country and centre-right political stalwart, Edward Seaga, also set up his own label. The latter's passion and skills soon drew him into the cauldron of national politics, but the former's path was tuned for musical success. With headquarters on Odeon Avenue, Blackwell led his campaign with an almost instant triumph, taking Laurel Aitken's "Boogie in My Bones" to the top of the charts in 1958 and laying open the musical airwaves for the modern sound of Jamaica.

Island Records, named in tribute to Alec Waugh's 1956 novel, *Island in the Sun*, was the label through which Chris Blackwell made his fortune and the fame of many Jamaican musicians. Having created a musical market niche for Jamaican sounds overseas, he moved to London in 1962, armed with an array of licensing agreements for Jamaican tunes. Three months later, while Jimmy Cliff's "Miss Jamaica" and Lord Creator's "Independent Jamaica" heralded the new national sovereignty, Blackwell had already plunged into the musical world of the former colonial metropolis, drumming up new artists and sounds for a new era.

One of the releases at that time was Bobby Martell's now highly-collectable "Judge Not". A transatlantic misnaming smudged the songster's identity, but that was soon corrected, as the same Bob Marley returned with the Wailers to claim Kingston's place in global music. In 1971 Bob Marley, Bunny Wailer and Peter Tosh signed up to Island Records, which was by then the leading independent label in the United Kingdom. Chris Blackwell, keen to build on the success of the recently released soundtrack to *The Harder They Come*, greeted Marley as the authentic rude boy striding into his office. Still in London, but with Kingston's musical mix in the air, the Wailers' final line-up brought in Earl "Wire" Lindo, Aston "Family Man" Barrett and his brother Carlton.

Back in Kingston at Dynamic, Harry J's and Randy's studios, the group produced the groundbreaking album "Catch a Fire", released with the "rock" format and publicity trappings to woo an audience well beyond Kingston's yards. The original three Wailers had been coached to sing harmonies at the start of the 1960s by Joe Higgs, amidst the crowded, dusty bustle of his yard on Third Street in Trench Town. A decade later, the Wailers rolled back to town and played the Carib Theatre and the National Arena. Their sound had shot beyond the domestic, but was simultaneously to remain rooted in West Kingston and the tenement yards of Trench Town

Kingston Sound
The first international hit by a Jamaican performer was Millie Small's "My Boy Lollipop", produced by Chris Blackwell in 1964. But it was Bob Marley and the Wailers who projected more definitively the

sounds of contemporary rebel Kingston to the world stage. Not only the music, but the city itself and the names of downtown neighbourhoods became known well beyond the island, conjuring up specific images of Jamaican urban cool or freestyle rebellion. Marley's "Concrete Jungle" referred specifically to a 1970s redevelopment project near Greenwich Park Road. The crowded tenements of Arnett Gardens and Newland Town were razed to the ground in West Kingston, to be replaced by the grey, modern blocks of urban living: "Concrete jungle, what do you got for me now?"

Kingston's neighbourhoods attract not only lyrical attention, but themselves have exuded a magnetic draw for musicians. Greenwich Town, abutting Spanish Town Road in West Kingston, was feted by Cornell Campbell on vinyl in 1975, but also served as a meeting point for aspirant musicians. Steve Barrow and Peter Dalton have recorded one-time resident Max Romeo's memories of the neighbourhood's 1970s music scene. Young artists would come into town from the country areas, sell farm goods, but also ply their musical wares and hope to be spotted by local producers. The two big names on the block were Bertram Brown and Errol "Don" Mais. From 14 East Avenue, the former operated Freedom Sounds, linking up Greenwich Town talent with the big recording studios of Channel One on Maxfield Avenue and Randy's on North Parade. Within little over a square mile, the urban reggae rhythms of Michael Prophet, Philip Frazer, Earl Zero, Rod Taylor and Prince Allla were created, recorded and produced.

Errol "Don" Mais, developing the Greenwich Town sound, soon fashioned new dancehall and dub trends, promoting Hopeton "Scientist" Brown as the mixing engineer at King Tubby's studios on Dromilly Avenue, a couple of miles along Spanish Town Road. These new tracks, springing fresh from Greenwich Town, bridged the transition from 1970s roots reggae to 1980s dancehall cuts. Dancehall and then ragga brought the buzz of computers to the late reggae scene. Singers and DJs increasingly worked over pre-recorded instrumentals, the rhythms flowing from high-tech chips, rather than fingered fretwork. Lyrics moved from Ras Tafari and radical political or social concerns to the clash of slackness and the hedonistic self. From the very first recordings, the changing musical landscapes of Jamaica have been etched on the patchwork of local studios and artists' residences dotted throughout West Kingston.

Trench Town Rock

Bob Marley perhaps most famously sang of his own Trench Town roots. Many of his lyrics concerned the plight of the "ghetto" and the troubles instilled from outside. As *de facto* community leader, he woke up one morning with his wife Rita in their tenement on Second Street, surrounded by police and snarling gun barrels. Local youths had rioted the night before, throwing Molotov cocktails at the police, and Marley was to be questioned by those "all dressed in uniforms of brutality". "Burnin' and Lootin'" recounts that morning: "This morning I woke up in a curfew/Oh God, I was a prisoner too." The issues were resolved, but even after Bob Marley had left the neighbourhood, his experiences reflecting on the community's tensions and resilience remained lyrical reference points. The 1980 tribute "Trench Town" realized the metaphorical strength of the neighbourhood to rally the urban poor.

His children, notably Ziggy Marley and the Melody Makers, have sustained the international voice of reggae's first family and have kept Kingston and its urban landmarks in the wider musical consciousness. Damian "Junior Gong" Marley won the Reggae Grammy in 2002 with "Half-Way Tree". The youngest of Marley's sons gained his nickname from his father, who was affectionately called "The Gong". Combining this popular affection with the toughness required for surviving in the Jamaican music industry, Tuff Gong Records evolved as Bob Marley's downtown recording enterprise.

The initial studio was established in Orange Street, just north of the Parade, before moving to 56 Hope Road, now the home of the Bob Marley Museum. The recording studio then moved back downtown to 220 Marcus Garvey Drive, expanding to become one of the largest and most influential Caribbean studios. Bob Marley's early mixing board travelled with the studio and remains at the heart of the complex, which includes the recording studio, mastering room, stamper room, pressing plant, cassette plant, record shop, booking agency, as well as the offices for Rita Marley Music and Ghetto Youths International.

Bob's Place

Few sounds have captured as many hearts and minds as Bob Marley's music, and few places have been visited as much in Kingston as his uptown home and former recording studio at 56 Hope Road, just east of King's House in Liguanea. The tall, detached wooden house stands secluded off the main road heading east to Papine and the University of the West Indies, shielded by a colourful wall of Rasta murals and an ever present sentry duty of brethren and sisters. Today the compound flows with visitors and staff, but much remains as was, both outside and within. The impromptu pitch on which Marley played in the garden is occasionally the scene of kick-around football. More often he would be holding court on the steps of the house, seated under the shade of an awning, dealing with Tuff Gong music business while reasoning with rankings of the Rasta reggae order.

Bob Marley died in 1981, aged 36, a victim of cancer. His death was a local and international tragedy. The funeral was marked by a day of mourning, as thousands filled the streets and followed the procession through Kingston and out to the hills. Rachel Manley, whose father was one of those politicians who perhaps genuinely connected with Marley's message, wrote of the significance of his death in Kingston in "Bob Marley's Dread (for Drum)":

> *BM dies, King dies, but*
> *Kingdom lives on*
> *...*
> *The Kingdom lives*
> *a heart of drums*
> *a small town throbs,*
> *we have begun*
> *the phoenix*
> *from a mulch of bones*

The impact of Bob Marley's life remains locally enshrined at the Hope Road museum. Rooms in the old house breathe 1970s roots reggae and Rasta reasoning, combining a mixture of total reverence and product placement, as preparations for a first-time wave of cruise ship passengers are mustered. An add-on shopping court has been reorganized, offering Ital Pamper hair-braiding, Herbs and Spices' rawmoon, bisey, Irish moss and dandelion tea. Bob's Honey makes an appearance, collected from bees that the musician adopted on moving to the Hope Road compound.

Part museum and part shrine, the Bob Marley Foundation has renovated, revised and re-branded the site as a "tourist experience", but despite attracting tens of thousands of reverent visitors each year, an intimacy with legend remains. Ms. Rosemarie Rowe, who has been a cashier from the start of the museum in 1986, remarks, "People burst into tears when they see Bob's bed, like they've come to the Promised Land." Chris Salewicz likewise describes the museum scene as "a sea of khaki-garbed dreads of both sexes... A palpable aura of sincerity, righteousness and reverence hovers about them like a rich metaphorical soup, enriching and nourishing the parts of our souls few other experiences can reach."

56 Hope Road was formerly the home of Island Records, until Chris Blackwell gave the property to Bob Marley in 1974 as part of a contract renewal. Only two years later, on 3 December, unidentified gunmen attacked the premises, seriously wounding the manager Don Taylor and shooting Bob Marley in the arm, while a bullet grazed the brow of his wife Rita.

On the night of the shooting, Bob Marley insisted on playing at a scheduled concert in town, but it was to be his last Jamaican performance before he left the country. This self-imposed exile from the politics, troubles and violence of Kingston in the 1970s, however, served to spread his music and the sound of the city to even wider audiences. While not designated officially as a National Hero, he must be considered as Jamaica's most celebrated and influential international ambassador. His musical trajectory spanned early reggae, rocksteady and ska sounds, while Marley's religious adherence to the Rastafarian faith rooted his presence at the forefront of contemporary Jamaican social and cultural transition. Many saw the brutish attempt on his life as an indicator of his powerful presence, caught as an iconic target in the crossfire between warring political clans and business interests.

"Exodus", voted as *Time* magazine's album of the century, evolved out of exile. With equally ironic praise from the establishment, "One Love" was judged to be the song of the century by the BBC. Included in the former album, "Ambush in the Night" denounces those who rely on the ignorance of the many for their own political games, "bribing with their guns, spare-parts and money/Trying to belittle our integrity." Similarly, aware that the Kingston he left behind was falling into political and social disarray, he foretold of the "Rat Race" in which "Political violence fill ya city."

One Love

Marley left Jamaica for 18 months after the shooting, before returning to the house and staging the "One Love" peace concert 1978 to commemorate the 12th anniversary of the visit of the Emperor Haile Selassie to Jamaica. In an emotionally charged National Stadium, he invited the two party leaders, locked in political and personal conflict, to join him on the stage in a gesture of reconciliation and peace. In

front of thousands, under the glare of lights, the piercing energy of clan-fuelled politics and the emotional tension of the Kingstonian throng, all long-time sufferers of the troubles, he held together the hands of Michael Manley and Edward Seaga, singing "One love, one heart/ Let's get together and feel all right."

Under the rawness of the spotlights and crowd's close-up attention, the leaders looked unsettled, but both had surprising connections with the scene at which they were now centre stage. Edward Seaga's early days as a music producer were behind him, but not entirely forgotten, and Michael Manley had quite evidently incorporated symbols of Rastafarianism into his popular political campaign. In 1972, en route to winning the election, Manley openly employed his Biblical nickname of Joshua, gained almost a decade earlier as a trade union leader when he spoke to strikers outside the Jamaican Broadcasting Corporation's "walls of Jericho". Now clasping a staff given to him by the Emperor Haile Selassie during a visit to Ethiopia, his "Rod of Correction", Manley combined a political zeal for social change with the "rebel music" of the current era. The voice of the downtown sufferer came into the political limelight, as Manley sought council with Rasta leaders and visited a "dunghill" commune for advice on quelling youth violence.

Max Romeo explicitly connected politics and reggae to focus on the wealth gap of Kingston: "Uptown babies don't cry, they don't know what suffering is like." In similar revulsion at Kingston's inequalities, Bob Marley voiced the biting lyrics of Legon Cogil and Carlton Barrett's "Dem Belly Full", warning that "A 'ungry mob is a hangry mob."

Such musical interventions and the symbolic concert were potent expressions for peaceful change. Seldom has such an image gripped the Jamaican nation in recent times: an international music icon and local hero clasping tight the uneasy, stiff palms of warring politicians. It remains one of the most influential visual symbols and acts since independence. Of similarly stunning impact, and an event that the concert commemorated, was the visit of Haile Selassie to Kingston in 1966.

Haile Selassie and Rasta Connections

The Wailers as a group first connected musically with the Rastafarian faith during their early rocksteady phase, but it was perhaps the lyrics and image of Bob Marley himself that captured international attention to the greatest effect. He was seen by many adherents as an appointed messenger from God or Jah. As Roger Steffens remarked, "Bob Marley is the most famous Rastaman who ever lived. On stage, with his Medusa locks spiralling outward from his head in wild abandon, he was a wraith from out of time, preaching timeless truths of a God that was black and incarnate in living flesh." As the reggae sound waves rolled, so did the message of Ras Tafari. Mervyn Morris' poem, "Rasta reggae", relates the roots of religion, reggae and resistance:

> *out of that pain*
> *that bondage*
> *heavy heavy sounds*

Ras Tafari belief and practice, however, developed at first in Kingston during the 1930s without such a clear rhythmic accompaniment. Count Ossie was among the most acclaimed Rasta drummers to bring nyahbingi music to wider audiences since the 1950s. He encountered the Burru community at Back-o-Wall, a former neighbourhood in downtown West Kingston that was later to be redeveloped as the concrete towers of Tivoli Gardens, and brought in the akete and funde drums as the Rasta musical heartbeat. This relentless percussion and chanting developed as perhaps the "purest" form of Rasta musical expression, evolving into the aural backdrop for "grounations" or spiritual meetings. "Grounation" by Count Ossie and the Mystic Revelation of Rastafari then brought together the mixture of bass, funde and repeater hand drums with horns and bass to an audience outside the Rasta community.

Yet the original musical Rasta prophet was perhaps Leonard Percival Howell, who incorporated the drumming, songs and ritual of kumina into his religious worship during the 1930s. He also preached the message of black nationalism and elements of Garveyism, stating that black Jamaicans should swear allegiance to the Ethiopian emperor, Haile Selassie, who had come to power in 1934 as a black monarch and the 225th descendant of the line of King David. The beginnings of the Ras Tafari faith emerged at this time. A principal tenet was that black Africans were God's people, oppressed by a largely white, capitalist world. Slavery had removed many from the Promised Land to a godless

Babylon, but redemption and repatriation would enable many to return across the Atlantic within their lifetime to an African homeland.

In the then British colony of Jamaica, Leonard Howell's radical black evangelism was clearly an anathema to the authorities and their vision of orderly development. He was sentenced to two years' hard labour for selling pictures of the Emperor Haile Selassie, an act judged to be seditious by the courts. On release, he continued to follow a radical path, founding a Rasta settlement just north-east of Spanish Town. In 1941 this community at Pinnacle Hill was raided by police. Ganja was seized and residents were charged with possession of illegal arms and drug offences. In the same year, Italian occupying forces were expelled from Ethiopia and the Emperor Haile Selassie was returned to power. In the capital itself, there were up to 15,000 Ras Tafari living in Back-o-Wall by the end of the 1950s.

The Ras Tafari in Kingston foretold of imminent change, and sympathetic elements of Jamaican society were gradually waking up to their message of redemption as the end of colonial control seemed nigh. In March 1958 three hundred Rastas met at Victoria Park and announced an island take-over, clashing with police at Coronation Market. Three months later, another group occupied King's House, the governor's residence, and were forcibly removed. Again in Kingston, within the year, hundreds spent their savings on buying a passage to Ethiopia from Claudius Henry, a Rasta leader whose house was raided by police. The authorities discovered detonators, firearms, ammunition, machetes and dynamite, blowing away any legitimate travel plans. Ticket holders were left on the spot with expensive souvenirs of a misguided venture. His son later mounted an armed counter-attack, which required the response of over one thousand Jamaican and British soldiers, aircraft and mortars. Religious and political tensions were bubbling over, and the Ras Tafari evidently meant business.

The Emperor Haile Selassie himself entered this cauldron as he arrived in the capital on a sweltering day in April 1966 at the start of a state visit. Thousands of Ras Tafari and interested bystanders crowded every space of Kingston's airport. A steady trail of trucks, buses, bikes and cars crawled east out of Kingston and along the narrow road of the Palisadoes to await His Imperial Majesty's arrival on Jamaican soil. The growing impact of the Ras Tafari had led to the commission of a report undertaken by the University of the West Indies in the late 1950s in an attempt to understand the basis of their faith. Leahcim Tefani Semaj, a Rasta scholar today, paraphrased a typical public response during these times: "The damn Rasta dem, wey de Rasta dem want, we just put dem in a damn boat and put dem out in the sea and sink the boat—say dem want to go to Africa!" But earlier fears among the authorities that the group was merely a militant, anarchic band of troublemakers—dreadlocked, doped-up and dangerous—were assuaged and the findings were sympathetic and well received.

The importance of Haile Selassie's visit stemmed from the primary belief among Ras Tafari that the Emperor Haile Selassie was a messianic manifestation of the only true God and Ethiopia, the true Zion. His arrival on the throne in 1930 was a crucial moment for the beginnings of the Ras Tafari faith. He remained in power until 1974, dying a year later, but his perceived earthly role as the "Might of the Trinity", the "Conquering Lion of the Tribe of Judah" and the "Elect of God, King of Kings" had been pivotal.

As the morning heat simmered, the expectation of the diverse audience rose likewise at Kingston's airport. Drum beating, chanting, the hubbub and folds of red, green and gold banners greeting the Lion of Judah, mixed freely with the haze of ganja smoke, droning abeng horns and the electricity of his coming. Rain splashed lightly on palm leaves carried by those among the crowd, but as the aircraft came into view, the showers uncannily ceased and an uncontrollable mass surged towards the taxiing plane.

Locked in the plane and surrounded by a passionate, euphoric mob, the Emperor took some time to disembark—clearly taken aback, and understandably unsure of what was going to happen next. He emerged, tearfully overwhelmed, and greeted the crowd from the steps of the plane. With some difficulty he was extricated from the airport and whisked away under escort to an equally packed and emotional audience at the National Stadium. The interest in his visit was immense, and lasted for much of his brief visit. The following day the Emperor laid a wreath at the War Memorial in the then King George VI Memorial Park, before visiting Vale Royal, the home of the prime minister, to view a Ras Tafari-inspired arts exhibition.

Bob Marley was off the island, staying with his mother in Delaware, during the visit. His wife Rita, however, was among the worshipful throng and later related her dramatic experience. As the Emperor's cavalcade passed by her viewing point, she caught his eye and as he waved his hand in greeting, she had a vision of the bloody wounds of nail marks on his palm. On Bob Marley's return to Kingston, both he and Rita engaged further in a committed pursuit of faith. Without a defining hierarchy, various Ras Tafari sects had already developed since the 1930s. The Twelve Tribes of Israel was formed in the early 1970s and attracted their allegiance. Today, there are over a million faithful adherents to Rastafarianism, and many, many more sympathisers, if only via the sound system and appreciation of reggae. Bob Marley, more than anyone, did much to spread the word through his music. Indeed, as a chosen prophet, he more than fulfilled the role of messenger.

Ganja Culture

The global popularity of Bob Marley's music and his Rastafarian faith have spawned a lasting stereotypical image of the religion. But not all of Kingston's Rastafarians view smoking marijuana as a religious act, and clearly not all who wear dreads, smoke ganja or take on the red, gold and green tricolour are strict or even casual adherents to the religion. Many of the so-called "designer dreads" or "wolves" (in sheep's clothing) who take on the Rasta look are derided by the devout. Guy Kennaway's light-hearted account of Jamaican life *One People* (1999) glibly suggests some variants to the faith:

> *Humble Dread, a silent, dreadlocked Rastafarian from deep back a bush, with a deeply lined face, matted grey locks and a mouth of empty teeth. Omble Dread was a Bongo Dread—that is, a real Rastaman who kept strictly to the salt free, pork free, ital diet, sang incantations to Jah, smoked ganja religiously, and led a peaceful, harmless, meditative life. There were two other kinds of Dread. The Commercial Dread, like Busta or Blender in Beach, who had dreadlocks and knew all the Rasta rules but liked Dragon Stout and jerk pork too much to observe them all the time. The other kind of Rasta was the Rental Dread, to whom the whole thing was little more than a hairstyle which white wuman dem*

found sexy. They ate anything, smoked coke and tief money without hesitation.

A voyeuristic focus on dreadlocks, originally a visual declaration of opposition to corrupt Western ways, is often matched by a similar engrossment with ganja among casual observers. Opal Palmer's poem "Ethiopia Under a Jamaican Mango Tree", however, simply relates the ruminative reasoning of Ras Tafari, assisted by the calming effect of smoking:

De babylon refuse fi
gi him wuk cause
him is dread locks.

But jah Brown nah
frown, nat cut no
strut, weed cool him
down as him sit-down
unda a Jah mango tree.

The image of weed in Jamaican society is a strong as ever. In the 1940s, Patrick Leigh Fermor came across his first taste while visiting downtown Kingston:

The air in the hut began to smell very strange—a sweetish, vegetable reek that awoke memories of Piraeus and Beirut. I noticed that the boy on the end of the bed was smoking a home-made cigarette as blunt and as unwieldy as an ice-cream cone. He smiled as my eyes fell on it, and waved it in the air. 'It's the wisdom weed, boss,' he said. 'This makes us see everything ever so clear...' He hospitably rolled me one, and handed it down the bed. I asked him how he got the stuff—didn't the police put a stop to it? They all laughed and pointed to a clump of weeds outside the door that turned out to be, on closer inspection, hemp.

Fifty years on, Guy Kennaway provides a whimsical account of attempts to control the ganja trade by the Jamaican and United States governments:

In the 1980s the Reagan administration declared war on drugs and made Jamaica a front line. Two United States Air Force helicopters were to recce for ganja plantations. They did not represent a threat to the Jamaican industry which was formed by numerous small growers with crops too insignificant to be spotted from the air. Ten dozen goats would have harmed the trade more, and saved the Pentagon a few bucks to boot.

In Angel Beach the arrival, each week, of the helicopter, was a keenly anticipated event. It made them feel important to be the object of American interest. On top of this, items dropped from pockets of the airmen as they leant out to survey the bush. Maxwell sported a pair of Ray-Ban shades that fell from the aircraft, and for a week, Busta built spliffs with a packet of American cigarette papers that wafted down beside his bar after the chopper had clattered away over the hills.

While the popular ganja-wreathed and dreadlocked images of Ras Tafari and reggae remain firm, many Kingston-based musicians have committed their work to the faith and continue the message. Bob Marley's "Africa Unite" and "Zion Train" first introduced Rasta spiritual beliefs to the international commercial sphere and mass audience. Little Roy, Fred Locks, Pablo Moses, Burning Spear and Luciano are but a few of those who have maintained the ethical and ideological continuity of the Ras Tafari message.

Sound Beginnings

Aunty Maisy's beer bar on Roosevelt Avenue is an unobtrusive wayside shack, sandwiched between Old Hope Road and Mountain View Avenue. A small, but regular clientele has rolled up for Red Stripe or rum night after night, year after year. Juttering and jiving via the fuzzy electronics of two speakers nailed to sloping shelves in two opposite corners, varied musical offerings have accompanied Aunt Maisy's liquor for decades, flowing from style to style as methodically as bottles are emptied and racked up for return. In the 1950s small-time bars such as these were the starting points for the prototype sound system, an amplified record player watted to the hilt, which would provide the platform for the Kingston sounds over which global recording labels now squabble.

Jamaica has highest output of records *per capita* of any country in the world. Over two hundred new recordings are produced weekly in Kingston alone. Most never leave the island, but this vibrant local music has kept the capital's pitch at the cutting edge at home and abroad. The local industry first started when records were pressed to make up the transition from rhythm and blues to rock 'n' roll in the North American market during the 1940s. The new sounds from the States were not what the Kingstonian music lovers, still fast shuffling to boogie-woogie, demanded for their nights out. So it was that early record producers were feeding a domestic demand, making up a shortfall in supply to hungry local consumers. Kingston's musicians made their own changes and a specifically Jamaican sound evolved. The rhythm guitar played up, the bass boomed and beats were dropped and added. Ska duly emerged—the first tunes putting the city on the international music map.

Although reggae and its association with the Ras Tafari creed have most successfully exported Kingston's music to the outside world, the modern sound messengers of the city had their roots planted earlier in the Jamaican folkloric genre of mento and North American rhythm and blues. Live big bands kept the hip crowd at Coney Island on East Queen Street buzzing during the 1940s, but the recorded tunes at liquor stores were steadily amplifying. Larger wattage and bigger sound boxes spread the new sounds and started replacing the big band orchestras. By the mid-1950s monstrous 40,000-watt engines of noise rolled along the blocks downtown and the sound system era had begun.

New dancehalls or "lawns" sprang up, such as the Bull Head on Central Road in Trench Town and the Pioneer in Jones Town. These venues were fenced off patches of land, generally next to a liquor store or bar. Chris Salewicz in his lively account of the Jamaican music scene, *Rude Boy: Once Upon a Time in Jamaica* (2000) writes that, "On the 'lawns' of Kingston, at venues like Chocomo on Wellington Street and Jubilee on King Street, jitterbugging audiences danced until dawn to tunes adopted from such American artists as Count Bassie, Duke Ellington and Glenn Miller."

The big bands developed alongside and fused with strains of mento, derived from Jamaican folk music, and the new sounds of bop and shuffle-boogie. Mento, however, had lost popularity in Kingston during the 1940s, increasingly seen as "ol' time music". Ska accordingly emerged during the 1950s as the new beat, echoing kumina, burru, mento, call-and-response revivalism, and shouting back a resounding Jamaican response to North American musical hegemony.

Whereas mento and folk music had come from the country, the new sounds were urban to the core. "Beat Street" was now the place to boogie downtown. Partisan, and occasionally vicious, rivalries developed between the sound systems and their followers. Forresters' Hall on North Street and Love Lane had long been a live-music, big band and dance venue. Now it became one of the leading dancehalls, challenged every weekend night by gigs at Chocomo Lawn and King's Lawn on North Street.

Recording Kingston

With new rhythms emerging downtown and sound systems carrying the tunes across the neighbourhoods, it was not long before the city's musical energy needed a recording industry to score the compositions onto acetate or wax. Vinyl was not pressed until 1959, and soft wax still remains the medium of choice in many dancehalls today. A decade earlier, on a verandah at 8 Merrion Road in Vineyard Town, Ken Khourie first started recording local voices on an audio recorder that he had bought while in the United States. People came to register their voice messages to send to relatives overseas. Later he began to record mento and calypso tunes, with the help of Alec Durie of Times Store on King Street, which were then sent to England to be made into records. On return, these "Times Store" records became Jamaica's first record label. On the release of new tunes, queues formed along King Street to get upstairs to buy them from the first floor of Times Store. A domestic record industry of sorts had started.

When ska hit the scene, the Kingston landscape was truly given its own musical identity. Jerry Dammers, who led the British two-tone movement with The Specials, writes that Jamaican producers created their unique sound by using "the whole recording studio like a musical instrument... They forced people to dance whether they liked it or not, by shaking the whole building with the amount of bass on a record or, if the sound system was outdoors, by creating the effect of an earthquake." This skill has not been lost today, as bashments let fly and downtown districts shake to mobile boom boxes, or a quivering plot of advertising hoarding props up a wall of speakers. Laurel Aitken, still dazzling the stage forty years after his first hit, is commonly referred to as the "Godfather of Ska", fusing calypso and boogie-woogie when he released the double A-side "Little Sheila"/"Boogie in My Bones" in 1959. Unbelievably, this was the first record by a Jamaican artist to reach number one in the Jamaican Broadcasting Corporation music charts, which had previously been dominated by North American music.

Then rocksteady stole the scene, and as Chris Salewicz comments, this sultry, languid tune "sounded like trouble... it became the soundtrack for Jamaica's first youth tribe, the ratchet-knife-wielding rude boys—the cooler than cool, hotter than hot Johnny Too Bads of downtown Kingston." Myth holds that the intense heat of the summer of 1966 allowed rocksteady to unwind as the ska beat became too fast to dance to. Towards the end of the decade, however, the reggae revolution had rolled into town, bringing new producers, styles and listening to the public.

The Big Three
Sound systems, a portable conglomerate of two dozen or more speakers boxed into a monolithic block of noise, were ruling dance floors by the mid-1950s and have remained the core element of the bashment set-up. Dee-jays played domestically produced records and added their voice to the tumult, putting their original mark on Kingston's music stage over half a century ago. For the first time, voicing over a record, introducing, jibing, whooping up the crowd with fast talk, set the Kingston scene ahead of the rest. Behind these dee-jays and massive sound system fronts were the real players, the owners who jostled for the number one spot, through decibel barrages and occasionally physical intimidation.

Tom the Great Sebastian is credited by many to be the forerunner of today's sound system specialist, pioneering his corner at Charles Street and Luke Lane. In the 1950s his powerful assemblage, original sets and hip tunes invariably outshone competitors during the early sound system battles. But the so-called big three were soon to challenge

Tom the Great Sebastian, forcing, or enabling, him to move upmarket to the swish Silver Slipper Club at Crossroads.

The first leader of the downtown triple pack, and arguably the most aggressive, was Arthur "Duke" Reid, a former policeman and top marksman. Having won the lottery and retired from the police force, he and his wife set up the Treasure Island liquor store, initially at Pink Lane, then at 33 Bond Street. A sound system and recording industry evolved around the bottle shop and Duke's bold personality. With pistols in side holsters, and a rifle close to hand, Duke was the original tough guy of music, never failing to fire off or use his physically adept enforcers, often recruited among criminal acquaintances from police days, to intimidate the opposition. His sidekicks would hurl rocks, and occasionally shoot bullets, at rival sound systems during their performances. It was, of course, a sure-fire way of calming opponents' musical clamour. Nevertheless, legitimate if unrestrained times at the Success Club on the aptly named Wildman Street ensured that he gained the crown of "King of Sounds and Blues" in the late 1950s.

Duke Reid was also nicknamed "the Trojan", after the Bedford Trojan truck that he used to shift the tools of his trade between gigs. Chris Salewicz notes that he was "an especially contentious figure", the subtlety of his operations matching the finesse of his ten-ton rig:

> *Sporting a trio of revolvers in his belt, from which he would indiscriminately fire shots, he was more inclined to destroy the opposition through violence than talent… Much of the gangland-style behaviour that later became a feature of the Jamaican music business can be attributed to him. Instead of mashing up the sound-system opposition by playing the heaviest, loudest tunes, he would simply charge into rival dances with his gang, beating up or stabbing people and destroying their equipment.*

The second to hit the scene, but with cooler dexterity and a quieter splash, was Clement "Coxsone" Dodd, nicknamed after a stylish cricketer of the time. Clement Dodd's first performance came early on, spinning records on a phonograph in his mother's liquor store, the well-frequented Dodd's store on Laws, then Beeston Street. As his technical and performing prowess grew, he built up the Coxsone

Downbeat sound system, a certain match for Duke's Trojan tune machine. Loaded with the first credited dee-jay, Count Machuki, the Downbeat system started to "flop" or beat all rival shows in terms of volume and sharp sound selection.

Duke's heavies set out to mangle Coxsone's sound, so in turn, the latter sought "protection" for his gigs to counter Duke's "security". One sharp-fisted boxer and talented dee-jay hired by Coxsone was Prince Buster, who came to be known as the "Voice of the People". Buster soon moved on from his role as a heavy to be one of the bright sparks in the sound system set-up, working with Coxsone and producing an array of classic ska sounds, including his own popular "They Got to Go". He worked out of Orange Street, not far down the road from Sonia Pottinger, the first and most successful woman to challenge the male monopoly of music production in Jamaica. She ran the Tip Top record store and produced a succession of best-selling rocksteady and early reggae records, such as Ken Boothe's "Say You" and the Conquerors' "Won't You Come Home".

Vincent "King" Edwards was the third major player, his sound system playing a formative role in early popular music. But he tired of working the music business and took his energies into politics, then progressed to a third successful career as a racehorse breeder. While not lasting the musical distance compared with the former two, he certainly made his mark on the town. Many tunes came to be known after the place at which they were regularly played. Derrick Morgan's smash hit "Lover Boy" was transformed to the "S-Corner Rock" after the "King" regularly toasted the tune to the dancing crowd's delight at a lawn off Spanish Town Road.

The Duke-Coxsone rivalry in Kingston progressed quite naturally to studio ownership. When Coxsone expanded his musical empire and moved into the recording business, Duke followed suit. Having shared the spoils of the sound system, both set up successful studios that shaped Kingston's musical output for the following decades.

In 1963 Coxsone opened a recording studio on 13 Brentford Road, close to Slipe Road in Crossroads, and launched a new label called Studio One. A prolific few years followed during which Studio One was the hub of Kingston's recording world. The Skatalites and later the Heptones forged their hits on Brentford Road, while one morning a group known as the Wailers turned up for a session. Their first big hit "Simmer Down" emanated from Studio One and soon they were on their way. Meanwhile, Duke had built a recording studio over his liquor store on Bond Street and was steadily harvesting the best of the rocksteady years, later producing U-Roy, the "Originator" dee-jay who dominated Kingston's radio waves in the 1970s.

Alpha Plus Buzz

While the big guys were bashing out tunes, and occasionally each other, on the sound system scene, an orphanage and home for the underprivileged founded in 1880 was making its own unassuming mark on the future of Jamaican music. The Alpha Institute still stands where it was founded, on South Camp Road opposite Sabina Park, and still keeps music and the school band at the heart of its curriculum.

The dusty look of the school buildings on the outside is blown away by the musical outpourings and big band sound from within. Classical music, jazz, brass ensemble and rhythm and blues are brushed up and dished out with trademark style. Since the 1890s, the school has maintained an orchestra and came into prominence particularly during the 1940s and 1950s when many of its former pupils, such as Tommy McCook, were leading the big band scene in Kingston's dancehalls. A few years later, major names of the rocksteady, ska and early reggae days, such as Roland Alphonso, Lester Sterling and Rico Rodriguez, underwent the rite of passage from the school on South Camp Road to the main stage of Kingston's music world. They would often return to the school as instructors, helping out where they had been guided along the way. Trumpeter Johnny "Dizzy" Moore, a leading member of the Skatalites, claims that the martial drumming from his time at the Alpha school influenced his style and the ska beat at least as much as folk-learned rhythms.

Don Drummond was among the leading lights of the Alpha alumni, but holds one of its most anguished memories. An exceptional trombonist of original chords and devout Ras Tafari faith, he was an early member of the revolutionary Skatalites, the cutting edge of ska in the mid-1960s. In the persona of a troubled genius, Drummond frantically murdered his girlfriend at the height of the group's fame, and died a few years later just down the road from his alma mater at the Bellevue Hospital for mental illness in Bournemouth Gardens. Lorna Goodison wrote this lament for his distressed brilliance:

For Don Drummond by Far far East
past Wareika
down by Bournemouth
by the sea,
the Angel Trombone
bell-mouthed sighs
and notes like petals rise
covering all a we.

The sadness of Don Drummond's life casts its own shadow over Kingston's musical history, which happily has more stories of genius, eccentricity and unrivalled buzz than tragedy. Among these must be the career of Lee "Scratch" Perry, so-called for his childhood skill at dancing the "Scratch Chicken", but with a nickname which also suits the freshness of his penchant for starting new sounds, mixes and musical beginnings. He was born outside Kingston in 1936, coming to the city in the 1950s and working with Coxsone's sound system. His unique talents poured through, producing new cuts and working at the end of the 1960s with the Wailers. Many credit his voice training skills for developing Bob Marley's vocals and uniquely lyrical turn of phrase. His innovative, if sometimes erratic, authorial style was a major factor in Kingston's evolving sounds of the seventies. Having developed his own production methods and the "kinky" sound of the Upsetters, he also built a recording studio, the Black Ark, in the yard of his house in Washington Gardens. Feeling the "pressure", however, he burned it all to the ground in 1979 and left Jamaica the following year. He remains perhaps the most original, enigmatic and wildly eccentric, yet to some extent under-feted, of all Jamaican music producers.

Dance Madness

Today Kingston retains its peerless musical heroes and plethora of recording places, despite the presence of the international giants of the music production and marketing world waiting in the wings. The early

1970s saw the explosion of dub, the remix of dance tracks that had started with the quest for new sound system manoeuvres during the late 1960s in Kingston, and which now fronts much of the dance music scene world-wide. King Tubby led the way in the back room of his house on Dromilly Avenue in Waltham Farm Park, just north of Spanish Town Road, in what seemed like inauspicious beginnings for a global sound. Meanwhile, in the centre of town, Errol "ET" Thompson was forging an alternative dub style in Randy's Studio 17 on North Parade. Drum and bass was born.

Whereas Kingston's original rude boys of the 1950s and 1960s packed style with guile, the heavy rudeness of later decades sharpened knives, pointed guns and brought a new measure of toughness to the musical scene. Gangsta lyrics and living could be correlated squarely with Kingston's political violence since the 1970s and the troubled mix of drug money, turf disputes, downtown territorial battles and a collapsing economy. Homophobic and violent lyrics have pandered to aggrieved niche markets. Bounty Killer's "Look Into My Eyes" was banned for running too close to Kingston's real streets: "…in this part of town, survival is my will./In order to survive I have to rob and kill." Shabba Ranks has similarly pushed the edge, homing in on domestic violence and false misogynistic self-belief.

The first dancehalls were the logical creation of what many writers have viewed as Jamaica's national passions: dance and music. In the mid-nineteenth century Anthony Trollope conveyed this idea in his haughty style: "Dancing is popular in England—is popular almost everywhere, but in Jamaica it is the elixir of life; the Medea's cauldron, which makes old people young; the cup of Circe, which neither man nor woman can withstand." Less that a century later, Kenneth Pringle lyrically recounts a Kingston eve in a similar, if more romantic, vein:

In the evening especially you feel it is one Kingston. Life is too strong for the barriers. In the transparency of dusk in this lucid climate the bright trams jazz down into the crimson and green of the smokeless city night. The dry radiance spurts from the electric lamps. Sheets of ruby and topaz and emerald fire glow from the tall advertisements. The bars fling out sparkling shafts. The soft and brilliant stars crowd over the palms and

roof tops, and while the drum beats from the darker regions and the
banjoes whine and the radios roar at full blast, you feel that the whole
city is united in its lively and infectious dance.

More recent writing, such as Rohan Preston's "Deep-sea Bathing (Inna
Reggae Dancehall)" have echoed the louder, spicier style of nights out
on the town:

Between each bass-blast
the woofers inhale like cartoon gods
ready to deliver one more blow.
The boomers gasp and pant with the plop
of a bobbing person every time
she pushes up, up, up above the waves

Dancehalls and clubs have merged. Every night Kingston has a
place ready for action, with notorious, naughty and noisy scenes of
revelry. The Asylum on Knutsford Boulevard, in the midst of New
Kingston's financial and residential high-rise towers, has been the
buzzing place of recent years. The infamous madness of the Cactus
Club, its partner in the outer suburb of Portmore, has now closed
down, leaving the Asylum to hold the floor as the city's most
celebrated hotspot. Sidewalk vendors hustle punters outside the club's
entrance, opposite embassies and adjacent to high-price hotels. Inside,
the wining of the crowd and throb of the sound system shake up a
sweat-filled, ganja-fuelled chaos of dance, where, writes Chris
Salewicz, "Moët flows freely [and is] drunk by large men with shades
and girlfriends who look like Caribbean Christmas trees." Carlene the
Dancehall Queen or Lady Saw, sprayed in satin-lycra, humping and
crotch-grasping, cut new sex-filled sounds for the dancehall crowds.

Zenga Longmore clearly missed this slackness on her Kingston
visit, finding a less frenzied alternative:

Pins and Needles, the Ultimate Disco Experience, was a small, poky
club with peeling wallpaper and dangerously rickety furniture. Two old
men sat by the bar, drinking white rum, staring at us unceasingly. The
music was a blend of syrupy ballads, and country-and-western. Reggae

is not played as often as one might think in Jamaica. It is looked down upon by 'respectable folk' as the music of the quashie dem. So, with two old men, Jim Reeves at low volume, and a bar that could only boast rum and Cocoa-Cola, the evening got off to a somewhat dismal start. The place was plunged in almost total darkness, thus saving me the trouble of not having to look at Big Mannie's gold medallions.

Dubbed Up

Mixing music and poetry, the speech and sound of reggae and Ras Tafari, led to the rise of dub performance, bringing leading lights such as Dread Talk, Dub, Sermon, Prophesight and Prophesay to centre stage. A part of the old toaster tradition, dub involved a dee-jay talking with wit and verbal dexterity into the microphone, introducing musical acts and keeping the gig going. Over-dubbing techniques and new technologies gave the dee-jays more gadgets and more power to play and score with the audience. As Gordon Rohlehr lucidly remarks, "The DJ became high priest in the cathedral of canned sound, fragmented discotheque image projections, broken lights, and youth seeking lost rituals amid the smoke of amnesia." Key among the performance poets in recent years have been Linton Kwesi Johnson, Oku Onuora, the late Michael Smith, Jean Binta Breeze and Mutabaruka. Voice and rhythm are the dominant ingredients of dub poetry; the message of the voice coming out above all else over the instrumental accompaniment. Oku Onuora outlines the melding of social comment, faith and voice in his dub:

I am no poet
no poet
I am just a voice.
I echo the people's
    thought
    laughter
    cry
    sigh...

Similar in depth and breadth and a hallmark of dub poetry, Mutabaruka sets the questions to the world around in "You Ask Me':

You ask me if I have ever been to prison.
Been to prison?
Your world of murderers and thieves
of hatred and jealousy
and… you ask if I have been to prison?

I answer
Yes
I am still there
trying to escape…

Carnivalesque

In contrast to the vexatious rhythms and words of dub, but just as carnal, "Downtown Carnival" high-kicked and wined its way for the first time along Kingston's streets in April 2001, drawing hundreds to partake and thousands to watch. The inaugural Carnival, suitably sequined, feathered and lycra'd to the hilt, marched off from National Heroes Circle, wound round to Ocean Boulevard, danced along the Waterfront, reaching a halting crescendo at the Inner-City Unity Lawn on the corner of Beeston and King Streets. This new Downtown Carnival is exactly that, and quite remote from the alternative "Bacchanal Jamaica", which is essentially an uptown, New Kingston affair. The difference is also largely economic. Carnival costumes cost many dollars to hire, or to make, and the larger Bacchanal Carnival has fancier costumes, big time sponsorship and seemingly endless nights of warm-up parties at the Mas Camps, the playful nightly Carnival preparation ground, on Oxford Road. The J$500 entrance fee for Blow-outs make this scene a pricey event, but somewhere for the less timid middle classes to shake a collective ass. Both Carnival parades, Downtown and Bacchanal, unite, however, for the grand partying finale during the last week in April.

The Kingston pre-Lenten celebrations are something of a copycat version of Trinidad's world-famous Carnival. Byron Lee first brought Carnival to Kingston in modern times, inspired by the commercial success of Port of Spain's costumed fiesta. Although originating from the winter-season festivities permitted within the repressive structures of colonial slavery, contemporary Carnival has migrated across the islands as a dress-up, dance-up, lucrative street party. With his band the Dragonaires, Byron Lee has long been the main exponent on the island of soca, the traditional sound of Carnival. Yet since starting the Bacchanal Carnival in 1989, the Kingstonian music maestros have also fused reggae, dancehall, salsa, rock and Dominican merengue into their local medley. Each year Carnival songs are aired at the Mas Camps to rehearse and warm up the crowds' appetite for the big soundfest at the end of the week. Thumpingly popular tunes such as "Old Woman", "Carnival Come Again" and "Kitty Kat" are bashed out regularly on the city's nightwaves.

Whereas soca tunes run the rhythm in Trinidad, dancehall is master for the Jamaican affair. Old-time soca has been blown away, as the Jamaicanized Carnival has its own home-grown musical flavour. On the last day of the week, the Carnival crescendo includes two lorry loads of bass-heavy sound systems that boom out hardcore dancehall and dub as they trundle along the spectator-lined route. Pursuing the trucks, performers in fierily bright costumed clans pump and wine for the top prize. Bashment Girl, Seaview Beauty, Silverado and Blue Diamond are regulars among the contending revel groups.

The Gleaner newspaper's "Carnival watch" charts the course of the Mas Camps on Oxford Road, listing the night-long bashments and blow-outs in the run-up to the final blast-out. The main parade cavorts through New Kingston to finish on the dusty football field at southern end of Knutsford Boulevard as a throbbing, reckless spectacle of energy.

In earlier times, the carnival season erupted in late December, in particular for the John Canoe or Jonkanoo celebrations, which incorporated African dance and European masquerade. The essence of revelry was a temporary release of enslaved workers from their owners' physical and cultural shackles, a moment that focused on West African yam festivals at the end of planting season. Fertility rituals became amalgamated with Christian notions of the Devil and the Yuletide festivities of excess. During the main days of Jonkanoo, great parades swept through town and country, filled with costumed actors and dancers who mimicked the central characters of Cowhead, Horsehead and the Devil.

For a brief moment, colonial power hierarchies were upturned and ribaldry was let loose during the Christmas festivities, much to the chagrin of sections of the elite who regarded it perhaps reluctantly as a necessary evil or safety valve for the enslaved majority. Lady Nugent, the diligent wife of Governor Sir George Nugent, kept a diary during her Jamaican sojourn between 1801 and 1807 in which she describes life at King's House in Spanish Town. She loathed these festivities since her household, "the family", would be upturned: "We don't like to drive out or employ our servants in any way… a bad dinner, no servants to attend, and I am sorry to say more than half the family tipsy… nothing but pipes, drums and tom-toms, going all night, and dancing and singing and madness all the morning." Even Matthew Gregory Lewis, known as "Monk" Lewis after his notorious novel *The Monk* (1796)—which told of religious ambition, murder and incest in Rome and was written when he was nineteen—raised his eyebrows at the activities. After inheriting plantation lands, he produced the equally famous *Journal of a West India Proprietor* (1834) in which he wrote: "My own heart which I have so long been obliged to keep closed, seems to expand itself again in the sunshine of the kind looks and words which meet me at every turn." As friend of the abolitionist Wiberforce, Byron and the Shelleys, his overly sentimental, self-mocking and liberal views still found little sympathy for the frenetic Christmas parties.

Michael Scott in *Tom Cringle's Log* gives some idea of the sonorous chaos: "This day was the first of the Negro carnival or Christmas holidays and at the distance of two miles from Kingston the sound of the negro drums and horns, the barbarous music and yelling of the different African tribes, and the more mellow singing of the set girls, came off upon the breeze loud and strong." Almost two centuries later, these same drum rhythms have been released to new local and global audiences by mixing into digitized ragga recordings.

CHAPTER SEVEN

City Visions

"My dear wife… is taking a trip to the West Indies."
"Jamaica?"
"No, she went of her own free will."
          P. G. Wodehouse, *Uncle Dynamite* (1948)

"National culture is national consciousness reflected in the painting of
pictures of our own mountains and our own womenfolk, in building
those houses that are the most suitable for us to live in, in writing plays
of our adventures and poetry of our wisdom, finding ourselves in the
wrestle with our own problems."
          Norman Washington Manley, "National Culture and the Artist"
          (1939)

Some of the first photographic visions of Kingston emerged from a
crowded studio on Harbour Street during the 1860s. While most
wharfside activities of the day were robustly gauged by tonnage,
Adolphe Duperly and Sons carefully measured chemicals and blocked
out the blistering sea air to produce their finely framed prints.
Beginning with his state-of-the-art *Daguerrian Excursions in Jamaica*
twenty years earlier, Duperly Senior was now encouraging and leading
his sons onward to the modern era of albumen print photographs. By
the turn of the century, *Picturesque Jamaica* captured in freeze frame the
huddled sidewalk meetings of townsfolk or the Parade's luxurious
expanse of peopled space, and brought quiet corners of the island to a
new generation of postcard hunters and coffee table tops.

A century later, the timepiece prints of the Duperlys' were brought
out of the quiet salons of private collections to face again the public's
eye at the National Gallery of Jamaica on King Street—a shutter snap's
hop from their original site of production.

This chapter seeks out these urban visions, not only those trapped by the lens, but also the vast array of performances and pictures that shape the city's art scene. Far removed from, and far more rewarding than, the images fleetingly conjured up in the ballroom of a visiting cruise ship or within the confines of a hotel lobby on the North coast, Kingston's visual and performing arts have a dynamism and international outreach that quietly parallel the louder claims of reggae and dancehall. Up until the early decades of the twentieth century, the style of Jamaican letters, painting and plastic arts was imported direct from or strongly influenced by British trends. The genteel humour of Wodehouse, the Brontës' romances and Hardy's Wessex, for example, formed the literary landscape of the day.

Edna Manley and Cultural Nationalism
Norman Manley's concerns for a national culture, ever more apparent as independence reached the shores of the island, were increasingly echoed by the cultural aesthetes of the 1930s and 1940s. Few pursued the call for a politically inspired aesthetic more robustly than his wife, Edna. She has been credited as being if not the source of a national Jamaican arts movement, then at least one of its foremost catalysts. Eurocentrism had framed the elite artistic vision of colonial and contemporary Jamaica. Edna Manley, among others, drummed up enthusiasm, patronage and a new place for "indigenous" Jamaican art. She bitterly opposed the "anaemic imitators of European traditions" who rendered dull ersatz for art: "Nothing virile, nor original, nor in any sense creative, and nothing, above all, that is an expression of the deep-rooted, hidden impulse of the Country—that thing which gives it its unique life."

Drumblair, the Manleys' family home, became a walk-in studio and talk-shop for painters, sculptors, photographers, writers and poets alike. Edna Manley's mother was born in Hanover, in the western part of the island, and her father came from northern England. Her own work, brushing by her Yorkshire roots, grasped African Jamaica. In 1936 she premièred her sculptures in an insurance office in Kingston, deliberately denying an expectant London gallery a first look at the new work. The metropolitan critics were nevertheless impressed and ushered her into the London Group with the likes of Henry Moore.

Just as significantly on the island, however, she had set a ball rolling that was soon to bowl over the old cultural order. Her iconic sculpture, "Negro Aroused" (1935) was the first piece of "modern art" to be bought by public subscription for the stuffily renowned Institute of Jamaica on East Street. A copy now rests just a gentle walk down from the modern National Gallery, which houses many other of her pieces, and defiantly stares out across the waters of the harbour. The Institute was founded in 1879 and had soon become the high cultural voice of the establishment. Ironically, it was here just two years later that the *ancien régime* would be rapidly shaken up.

Norman Manley first met his future wife on the far-off English coast of Cornwall. He described her as a "strange, shy and highly individualistic person... unlike anybody I have ever known." While this sensitivity inevitably fed into her artistic work, so did a robust energy that belied her husband's initial impression. This passion took the form of stormy sessions on the piano, played with "great expression" according to biographer Jackie Ranston, during a childhood "given to rebellion and sudden rages." Her school-leaving reference from the head teacher advised: "For anyone who desires not to be dull... I recommend this youngster as a companion." Norman and Edna were married in London in 1921, before settling down in Jamaica. Between them they shaped many of Kingston's contemporary political and cultural trends, carving original paths as perhaps they had done from the very start of their married life. As Ranston recounts: "For the first part of their honeymoon they bicycled south to the New Forest where they stayed a fortnight, sleeping in a tent that Norman had built himself."

Once installed in Kingston, Edna's dynamism was devoted to the arts. Her work gave full expression to perceptions of African form in sculpture, moulding Jamaican archetypes that shaped a new awareness away from the traditional norms and towards what she termed, "a still unrealised Island consciousness". Just as "Negro Aroused" became symbolic of this transition in the national arts scene, her other works such as "Pocomania" (1936), with raised fist and entranced, glaring eyes, were inspired by the times. Less political but just as passionate, her work during the 1940s for the *Dying God* series employed sun, moon and horse motives, feeding off the romantic majesty of the Blue Mountains lying ruggedly to the east of Kingston. Later in life, on completion of "Jacob and the Angel" (1982), her diary entry reveals the enthusiasm and nervous energies that electrified her life's work:

> *So tomorrow we will lift the clay model of 'Jacob and the Angel' down from the wall to cast it. It is now 4ft 2ins and very heavy—and if they shake it, it will crack all over!! So let's hope there's enough left on which to do a repair job!!*
>
> *I have loved doing it—to me it's the inner struggle—elemental, earthy man at war with the light that would lead him.*

Manley's passion for the Jamaican arts pushed her enthusiasm towards radical action. Beyond the regular Drumblair soirées, an indigenous movement was taking shape. In 1939 a group of around forty liberal thinkers literally took the establishment by storm, inviting themselves to the annual general meeting of the Institute of Jamaica and demanding "Jamaican art for Jamaicans". The Institute had been until that day a bastion of colonial taste, taking an exclusive and Eurocentric stance on the task of promoting "the encouragement of arts, science and culture in Jamaica". Robert Braithwaite, who had led the rebels into the thick of the directors' gathering, demanded that the heavily oiled portraits of plump English governors be torn down from the surrounding walls.

This mandate for new artistic expression was as explosive in this context as the labour riots and strikes had been in the streets outside during the previous year. Marcus Garvey's calls for black awareness in Kingston during the 1930s had undoubtedly charged the ideological atmosphere and readied critics for cultural change. Edna Manley's free art classes and volunteer-run training courses brought practical sensitivity to the burgeoning spirit of nationalism, which her husband and others were to lead in the political arena. For over four decades, Frank Cundall had conservatively steered the Institute away from new artistic expression, relying on a colonial and European heritage for guidance. However, his more outgoing successor, Delves Molesworth, came to the helm in 1937 and proved to be the right person at the right time. Clearly boosted by the liberals' brash entrée into the inner sanctum of the Institute's affairs, he ran with the young nationalists and was instrumental in founding the Institute Group of leading local artists.

Art classes at the Junior Centre of the Institute of Jamaica formed the structural basis for the development of a nationalist, extensively post-Impressionist core of talented "new" artists. Drumblair continued to provide an informal gathering point for both radical political and cultural debate. The buzz of an independent Jamaica was alive on Kingston's streets and in the talking-shops of private salons, even if the constitutional birth of freedom had to wait another decade. In 1950, the Jamaica School of Art was established to take on the pedagogical role that the born-again Institute had nurtured.

With the increasing production and acceptance of indigenous Jamaican art, a public showing space was soon required. Independence in 1962 gave stability to fledgling national institutions such as the schools of art and dance. A dedicated exhibition space for this new outpouring of regionally and internationally recognized Jamaican creativity became the priority, and it could only be located in Kingston, the point of convergence for so many artists. In 1974, the National Gallery was first established in the impressive rooms of Devon House on Hope Road, but it later migrated—against the general trend—to larger and lighter premises downtown.

National Gallery

Thankfully, it is usually only civil engineers who judge a gallery from the outside. The beige block of the National Gallery of Jamaica on the corner of King Street and Port Royal Street admirably mirrors its architectural siblings of Kingston Mall and the Jamaican Conference

Centre. Clearly a product of its time, the interior artistry is happily more transient, allowing the gallery to display its vast visual wealth of local and international artists with a regular series of exhibitions that underpin the importance of its status as a leading arts centre.

The move downtown was questioned, particularly by the wealthier classes who were heading north, away from the troubles of the "common folk" and political hoodlums who governed their votes and livelihoods. Why move the artistic treasures downtown, when those with "cultural taste" were shifting uptown? Bigger, brighter display areas and a progressive vision to create a modern arts centre lay at the heart of the choice. The finely decorated corridors of the National Gallery are in stunning juxtaposition to the surrounding streets: material visual wealth encircled by a failing urban development plan and the impoverished neighbourhoods of downtown. To arrive at the gallery, most visitors must step out of the uptown or beach hotel existence to which they may be accustomed and into the Kingston of the majority.

One of the most buzzing works within the gallery is Sidney McLaren's "Parade Square" (1970), a vital viewpoint of central Kingston. Primary colours splash flashes of buses, cars, hurried people and a banner of "Beautiful Jamaica Land of my Birth"; all traced in enamel on hardboard. McLaren simply captures the essence of the urban landscape just outside the doors of these eighteen galleries-in-one, covering 25,000 feet of floor space. A. D. Scott's collection of Jamaican art; the Cecil Baugh gallery of ceramics; the Edna Manley Memorial Collection; pre-twentieth century exhibits—all add to an impressive whole at the heart of downtown. Many of the artists painted, sculpted and lived within a few blocks of where their works are now housed in immaculate conditions.

Seventy-years ago, on wandering into Issa's china shop on Peters Lane just behind King Street (in what was a less stark part of town than now), the visitor would have noticed an array of brightly coloured plates. In Taylor's stores on West Queen Street, Heyward Street or Princess Street, similar hand-painted decorations were enlivening the shelves of porcelain and leading an upturn in sales. The same brush strokes now grace the rural landscapes and portraits of National Gallery or the homes of the very wealthy or very lucky. Delves Molesworth,

Secretary of the Institute of Jamaica, aided the journey of Albert Huie's art from sideboard to exhibition piece, via a change in medium to oils and canvas. He met with the young painter, admired his out-of-work-hours paintings and sponsored a series of art lessons for him with the respected artist, Koren den Harootian, who was living in the city. The latter was a close friend of the Manleys, who helped Edna to encourage new Jamaican artists. Born in Armenia, he lived in New York, but shuttled to and fro between the city and Jamaica, where he spent much of his time supporting the incipient art scene and producing his own drawings, which celebrated the beauty of local landscape, people and the island flora.

Albert Huie had moved from the countryside as a young teenager to live on East Street with his uncle. A keen artist, he paid his way initially by painting plates—rapidly, but very well. Molesworth, who spotted his talent, was great friends with and lived near the Manleys. The young artist was soon drawn into the Drumblair cultural circle and sold his first painting, "The Lace Girl" (1937), to the family. His works were detailed, finely composed rural scenes depicting a life far removed from the turbulent times of urban strife in the 1930s. Fully reflecting country Jamaica, his studio was nevertheless situated in the thick of downtown Kingston, overlooking a yard with fruit trees and flowers. His first exhibition, well received by the burgeoning band of "new" Jamaican artists, was held at the YWCA on North Street in the early 1940s. He became a stalwart of the liberal Institute Group, painting everyday Jamaican scenes and people. In his latter years he was affectionately dubbed the Grand Old Man of Jamaican art, painting with the same mix of care and enthusiasm that had pushed him into the limelight six decades previously.

While Huie lived in town but painted the rural surrounds, David Pottinger used his immediate environment as the subject of his work. His paintings, such as "Trench Town" (1959), depict the moods and light of downtown living. With no formal training other than a day-job as a sign painter, the subtlety of his work is all the more impressive. His series of downtown paintings reveal the drab melancholy of poverty in hues of grey and brown, yet capture the life of lithe figures gathered at street corners or in a yard. Standing in front of these images of West Kingston, cooled by the gallery's air conditioning and calm surrounds, the contrasting proximity of those desolate lanes is all the more revealing.

With similar scenes from peoples' lives, but coming from a classically trained background, Barrington Watson's paintings catch the mood of domino games and water-coloured rural squares. His technical style, clear and direct, ran counter to the growing trend to recognize and pursue an "intuitive" feel for art. While staunchly a Jamaican artist, he reacted to some extent against the "Africanization" of Jamaican painting. When asked if the African element should be the main focus of Jamaican arts, he retorted, "Hell no! We are part European and part African. You can't put down Europe. I mean, why are we talking English? We are not complete Africans. I believe that we in the Caribbean have the unique opportunity of producing art that embodies world culture as we are a mix of many races and nations." His work therefore ventures away from the early intuitive painters such as John Dunkley, whose work was among the first to capture a rawness and sombre mood within Caribbean surrealism.

John Dunkley and a Jamaican Tradition
Dunkley's work is very much the forerunner of those specifically island-grown visions that Edna Manley sought to encourage. Born in 1881, with no significant schooling behind him, he left to work in Central America for many years before returning to set up a barbershop in 1930 in downtown Kingston. His dark paintings such as "Back to Nature" (1939) and "Jerboa" (1940) focus the eye against the white wall space of the National Gallery. Entangled trees, scrolled vines and voluptuous herbage, dowsed in greys and browns, light and dark, evoke lush, tropical vegetation. Repetitive images of wide-eyed frogs, furtive rodents, sharp ravines and twisted, chopped branches create an unnerving spectacle. This unusual style limited sale of his work during his life, but his radical and discerning move away from the contemporary norms now underpins its material and visual value. He was "discovered" by Edna Manley, whose diary records her amazement, gasping at the sight she saw on entering his barbershop on Princess Street, which operated by default as an exhibition space:

As I stepped through the door and windows of the little room he had painted in gay brilliant colours in enamel, the most lovely designs of flowers and leaves and fruits—the furniture too, each piece a gem of design and colour, was decorated. But the masterpiece in the centre of it all was the barber's chair. Never in all the world I think could there be another barber's chair like this. It was covered with designs—the back, the sides, the base, everything except the seat. The whole room was aglow with colour… and against the walls his pictures were stacked.

The National Gallery charts not only the artistic evolution of the country, but visually reflects a nation in political transition, changing identity from colony to state. Rex Nettleford, Jamaica's cultural polyglot, has said that after independence "the question of national identity shifted to definitions about who comprised the 'native population' and, by implication, what constituted the 'nativeness' of society." The gallery walls explode with ideals and spiritual dynamism from the 1960s, a decade which reflected this change. The extrovert Karl Parboosingh exudes a sensuous abstract style—eclecticism mixed from the art circles of New York, Paris and Mexico City. Heavy and intense colours, sliced by thick dark lines, upturn the classical forms that had gone before.

A similarly vigorous approach emerged from the failed political promises of following decades. The intensity of Eugene Hyde's "Casualties" (1980), painted just before his death, addresses crumbling social surrounds, while perhaps some of the most strikingly surreal work in the National Gallery is that by Colin Garland. The bright and bold "Fairy Scape" (1975) eerily compliments David Boxer's assemblage "Rack With Seven Heads" (1971). The two works respectively employ vivid oils and covered skulls in painted mesh and gauze, leading observers into thinking anew about their own social landscapes.

Expressionism finds a specifically Jamaican spiritual form in Milton George's pocomania scenes, such as "Back Yard" (1970), energized with figures gripped in exultation, kneeling and collapsing to the floor. Among the most impressive corners of the gallery is the Larry Wirth Collection—sixty-five carvings and paintings by Kapo Reynolds, a visionary intuitive artist and spiritual leader or Shepherd for a revivalist group in West Kingston, before his death in 1989. As with many of the most original Jamaican artists of the twentieth century, Kapo was self-taught. He left the countryside to settle as a preacher in West Kingston in the early 1930s, having heard the divine call from a visiting angel as a teenager. Intense and luminous primary colours symbolized the passion of his revivalist beliefs, while many of the sculptures were created as religious artefacts for his church. The originality of his work came to international prominence during the 1950s when overseas buyers discovered his talent via the Hills Galleries collectors. In 1981, "A New Spring" was chosen as the wedding gift for Prince Charles and Lady Diana from the people of Jamaica. Kapo's meditations on obeah and revivalism had found their way to the royal rooms. Among the pieces on display in the gallery, the beautiful mahogany carving "Obedience Covers All" (1965) illustrates four family figures, Mamsel, Demsy, Coolie and Turina, kneeling and facing away in spiritual devotion.

Another loyal patron of Kapo's work was Edward Seaga, whose support was matched by the eloquence of his praise for the artist's genius: "The best intuitive art has the ability to animate us because it makes us see things as if we were looking at them for the first time. Between the artist and the medium there seem to be no inhibitions and the imagination is set free to relate what it sees with an immediacy which brings us to the heart of the artistic experience." The sensitivity of this appraisal is made all the more poignant by its context—that of the early 1980s during one of the bloodiest moments in the long-running JLP-PNP political feud.

Within the same space, and likewise divinely inspired, Everald Brown's wall paintings, ritual objects and decorated musical instruments were initially made for the Ethiopian Orthodox Church. An example of the latter pieces, "Star Banjo" (1977), stands unstrummed in the gallery, a brightly painted, carefully crafted hybrid of ornament and musical instrument. The art of Kapo, Everald Brown, Alvin Marriot, Osmond Watson, among others, combines religious imagery, dream manifestations and visions of Jamaica.

The National Gallery remains one of the region's most substantial public art collections, and significantly provides a downtown space of international cultural importance. From its galleries emerges not only the history of Jamaica's changing artistic mores but also an intimate visual analysis of Kingston as a place of evolving urban landscapes. Formal viewing as offered by the National Gallery, however, is but one aspect of the artistic spaces that abound in Kingston. These encompass the commissioned friezes of Norman Manley International Airport, the bucolic community murals of Tivoli Gardens or Southside, gently bleached by the sun, and the originality of Utech's recent Sculpture Park of the Caribbean on its Papine campus off Old Hope Road. Here a range of pieces from Jamaica's leading sculptors, the majority having graduated from the Edna Manley School of Visual Arts, form an open plaza of technology and art in the midst of the new university. Each display, whether community mural or public acquisition adds another stage in the contemporary development of "Jamaican art for Jamaicans".

Private and commercial galleries are soundly scattered around Kingston, the majority located uptown, but carved, woven and painted artworks also grace downtown stalls and markets. Founded by Guy McIntosh, the Frame Centre Gallery at Tangerine Place has carved out its own important spot among the larger commercial galleries. In a similar league, on Oxford Road at the heart of New Kingston, the Mutual Life Gallery showcases some of the best of the city's and country's changing and original arts scene. Devon House shopping centre on Hope Road is home for the Wassi Art Gallery, which offers a varied palette of alternatively produced pieces. Further along the same road, Things Jamaican is a state-affiliated gallery for the promotion of Jamaican arts and crafts. Practical and precious products alike lead the consumer through the culinary arts to sculptured wood and bark baskets. Babylon Jamaica on West King's House Road houses Ras Tafari-inspired art, while Barrington Watson's Contemporary Arts Centre on Liguanea Avenue provides a master class of inspiration.

Ward Theatre: Popular Entertainment
P. G. Wodehouse's style of gentle merriment entertained the upper and middle classes for a large chunk of the twentieth century, but more robust, indigenous ribaldry now also draws a wider population to the capital's theatres. Roots theatre has captivated much of the stage action these days, but the various forms of its pantomime forerunner, notably more risqué than its British counterpart, has been attracting crowds for almost two centuries. Modern Jamaican theatre consistently adapts to please audiences who demand fast-moving, tuneful bawdiness, populist commentary and biting wit. A visit to any performance will be a memorable evening. On major opening nights, well-preened spectators pack theatre stalls and fill the venue with pre-performance chatter. With the public poised for entertainment, good-natured hoots, foot stomping and the occasional waft of ganja greet the inevitable delays while last-minute stage preparations are completed. Criticism and delight are seldom withheld during shows, which are lifted or buried by canny, expectant and attentive audiences.

Just a short walk up from the cool, calm spaces of the National Gallery, a similarly renowned locale for the arts, but one of much older vintage, dominates the northern side of the Parade's downtown cacophony. Overlooking the square's mishmash of buses, bikes, sellers, shoppers and wanderers, the theatre stands as a remnant of early twentieth-century artistic patronage. Behind its stunning cerulean and powdery white frontage, the Ward Theatre retains an iconic place in the Jamaican cultural landscape. The ornate and striking façade is matched by the majestically domed and once delicately fashioned interior. The ensuing decades have chipped away some of the sheen, but the theatre remains not only an architectural, but also a steadfast historical, symbol for the capital city. It was on this stage that Norman Manley launched the People's National Party in 1938, an event which was to open the way to a new political era and independence. A few years earlier, Marcus Garvey had roused the city's African consciousness from the same platform.

Arising out of the rubble of the earthquake in 1907, the impressive theatre owed its construction to the benevolence of Colonel C. J. Ward. An energetic performance of Gilbert and Sullivan's *Pirates of Penzance* shook the new auditorium into life on 19 December 1912, on the site of the previously destroyed venue. The atmosphere and attractiveness of the "new" Ward Theatre is far removed from earlier accounts of its predecessors. In his *Letters from Jamaica* (1873), a despondent Charles Rampini complained that:

> *Town life in Kingston is strikingly sombre and unexciting. There are few amusements either public or private. Dinner parties are rare events. The little theatre on the Parade is opened, on an average, twice a year—once for the performance of a local amateur company; on the other, for that of a stray professor of legerdemain on his way home from Panama. Not long ago it was taken by an itinerant performer on the flying trapeze. But the Kingston press was so shocked by the unfortunate man taking part in the entertainment, that after a couple of nights' performances he was compelled to close his doors.*

Theatrical presentations have clearly evolved and have routed the killjoy element, but the struggle for funding remains constant. A century before Rampini's recollections, Edward Long remembered a similar theatrical space, which while offering architectural daintiness, suffered from fickle finances:

> *In the lower part of the town is a very pretty theatre, exceedingly well contrived, and neatly finished. Dramatical performances were exhibited here during the last war; at which time there was considerable quantity of prize money in circulation; but in time of peace, the town is not able, or not disposed, to support so costly an amusement.*

Private interests and ticket sales still determine the Ward Theatre's fortunes, which are today managed by the Ward Theatre Foundation but without regular state aid or public endowment. The portrait of the founding colonel may hang somewhat forlornly in the foyer amid fading murals of Columbus' arrival in the Indies, but the theatre survives and continues to attract a range of drama companies and school or civil functions. Of these, the annual pantomime remains by far the favourite *grande dame*.

Each year at 6.00 p.m. on Boxing Day, the new season at the Ward is heralded by a burst of the national anthem, then the band takes sway and a heavy stage curtain unveils the fresh offering to an eager audience. The punctuality of the pantomime's opening is legendary, as is the crowd's enthusiasm. A broad cross-section of the city's families pay their annual visit to the theatre, today set amid downtown's troubles outside. The roots and tradition of pantomime have remained embedded at the Ward Theatre for over six decades since the first performance of *Jack and the Beanstalk* in 1941. As the New Year settles in, the pantomime moves uptown to the Little Theatre. In one sense, this migration forms a "homecoming" since the modern pantomime season was inaugurated by Greta and Henry Fowler, who founded the Little Theatre Movement in the 1930s. Following the Fowlers, the well-respected writer and director Barbara Gloudon ably took over the reigns. Since 1976, the Little Theatre Movement has provided the basis for a National School of Drama, which is part of the Edna Manley College for the Visual and Performing Arts.

The Little Theatre Movement is the oldest company in the Caribbean and consistently attracts the crowds to the annual pantomime, providing sexual innuendo, satire and sensation—all somewhat removed from the very first versions based on British fairy tales. By the third pantomime, African elements were introduced into

the story line of *Soliday and the Wicked Bird* (1943), but the biggest hit arrived a few years later with the pantomime première of Anancy, the spiderman-trickster whose web of guile and self-survival entangled him in the tale of Bluebeard. Busloads of school children and adults were annually ferried into Kingston for the season's treat, which soon became a hallmark of Jamaican theatre. Following the great success of *Bluebeard and Brer Anancy* (1949), the latter became a regular visitor to the Ward at Yuletide. His exploits jumped lightly from traditional oral narrative to the lights and greasepaint of the pantomime.

Among the many great performers who graced the stage of the Ward, Ranny Williams won a wide following for his renditions of Anancy. The much-loved and internationally successful poet and performer Louise Bennett, "Miss Lou", made her name at the Ward. Bringing Jamaica talk lyrics and logic to the stage, Miss Lou enraptured audiences with her popular folklore and social commentary. Brer Tiger and Brer Tacoma were regular caricatures of local figures of authority, whose superior power or material wealth were no match for the sharp wit and cunning intellect of the slightly built Anancy.

Miss Lou spent many, many hours performing and reciting at the Ward Theatre, and established herself and the theatre as icons of the nation's performing arts. The venue was the focus for the region's drama for much of the last century, attracting an array of stars. In many of her own appearances, Miss Lou captured the buzz of the moment and celebrated the theatre's success. "I' wut I'" rejoices at the visit of Todd Duncan, whose performance was worth every penny of the ticket price:

An den de man open him mout,
An den him start fe sing,
Me feel jus like de sweetes bell
A heaven was a-ring!

She recalls in "Him deh yah" the visit to Kingston in 1948 of another famous singer Paul Robeson, who was among the first to raise the call for equal civil rights from the modern stage:

Him gwine tan pon Ward Theatre stage
Real-real live, wat a ting!

Him gwine fe bow, him gwine de smile,
An den him gwine fe sing!

Again, paying tribute to the popularity of others over her own great success, Miss Lou marvelled at the multitude who queued up for tickets to hear the famous contralto Marian Anderson on the Kingston stage in "Monday Gawn":

But tan! De crowd noh tap yah so!
Se deh, bout ten line meet!
Some bruck de corna roun Parade,
Some bruck gawn up King Street

Tom Redcam and the Little Theatre

The Ward crowds have waned somewhat in recent years, as theatres in New Kingston seem a nearer and safer option for the uptown crowd. Among these, the Little Theatre on the wide curve of Tom Redcam Avenue heads the field, accompanied by its sibling offshoot the Little Little Theatre. As well as receiving the seasonal pantomime after its grand opening at the Ward, the former venue houses a year-round programme of performing arts. Built in 1961, on the success of the Little Theatre Movement, the white block of dramatic facilities has taken on the contemporary role as leader of the pack and home of Jamaican theatre. Lacking the grandeur of the Ward, the protégé has nevertheless outperformed its forerunner in terms of attracting the cutting edge of the nation's performing arts.

The road off which the theatre stands is named after a similarly progressive figure of Jamaican letters who wrote under the name of Tom Redcam. The author, Thomas Henry MacDermot (which when reversed reveals his *nom-de-plume*), was born on the island in 1870. Finding his way into journalism and then publishing, he started the All Jamaica Library, embarking on a crusade to promote local fiction and writers in a similar manner to Edna Manley's later success with the visual arts. The national literary corpus took many decades to extend beyond the efforts of the colonial elite, but Tom Redcam was among the first to encourage writing at all levels. The endeavour to widen popular readership may have run aground, but his own work nevertheless found more welcoming waters. The innovative use of creole in some of his poetry and his novel *Becky's Buckra Baby* (1904) charted new directions which others would follow and established him as the country's poet laureate.

The Little Theatre lies on an imaginary borderline between uptown and downtown, and provides a suitably eclectic range of productions, from classical music and contemporary dance to pantomime and roots theatre. The latter has gripped the Jamaica theatre scene, drawing out more everyday lewdness, slapstick and comedy for a wider audience. The productions promoted by Lloyd Reckford and Norman Rae in the 1960s have been replaced by ruder, louder, more grindingly farcical plays such as Balford Anderson's *Lovers Flex* or *Man fi get bun* (1999). Titillation hauls audiences from all parts of society to the Ward Theatre and mid-town venues, such as the dependable, welcoming Barn.

While roots theatre brought loud laughter to the stage, the progressive Sistren Theatre Collective made their mark in the 1990s by digging more deeply into Jamaican roots. Members of the collective also performed in Jamaica talk and were all working women, whose improvised productions sought to revise women's roles in a society leaden with machismo and patriarchy. Sex, guns and domestic violence were still elements of performance, but not framed as laughing fodder. In a similarly striking style, the Area Youth Foundation has gained an international reputation for productions relying on local talent from rival downtown communities, such as Tivoli Gardens, Denham Town, Trench Town and Rema. As political and territorial violence placed communities under curfew or cast members suffered threats as "informers" for mixing with the enemy, the regular rehearsals, often taking place to the sound of gunshots, have produced a series of acclaimed shows.

Even the crude vitality of roots theatre, however, has met its match in recent years as several former theatres have turned to offering more direct displays of flesh. The Playhouse II is now a strip club, along with other venues off Oxford Road such as the Palais Royal. Green Gables, a stalwart of the modern theatre scene, burned not with dubious desires but disappeared in flames and was razed to the ground. The Jamaican performing arts, rich in talent, ideas and originality, are facing threats from a variety of angles as venues have dwindled. The age-old battles between "low" and "high" culture, between "serious" and "superficial" art persist, but the rich seams of talent are not matched by a similar wealth of funding. However, just as the former Theatre Royal was rebuilt by the generosity and insight of Colonel Ward and local donors following the 1907 earthquake, so too optimism for the future of theatre on Jamaican soil is warranted. Errol Hill, whose incisive account of colonial theatre *The Jamaican Stage* (1992) is itself a significant step forward, argues "The dominant minority culture that reigned for three hundred years is no more; Caribbean theatre artists can march forward with confidence to seize and proclaim what is rightfully their own."

The Gift of Dance

Staged romance, lust and gunplay are not limited to roots theatre. Kingston is also home to perhaps the most successful dance company in the region, which has consistently provided world-class performances and innovation for a loyal public. For forty years, the National Dance Theatre Company (NDTC) carved out an international reputation through deft footwork and dazzling body movements. The Little Theatre plays host to the company's dynamic performances, juxtaposing light touch and fine artistry in a blackened auditorium, with the steady, cumbersome crawl of clogging traffic along the outside arm of Tom Redcam Avenue.

Formed at the time of independence, the NDTC has spawned a prolific offshoot of smaller companies, all jostling for prominence in the Jamaican dance milieu. The Stella Morris ensemble, l'Acadco, the Jayteens and the Company Dance Theatre and the Tivoli Dance Group, among others, have extended Kingston's dance scene well beyond the Little Theatre's annual dance season between July and August. Rex Nettleford, writer, educator, choreographer and university vice-chancellor, has long been Artistic Director at the NDTC, supported by the enduring creativity of Arlene Richards, Barry Moncrieffe, Monica Lawrence, Clive Thompson and Bert Rose, among many others. Imaginative acrobatics, strides, turns and whirling cascades enrapture reviewers from the *New York Times* to *The Dancing Times*. Bill Harpe exclaimed in the latter, "The greatest gift which can be bestowed upon a dance company is to be rooted in a society in which dancing comes as naturally as sitting down to a meal or going for a walk. The NDTC are the recipients of such a gift."

The unique dance vocabulary of the company offers a new syntax where, continues *The Dancing Times* in suitably florid style, Jamaican dancers "ripple like snakes and promenade like flamingos." The success of the dance company has spurred on the Jamaica School of Dance, a core component of the Edna Manley College of Visual and Performing Arts, located unobtrusively around the corner on Arthur Wint Drive. Jamaican dance has long attracted international professional interest. As early as the 1940s, the celebrated choreographer and dancer Katherine Dunham spent many months in Accompong, studying the myal- or spirit-inspired Coromanti dance. She returned several times to Kingston to assist dance companies, and incorporated a strong Caribbean element into her own performances. Writing in 1969, Rex Nettleford produced an impassioned plea for funding to maintain excellence in the performing arts, arguing that "inherent in the collective experience of Jamaica are universal values that can be given dance-expression for the greater enrichment of the people of their country and for dance itself." Over three decades later, his rich text and tribute to NDTC still holds strong.

Jahwood?

Island in the Sun (1957) with Harry Belafonte, James Mason, Joan Fontaine and Dorothy Dandridge set the course for a stream of classic Hollywood depictions of the Caribbean. Well after Errol Flynn tussled with elaborately coiffured villains on the prow of pirate ships in *Captain Blood* (1935), Johnny Depp brought the salty sea dogs of Port Royal back to modern screens in *Pirates of the Caribbean* (2003). Tom Cruise briefly shook box office ratings in *Cocktail* (1988) and the Hollywood industry even brought some Jamaicans into the frame with Disney's *Cool Runnings* (1993), which celebrated Jamaica's eccentric bobsled entry at the Winter Olympics of 1988. Most famous of all, James Bond pursued evil and a raging libido on the Jamaican north coast, while millions of cinema fans said yes to *Dr. No* (1962) and his dastardly entourage.

Although rose-hued silhouettes of palm trees, sea and sunsets have framed many film scenes, relatively few have been part of Jamaican-funded productions. As a largely urbanized island it is not a surprise, however, that the few wholly Jamaican films that have gained international attention have told tales of the city, predictably starring Kingston. Stephanie Black's documentary film, *Life and Debt* (2001) gripped international audiences with a gritty, insightful account of a Jamaican economy dragged down by international arrears. Just as provocative, but with the force of fiction to smudge an equally shocking reality, several feature films have also grabbed the limelight. Perhaps the most famous all-Jamaican production was one of the earliest, the perennially popular *The Harder they Come* (1972), starring the evergreen Jimmy Cliff.

Heading out towards the University along a dusty, heaving Old Hope Road, then veering sharp left past yet another pink and yellow shopping mall brings you to Confidence View Lane. Not the scene of a million dreams, but a hotspot for what was to become one of the world's cult music films. Produced, directed and co-written by Perry Henzell, the all-Jamaican hit *The Harder They Come* became an international sensation in the 1970s. The film tells the story of Ivan, a johnny-make-good country boy who rolls into Kingston seeking gold-paved fame and a musical fortune, but falls down dead after a brief and violent experience of reggae recording, ganja running, a graffiti-tagged manhunt and the final curtain hail of police bullets. A jam-packed action production, the rags-to-riches-to-ruin visuals are echoed by a shrewdly crafted reggae soundtrack and Jamaica talk dialogue. Chris Blackwell's Island Records recorded the best of the Jamaican music scene for the soundtrack, including Toots and the Maytals' "Pressure Drop" and the main man of the show Jimmy Cliff's classic rendition of "Many Rivers to Cross" and "The Harder They Come". The soundtrack was applauded by the *Rolling Stone* magazine as one of the most influential albums ever recorded.

Jimmy Cliff played the lead as Ivan, whose story seemed a very loose fusion of his own arrival at a Kingston recording studio from country Jamaica with that of Rhygin, a gun-toting ghetto outlaw from the 1940s. In a recent interview, the singer-actor explained:

I had hard times in Kingston and hard times in the music business just like the character. I got no money for my first two songs I recorded and I got punched up because I asked for money. But I think the entertainment world is just corrupt, so what can you do?

Ivan, a desperate figure, echoed the dreams and despair of Kingston's majority poor in the theme song of the film: "But between the day you're born and when you die/They never seem to hear you when you cry."

Lacking a script to transcribe, Michael Thelwell developed the visuals into a subsequent novel, interweaving the demise of the would-be music star, and later cowboy gangster, with telling descriptions of downtown life:

These ranches surrounded the lower city. On the hills to the east, in the gullies of the shantytowns of the centre, and in the swampy mangrove wastes of the west, young men and boys sat around flickering fires in places called Dodge City, Hell's Kitchen, Boot Hill, El Paso, Durango, and even Nikosia (there was terrorism in Cyprus at the time). They smoked ganja, dreamed valiant dreams, and cursed the rich, the 'high-ups' of society, and the police, especially the elite 'Flying Saucer Squad', their sworn enemies... Almost at predictable intervals, pulpits rang with denunciation of lawless youth and wrong-doers, and editorials would call attention to the dangers represented by gangs lurking in the cracks and crevices of the social fabric. The Flying Saucer Squad would stage their well-publicised 'lightning raids' and for a while the ranches would be deserted and the gangs scattered. Until society forgot.

Located mainly in the busy streets of West Kingston, the film also captures downtown's exasperated tensions and choreographs them on the big screen, tracing the city's sounds and senses in a local narrative of good, bad and ugly. As Perry Henzell recalled, during the two years of the film's staccato on-off making, "Everything happened here, from rain to riot." The script, which barely existed as one complete scroll, acted more as a hopeful guide to possible proceedings. This became a necessity, not as the result of an intense pre-Dogma cinematic experiment, but due to the reality of piecemeal funding and the scattered availability of leading actors. Jimmy Cliff was pursuing international stardom on the musical front, while many of the cast relied on freelance work whenever and wherever. The camera rolled on all that greeted the lens in Kingston's streets and crowded neighbourhoods. Some Jamaican commentators reacted coolly to the film. Censorship demanded overly violent scenes to be clipped. Why try to reveal the city's tawdry underside to all and sundry? Best keep troubles covered and let things clear up, or at least hide them away from others' view. Kingston film-goers, however, were less reluctant to see their lives dissected on the big screen and primed themselves for a blockbuster première.

The film opened on 5 June 1972 at the Carib Theatre, which was besieged on the night by almost ten thousand Kingstonians. Six thousand squeezed inside, while thousands thronged outside, including a large chunk of the VIP guest list. Chaos reigned as thousands scrambled to assail the theatre. The lucky audience packed every space of the auditorium, soon hooting, howling, firing blazes of praise and screams of pleasure onto the screen's proceedings. Perry Henzell and his crew had hit the jackpot. The international film festival circuit transformed national approval to global acclaim. A cinema in Boston would go on to screen this first Jamaican film classic continuously for the next four years.

The Carib Theatre fared less well. Placed at the heart of Crossroads on Slipe Road, the single screen cinema was an iconic landmark and the scene of many matinee love matches and Saturday spaghetti western shoot-outs. A mysterious fire in 1997, however, burned down the venerable old building, which was replaced by Carib 5, one of only a few multi-screen cinemas in the country. The relative sparse scattering of Jamaican films matches that of Kingston's cinemas. Sovereign Centre's Liguenea Complex and Portmore's Cineplex pair up with that in the Island Life building off Knutsford Boulevard, while the Half Way Tree cinema is now gone.

Irrespective of location, all Kingstonian cinemas share the common cold, a tropical movie-going affliction which reveals itself through a variety of symptoms. In many cases, the cold is undetected and has limited impact on the film-viewing experience. In severe cases, however, those susceptible to cinematic chills arrive prepared for the Arctic; fleeces, super-puffy goose-down coats (wraps and gloves for the chronically afflicted) are the safest recourse to enjoy the film and fight off the overzealous air-conditioning units that freeze the auditorium's atmosphere. William Makin, living in Kingston during the 1930s, recalls the advent of this latest technology to a then state-of-the art theatre:

> *Greatly daring, the proprietors covered it with a roof and pumped frozen air into the auditorium, and called it 'air conditioning.' First impressions were that one was locked in the refrigerator and forced to see a film. At the end of the performance one had the paradoxical feeling when stepping out of the cinema of stepping into the unventilated atmosphere of another cinema...This particular cinema, after a few daring pioneers presented with free tickets had tested it and emerged alive, became a deserved success.*

Despite these frosty expeditions, Makin nevertheless relied on his frequent cinema trips as a social refuge. While his memoirs reveal a barrage of racial and gendered prejudices that were perhaps not that far removed from those of the colonial clubrooms of the time (and would certainly curtail his readership today), he reports, with a near angelic countenance, that for a "member of the respectable majority" Kingston offered little but movie-watching as an evening's entertainment:

> *There are clubs where one may drink oneself into a stupor and deposit the white man's burden while holding up the white man's bar. There are multitudinous churches capable of supplying highly seasoned gospels which would excite even the mildest mannered cut-throat to confession and exhibitionism. There are many other diversions, most of which take place in rum taverns, but need a sailor-suit for quick response. Being no beachcomber of such tropical delights, no transgressor in the tropics, I weakly chose the cinema as my dope.*

Since then, much has changed. The chapels and grog shops still ply their wares, but sailor-suits are less visible downtown and several uptown bars have imported the bland Formica and stainless-steel chic of domestic airport lounges or glossy furniture catalogues. Air-conditioning has also developed in technical subtlety and effect, but so too has the audience's ability to ward off the chills by wedging themselves between insulating mounds of popcorn and cardboard buckets of soda.

All cinemas, however chilled, were packed for the next all-Jamaican international cinema bonanza, which hit the screens and box office cash tills exactly a quarter of a century after *The Harder They Come*. *Smile Orange* (1975) had mocked the tourist industry, and three subsequent films, *Rockers* (1978), *Children of Babylon* (1980) and *Countryman* (1982) gained acclaim for their revealing visions of the ebbs and flows of Rastafarian lives. (The hero of Dickie Jobson's latter film lived on Hellshire Beach, a short ride to the west of downtown Kingston. To ease life's multiplying pressures, he swam out beyond the reef as far as he could manage.) But it was *Dancehall Queen* (1997) that was to capture international cinema audiences again. Under Don Letts' direction, the opening shot leads the viewer's gaze straight to a vendor-packed street market, knowingly next to the Carib Theatre in Crossroads.

Having made a mark with the reggae soundtrack of *The Harder They Come*, Chris Blackwell's Island enterprise now backed a video-shot tale of dancehall culture. Audrey Reid starred as Marcia, a Kingston street vendor who kits herself out and glosses up to win a club competition as the "Dancehall Queen"—the diva of Jamaican sound. Chris Salewicz interviewed Carlene, a real dancehall queen, who sports her own provocatively-pictured line of "Slam" condoms, revelling in the intensity and self-love required to remain at the top of the glittering pile: "People have tried to dethrone me... But I'll be Carlene the Dancehall Queen for life. I think I'm going to go down in history as the Dancehall Queen: there is no competition there."

A subplot of sex and the shudderingly lecherous figure of "Uncle" Larry structure the main plot of downtown lives poised on the edge, while big-time music stars such as Lady Saw, Beenie Man and Anthony B back up the musical input. Paul Campbell, one of the country's leading contemporary actors, stars as Priest, the sinister, bleached-headed, gold-toothed villain. Reviewers gauged the film's display of slackness to be lewd, but the driving human interest and thumping soundtrack brought this Jamaican original to an enthusiastic world-wide audience.

Dancehall Queen pushed Jamaican cinema, says author and cinema critic Keith Warner, towards the major leagues, but lack of funding and limited technical access stalled the country's successful entry into the big time. Cinematic portrayals of the trials and tribulations of contemporary Kingston, such as the action-stuffed *Third World Cop* (1999), have marked several attempts at reaching a global audience, but ultimately missed the mark. Even so, Kingston remains the star or backdrop of most Jamaican films, and the impact of the big screen on the city's denizens remains as vital now as it ever was, but thankfully not in the Hollywood form ironically evoked by Una Marson in her poem "Cinema Eyes" (1937):

> *My ideal man would be a cinema type—*
> *No kinky hair for me,*
> *No black face, no black children for me.*
> *I would take care*
> *Not to get sun burnt,*
> *To care my half indian hair*
> *To look like my cinema stars.*

She later casts aside this sickly apparition, pointedly emphasizing that people "fed on movie lore, lose pride race." Lloyd Richardson is similarly wary of the so-called "high culture" imported in colonial times and which lingered aloof from the majority. In "The Poet Sings His Painting", he warns fellow citizens to connect Jamaican art with Jamaicans, echoing Edna Manley's call fifty years beforehand:

> *But the little white tag*
> *that's stuck on the painting*
> *says the price is too high*
> *...*
> *And the writing's on the painting.*
> *....*
> *And the poet sings his song*
> *the singer writes his painting*

the painter sings his poem
the poet sings his painting
the singer draws his poem

and whatever fuck
de whole a dem
dish out,
we
all
still
dance along.

CHAPTER EIGHT

Roundabouts

"While somewhat unattractive in itself, Kingston possesses a beautiful birthright in its environment of hills and mountains, in its groves of cocoas, giant ceiba trees, and luxuriant gardens."
Frederick A. Ober, A Guide to the West Indies, Bermuda and
Panama (1920)

"...the diesel fumes and the noise and poverty unto death of Kingston are reduced to a hazy view of plain white buildings spread among the green trees that clothe and soften the city. Kingston, ringed by mountains, runs smoothly into the harbour and the wild blue horizon. From such a distance, the city can be almost be overlooked."
Vanessa Spence, *The Roads Are Down* (1993)

The northerly upward crawl from Half Way Tree along Constant Spring Road winds slowly into Stony Hill Road. Houses become bigger, flatter; gardens larger, leafier; fences taller and dogs fiercer. While New Kingston burgeoned with an influx of the middle classes during the 1960s, many of the wealthiest households headed to the westernmost foothills of the Blue Mountains. The crescent of ridges arc heavily around the north of Kingston, hemming the city to the sea, catching marine breezes by day and hurling them gently back at evening. Sinuous roads coil upward like vines from the dense grey thicket of the city, and within a few miles bushy scrub alternates with eucalyptus, boarwood, rose and orchid. Affluent mansions and simpler homes line the crest of Jack's Hill, hugging Skyline Drive that totters on the edge of the Grand Ridge. From these hills, folk like Katherine in Vanessa Spence's novel *The Roads Are Down* can be "close enough to Kingston to be glad—like me—that they did not live in it."

Escaping the push and shove, heat and grime of the busy city is an urge dreamed by many and pursued by the few who can. Christine Craig writes cleansed and refreshed from the murkiness of urban existence through her leading character who celebrates life *In the Hills* (1989):

Up in these hills the mornings bloom so gently moist, everything so wet with dew and wrapped in pale grey that you want desperately to hold your arms out, to pull it all to you and hold it there for an hour, keep it all with you for a space of time. But the sun, busy auntie, rushes out, rushes out and tidies it all away so quickly you can hardly believe your grey moment was ever there. Later, the busy, rushing sun will spread herself out and reign expansively throughout the hills.

Years before, I had left the heat and the noise and the warring of the city to build my small house here on my mother's land.

The hills' residents are a changing mix of affluent commuters and small hill farmers, living here by birthright, life choice and necessity. All share the same visual sweep of the city below; a hazy, ashen sprawl to the curves of the bay and the delicate finger of the Palisadoes. Approaching from the air, Kenneth Pringle savoured the reverse view in *Waters of the West*:

Four thousand feet below and westward, seen through the delicate, translucent, summer green of banana pennoms, the Liguanea Plain warms into a soft, flesh-like peach… And beyond the Palisadoes lies harbour, dove-grey, shining through a breath of mist, calm as a mill-pond, set as a mirror of mercury. In that pale, strange, bluish light one can just perceive in the billows of greenery which roll back from the water-front a white dome, a yellow tower, a red-shingled roof. Then the foliage of that hidden city, still as if reflected in glass, carries on the eye to a great snowy band of mist, above which there seem to ride the violet clouds. These are the impossible Blue Mountain crests.

Mountain Bound

The former colonial redoubts of Newcastle and Irish Town are draped from the folds of the Grand Ridge that shields Kingston's northern flanks. The sites were chosen for settlement in the nineteenth century by the British military and the labourers involved in working mountainside plantations. Field Marshall Sir William Gomm established barracks at Newcastle in 1841 as a cooler, healthier outpost for the sickly soldiers stationed on the Liguanea Plain below, who were battered by heat, tropical fevers and ill-living. As James Anthony Froude noted forty years later, "Having ceased to quarter our regiments in mangrove swamps, we now build a camp for them among the clouds."

Away from the humidity of the coast, the ridge of mountains gives welcome respite from the lowland heat trap. H. D. Carberry's poem "Nature" (posthumously published in 1995) lyrically bathes in the climatic benevolence of the surrounding hills:

We have neither Summer nor Winter
Neither Autumn nor Spring
...
The days when the rain beats like bullets on the roofs
And there is no sound but the swish of water in the gullies
And trees struggling in the High Jamaica winds.
...
But best of all there are the days when the mango and the logwood
blossom.
When the bushes are full of the sound of bees and the scent of honey
When the tall grass sways and shivers to the slightest breath of air
When the buttercups have paved the earth with yellow stars
And beauty comes suddenly and the rains have gone.

Wedged on the mountainside, residents of the upland towns are caught in the daily flow of cool mists.

Every evening a vapour descends from these summits towards the vales
below, and probably adds some strength to the land-wind, which sets
from this quarter after sun-set. In the morning the fog rises, and seems
to creep in a regular train to the higher grounds; so that, for a great part
of the day, it continues so thick, as to give the air a chill, even at noon,
equal to what is felt here before sun-rise. Where it is more broken and

dispersed, so as to admit the solar rays to pass freely, warm steams imme-
diately begin to be exhaled; and the mossy ground feels to the hand like
a hot bed.

Writing in the latter half of the eighteenth century, Edward Long
clearly savoured the occasional stormy coolness of his retreats to these
hills and his namesake mountain, which closely shields Kingston's
eastern flank. He continued:

The clouds assembling about noon gradually thicken, grow black, and
descend lower… Soon afterwards, the vapoury particles begin to
condense and fall in rain; the lightening flashes with great vivacity, as it
traverses along, in a variety of angular or serpentine directions. We hear
the majestic thunder rolling at our feet, and reverberated by a thousand
echoes among the hills. This tumultuous interlude continues until the
vapours, grown lighter by a plentiful discharge of their contents, begin
to re-ascend and disperse, climbing over the stately pinnacles of these
mountains, like flocks of sheep retiring hastily to their fold.

These surrounding uplands thus offered air "pure, temperate, and
salubrious, during the whole year" so that health and vigour were
almost guaranteed. Anthony Trollope was another ardent admirer of
the mountain-borne constitution, remarking that "I can imagine no
more healthy climate than the mountains around Kingston. 'Tis here
that bishops and generals love to dwell, that their daughters may have

rosy cheeks, and their sons stalwart limbs." Long specifically mentioned the fine stamina of the garrison billeted on nearby Stony Hill. Their descent to the barracks in Kingston conditioned a rapid decline, "where probably, not more from the change of air, than the greater facility of procuring spirituous liquors, they grew sickly, and reduced in their number."

Up at Newcastle, neat white ranks of houses are still terraced around the trim Gomm Square, which has miraculously been levelled from the steeply sloping pine and fern-covered mountainside. Polished regimental plaques garnish the parade ground, fuzzily viewed across the dewy black tarmac that soon begins to steam gently in the late morning sun. A restful quiet descends on the place after drill practice falls out. The British Army finally marched down the hill after independence curtailed a two-century sojourn. The Jamaica Defence Force now runs the show. The early days of colonial square bashing were also looked upon most rosily by Trollope during his island travels:

> But yet it consists now of a goodly village, in which live colonels, and majors, and chaplains, and surgeons, and purveyors, all in a state of bliss—as it were in a second Eden. It is a military paradise, in which war is spoken of, and dinners and dances abound.

Hunkering up amid the hills, if not every person's paradise, seemed the far healthier option for Kingston's foot soldiers, but the demon of drink was not bound solely to lowland dispositions and it was thirstily pursued where it could be found. Froude suggested that by the end of the nineteenth century the Newcastle garrison downed perhaps only a few quarts of beer, but had reached new heights of boredom and were wholly restless.

> With nothing to do, no one to speak to, and nothing to kill, what could become of them? Did they drink? Well, yes. They drank rum occasionally; but there were no public-houses. They could get it only at the canteen, and the daily allowance was moderate. As to beer, it was out reach alto- gether. At the foot of the mountains it was double the price which it was in England. At Newcastle the price was doubled again by the cost of

carriage to the camp. I inquired if they did not occasionally hang them-
selves.

With limited options for alcoholic escape, many took the more physical action and opted to desert in large numbers. On the way down the hill, the hamlets of Irish Town and Redlight provided welcome relief. The latter, as the name suggests, serviced the garrison with a brothel, while the former had sturdier roots as a settlement of Irish coopers who arrived in the nineteenth century to make shipping barrels for the surrounding coffee plantations. The coffee beans of the Blue Mountains further to the east remain among the most prized and hence expensive in the world.

High Life

While the Newcastle barracks still hover on the hillside as a paradise lost for some residents and their predecessors, more homely sites are scattered amid crumpled glens and precarious slopes. A much-repeated story tells that when Columbus was requested by the Queen of Spain to describe the appearance of his new-found land, he crushed a leaf of paper in his hand and released the folds upon the table, revealing a crumpled outline more elegant than his own words could express. Within these irregular contours small-scale farmers harvest coffee, bananas, yams, scallion and furtive bales of ganja. Rickety trucks transport higglers and their crops down to town on market days, spewing up dust or mud as the season dictates and the curves sharpen. Money-laden four-wheel drives chart the reverse route to the top, past discreetly hidden homes or quality hostelries. The founder of Island enterprises, Chris Blackwell, owns one of the most chic hideouts on the island: Strawberry Hill lies mid-way between Newcastle and the capital. Acres of bougainvillaea, bourbon and ice by the pool and a dozen shimmering white cottages cap the retreat's delights. Bob Marley sensibly first fled here following the attempt on his life in 1976 when it was the music producer's private residence.

Gazing down upon Kingston's hazy, deceptively beautiful sprawl when framed by burning crimson bougainvillaea, Dallas Mountain lies roughly to the east, while due south the careful, slow-motion flight paths of approaching planes are guided by the faint strip of the

Palisadoes. Peter Abrahams described the island as a mosaic of dazzling views and that of the capital below as "a miniature model city on the edge of the sea. The bright sun lit its buildings, gave them the look of newly-washed cleanness; and, here and there, the sun struck quivering reflections from roofs and windows." The white sands and sea of the Hellshire coast glitter to the west, backed by the sprawling suburban expanse of Portmore. The writer Chris Salewicz, while charmed to wallow within the hotel's leisure, muses: "Strawberry Hill is probably the most beautiful place in the world. From the verandah of my cottage I have a view of much of the south of Jamaica. Ten miles below, half an hour's switchback drive from the mountain, the grid plan of Kingston is laid out like a relief map, even the shantytown of Riverton City, from whose ceaselessly burning city dump a plume of smoke spirals."

The hills above Kingston are dotted with splendid houses, their blooming gardens straight out of a botanist's floral fantasies. Cherry Garden, another verdant suburb in the peaks, was much admired by Froude during days from a different era:

Cherry Garden was a genuine homestead, a very menagerie of domestic animals of all sorts and breeds. Horses loitered under the shade of the mangoes; cows, asses, dogs, turkeys, cocks and hens, geese, guinea fowl and pea fowl lounged and strutted about the paddocks. In the grey of the morning they held their concerts; the asses brayed, the dogs barked, the turkeys gobbled, and the pea fowl screamed. It was enough to waken the seven sleepers, but the noises seemed so home-like and natural that they mixed pleasantly in one's dreams. One morning, after they had been holding a special jubilee, the butler apologised for them when he came to call me, and laughed as loud as the best of jokes when I said that they did not mean any harm. The great feature of the day was five cats, with blue eyes and spotlessly white, who walked in regularly at breakfast, ranged themselves on their tails round their mistress's chair, and ate their porridge and milk like reasonable creatures. Within and without all was orderly.

Apparent domestic order jarred with the occasional chaos on the tracks and roads outside, even during Froude and Trollope's time. The latter embarked on a trip through the hills to ascend Blue Mountain

Peak, the highest on the island at over 6,000 feet. Needless to say, a train of servants, who at least made the most of the author's liquid reserves, hoisted along his weighty baggage for the eventful trip:

Every now and then we regaled the negroes with rum, and the more rum we gave them the more they wanted. And every now and then we regaled ourselves with brandy and water, and the oftener we regaled ourselves the more we required to be regaled. All such things are matters of course. And so we arrived at the Blue Mountain Peak.

Rather than follow the rum-soaked course of the writer and his indentured entourage, contemporary trekkers in the Blue Mountains are more likely to rise in the cool, dark hours before dawn to climb the slopes with backpacked trampers, chartered guides and hard-worked farmers. As myriad visitors have testified over the year, the summit-level views leave them in awe. In the eighteenth century Edward Long penned prose in enraptured terms, still enchanted by his hillside vapours:

No object of nature, I think, can be more pleasing and picturesque, than the appearance of the heavens about sunset, at the close of almost every day; when that majestic orb seems perched for awhile on the summit of a mountain: its circumference is dilated by the interposing vapours; and here, detained in view by the refraction of rays, it looks as if resting for some moments from its career, and in suspense before its departure: on a sudden it vanishes, leaving a trail of splendour aloft, which streaks the clouds, according to their different positions and distances, with the most lovely and variegated tints that the happiest fancy can imagine.

Two and a half centuries later, Kenneth Pringle was also transfixed by the phantom veils of mist and sheets of rain which often envelop the Blue Mountain heights for the best part of the day:

I often think of the Peak now as a crater of grey moving cloud and bitter winds driving towards evening into a wilder commotion of tempest. One could feel it brewing. The wind whipped and shrieked more savagely, the vapour became fantastic and ghostlier, the air grew

*darker. And suddenly from end to end the enormous, the limitless heav-
ens hissed with a sound like scissors slitting silk, and from their opened
flanks rolled and volleyed peal upon peal of extravagant thunder…
And below and around the ruby, green, and purple lightning jaggered
and crackled, illuminating vast ranges of terrible peaks, colouring tropical rivers, decapitating palms, crashing round citadels of cloud as if
they were capitals of marble.*

Rocky Rides out of Town

To scale these moisture-trapping heights, Stony Hill Road leads the
traveller north, over to Wag Water Valley and towards the northern
coast. Blueprints to modernize this road remain firmly pinned to the
drawing board, while the alternative north-easterly escape route, in the
direction of the Blue Mountains and John Crow National Park, still
leads to exhilarating negotiations with hairpin bends and sudden
gradients. Skirmishes with sharp corners and bottomless potholes
commence soon after Papine en route up, up and up via Gordon Town
Road. Today's market traffic descends from on high, and eyes are soon
trained to the road through a mixture of experience and justified fear.
A hundred years ago, Froude could take time to report on the
botanical feast of roadside flora as the track wound up to Gordon
Town itself:

> *Above the line the tropical vegetation was in all its glory: ferns and plan-
> tains waving in the moist air; cedars, tamarinds, gum trees, orange trees
> striking their roots among the clefts of the crags, and hanging out over
> the abysses below them. Aloes flung up their tall spiral stems; flowering
> shrubs and creepers covered bank and slope with green and blue and
> white and yellow, and above and over our heads, as we drove along,
> stood out the great limestone blocks which thunder down when loosened
> by rain.*

Danger loitered in the pendulous rocks, but early twentieth-century
travellers, within grasp of a double buggy for forty shillings or hiring a
brawny pony to plod the path, still arrived with wonder attached.
Frederick Ober's guidebook from the 1920s advised on several travel
modes:

*Either way, the route is picturesque, and from the trail, as it constantly
ascends, most glorious views are outspread... 'Delicious' is the word that
best describes the scenery along the trail, winding as it does by the banks
of tinkling streams with water so cool and clear that it seems as if the
speckled trout must haunt there.*

Portmore, the Young Pretender

Heading away from the hills and westward from Kingston may prove a
more challenging, and immediately less bucolic, excursion. Motoring
north-west from the Parade out along Spanish Town Road, the chaos
of dusty downtown existence edges towards the car windows.
Approaching Six Miles, Washington Boulevard trails westward to
Spanish Town. An earlier turn towards the mangrove-lined Causeway
leads directly to the modern low-rise growth of Portmore. During
daylight, rush-hour traffic reduces the Causeway to a metallic slow-
worm spanning Hunts Bay. Urban tales from recent years recount
occasional and unfortunate late-night drives during which the
homeward leg ends with a hold-up. Highway robbery returned in the
twenty-first century, but now handled with an Uzi.

Hemmed in by hills to the north and east, Kingston has outgrown
the Liguanea Plain. A brash urban upstart of the sixties now challenges
Kingston as the country's newest would-be city. Pastel and mirrored
shopping malls, waves of commuters and a cluster of clubs form some
the reasons for Portmore's claim to new urban fame. Planned as a fresh
settlement to absorb some of capital's demographic over-spill, the
burgeoning satellite has expanded at a spectacular rate as the metropolis
moves westwards.

Arrival at Portmore via the long bleak drive along Marcus Garvey
Drive, scoured by sun and dust, past the Newport West oil refinery,
docks and gantries and the free-zone assembly factories perched before
the Causeway lowers expectations to the level of the surrounding
mudflats that choke the estuary. Roadside shacks sell fish and crafts
from the narrow strip of landfill and beach, smudged by the harbour's
washed up line of oiled plastics. The low-lying beige bungalows
smoothed to the contours of the former coastal scrub do little to feed
further the vision of a bright new municipality, but turreted surprises
jut up out of the planned sprawl and colourful billboards announce the

weekend's visiting club acts. The "concrete castles" of Portmore—embellished domestic units splashed pink and ridged by mortared battlements—are commonly recognized symbols of social self-improvement. Equally well known is (or was) the wicked Cactus nightclub, which formerly drew good time party crowds to bump and wine from all of Kingston. When anything kicked off on the Jamaican dance scene, it started at Cactus or arrived there soon after.

Portmore prides itself as the pulse of a new Jamaica and successive councillors called for city status before this became a reality in 2003. With over 100,000 residents, its right to independence carries statistical weight. Likewise, the city-sized traffic problems demand attention as the populace crawls to and from Kingston via the Causeway crush. An expanding range of communities—Edgewater, Bridge Port, Garveymeade, Westchester, Passage Fort and the subtly named Independence City—form the constellation that is now Portmore. Port Henderson, an eighteenth-century village with restored buildings and the historic Rodney Arms, lays claim to be the heritage jewel in Portmore's otherwise modern crown. Further along the spit past Dawkins Pond lies the crumbling Fort Augustus, an eighteenth-century fortification built to defend the harbour and which now houses a women's prison. Even the British fleet first eschewed pre-Kingston soil when it landed at Passage Fort in 1655, before heading off on a six-mile march inland to seize Spanish Town and claim a new colony for the crown.

While Lime Cay attracts more than a fair share of flash boats and booming party cruises beyond the Palisadoes, the mass of the population from both Kingston and Portmore head to Hellshire for fried bammy and festival on the sands. A bus ride and shared car transport visitors to Hellshire's beaches without too much bother or expense. Dry bush and cacti crowd the barren hills behind the beaches, which come to hectic life at the weekends. The mass of people, crammed on the edge of a brilliant seascape, splash and revel in boisterous contrast to the semi-desert behind.

The Hellshire beaches lie to the south of Portmore, but are firmly part of the town's claim to city status, having been annexed as an unlikely Copacabana to Portmore's Rio. Late eighteenth-century expectations did not bode well for real estate ventures on a coast that was "for the most part so rocky and barren, as to not be worth inhabiting." But ever with a nose for invigorating vapours, and perhaps an early sense of a good sales pitch, Edward Long remarked that, "The air on these hills is extremely healthy: the rocks are concealed from view by innumerable aromatic herbs, shrubs, and trees, possessed of great medicinal virtues, though hitherto explored by only a few curious persons."

Over time, Long's "Healthshire" was corrupted to Hellshire and the rows of wooden huts and fishing shacks that came to line the shore traded mounds of fried fish and iced beer rather than herbal remedies. Bashments stir up the weekend crowd at Fort Clarence, but neighbouring Hellshire beach itself is the centre of local action. Having taken on the modified title, Chris Salewicz reports that even this beach is misnamed. Locals refers to the fishermen's beach more properly as Naggo Head, owing to similar reasons of phonetic slippage:

> *Naggo Head is named after the Naggo people, the original settlers. I had long assumed this to be the name of, say, an obscure African tribe. Then I learned the truth, which has as its own inevitable Jamaican simplicity. The Naggo people were displaced plantation labourers who were moved to the area from their original homes after slavery was abolished, protesting loudly, 'Wi nah go!'*

Spanish Town: Old Time Rival

While the weekend beach crowds threaten to boil over, there are quieter moments in the shady corners of the island's former capital. Viewed from the distant heights of the Grand Ridge, Spanish Town lies to the west of Kingston, loosely corralled beyond the sprawl of Portmore on the Nelson Mandela freeway. As the name suggests, the settlement was the centre of Spanish operations while Spain governed the island from 1520 to 1655. The Spanish called their town Villa de la Vega or St. Jago de la Vega, and according to a report of 1628 the site was "marvellously attractive... very well built and laid out." Only a few relics of this era remain and these are carefully housed in the Institute of Jamaica. Traces of a Hispanic and Catholic past rest only in the solitary names of Red Church Street, White Church Street and Monk Street. Having sparred with the neighbouring port to retain its role as the seat of colonial government, the town was pushed aside in favour of the bustling, mercantile hub of Kingston.

Today it might prove difficult to envisage the town as a former holder of and vigorous contender to Kingston's capital title. Less than four decades after it relinquished its crown, vestiges of the city's past were effectively subdued. Writing in 1908, Sir Frederick Treves noted the comfortable sleepiness of the settlement:

> *It is a small, sweet place, quaint, quiet, and sound asleep. It is a village where there is an eternal summer; where the trees are always green, where flowers are ever in bloom. Most of the houses are of wood, with ash-coloured shingles on the roof; many are old, made exquisite in tint by centuries of sun. All are gay with jalousies or verandahs, with balconies or breezy porches, for it is hard to keep out the flood of light which pours down upon this "level mead." After three centuries of strenuous life Spanish Town would seem to have resolved to doze out the rest of its life in the sun.*

Even the dramatic events of the previous year's earthquake failed to revive the urban pulse, beyond the immediate unkind shock, which was "as if an opium eater, asleep in a field, had been suddenly tossed into the air by a rabid bull."

Retiring gracefully for the most part from the administrative fray, Spanish Town still houses the bulk of the nation's archives. A few steps from the parishioners' petitions, crumbling parchment and cracked leather, the central Georgian square dominates the city's few attractions. A quiet walk through the ruins of the old court, scorched and razed to the ground by public revolt against century-old imperial injustices, conjures up something of a turbulent, ill-governed past. Anthony Trollope scythed mercilessly through the decline of Spanish Town with a cursory slice of his nib:

> *It is like the city of the dead. There are long streets there in which no human inhabitant is ever seen... The Governor's house—King's House as it is called—stands on one side of a square; opposite is the house of the Assembly; on the left, as you come out from the Governor's, are the executive offices and house of the Council, and on the right some other public*

buildings. The place would have some pretension about it if it did not seem to be stricken with an eternal death. All the walls are of a dismal dirty yellow, and a stranger cannot but think that the colour is owing to the dreadfully prevailing disease of the country.

The author was unable to note the most delicate attraction of the square on the north side, upon which later visitors, notably Patrick Leigh Fermor, have waxed lyrical. The Rodney Memorial, designed by John Bacon, is laced with the pomp of empire. The central marble pedestal, shielded by ornate decorations, Corinthian pillars and a canopied rotunda, celebrates brute naval force and the persona of Admiral George Rodney, who routed the French fleet off Guadeloupe in 1782 and saved Jamaica from foreign occupation:

Britannia, drawn by a team of dolphins in a cockle-shell, travels victoriously through a bas-relief of destruction. Fleur-de-lys banners trail humbly in the water and brigantines and frigates and men-o'-war, the wreckage of the entire French fleet, litter the marble background; tritons emerge, and a fanfare of conches wafts her onward while sea-lions and porpoises and strange sea-monsters gamble beside the vainglorious car. The fishtails of marine unicorns uncoil through the breakers, and an alligator, anonymously basking here, reveals its teeth in subtle approbation. Olympian above his attributes stands Bacon's statue of Lord Rodney himself. There he postures, the intrepid admiral, brilliant sailor, confirmed gambler and philanderer; fantastically dandified, eaten up with vanity, racked by gravel and the gout and bowed down with premature old age; changed here, by apotheosis into a Greco-Roman hero in toga, chlamys and kilt, and a thorax embossed with the Medusa's head.

Today's calm is a far cry from the exuberance and delight that must have rung around the square when the end of slavery was proclaimed here in 1833. The Rodney Memorial still decorates the square, but with decidedly less polish than during the old days. Compared to the rush of Kingston the heart of Spanish Town now barely murmurs:

The streets were almost empty of citizens. But they were full of sunlight and heavy with that late-afternoon atmosphere which is peculiar to towns that have lost their importance. For Kingston, with its outlet to the sea, its docks and its trade, was too much for the old island capital. The languid mechanism of Spanish Town came to a halt and the government was reluctantly transferred to its urchin usurper.

Little has changed since Leigh Fermor's visit in the 1940s, save for the frequency of shootings in the outlying yards, mirroring Kingston's political and latterly drug-fuelled conflicts. Just off the main square, tranquillity still reigns within the cathedral. Inside the solid walls, which do well to muffle the incessant traffic streaming along the bypass, glimpses of Spanish Town's fading antiquity rest entombed:

Grandiloquent Georgian epitaphs to dead governors and administrators have thickly silted up the walls of the interior. Bulging and inadequately pinioned brats in marble pine over torches reversed, or shrouded urns, and pale sibylline figures mourn in attitudes of pensive melancholy beside the stately eighteenth-century obituaries. The floor of the nave is virtually paved with memorial slabs of black and white marble. The charges on the shields that nest there in a whirlwind of carved mantelling have been rubbed smooth by the tread of generations, and the seventeenth-century lettering of the brief biographies beneath them, telling the tales of early colonists from York or Somerset or Connaught, is all but indecipherable.

Writing in the 1870s, Charles Rampini also failed to conceal his despair at the town's decay:

Everything connected with it is dull and languid. The few officials whose duties keep them there are gloomy and dispirited; and the occasional balls, which like angel's visits are few and far between, waken the echoes in the old ball-room of Government House, only by the contrast render the desertion more marked and the solitude more appalling.

His account looks wistfully to the livelier days of decadence when the once grand mansions brimmed with privilege and fun:

What visions of jerked hog and black crab, of turtle-soup and old Madeira, does the sight of them produce! What pictures do they conjure up of those wicked old times when aides-de-camp used to ride alligators through the streets, when admirals used to give balls to the brown girls of the time, when vice in every shape was more reputable than it is at present! Is there a single bottle of the old Madeira extant? Does any one remember the Hell Fire Club? Is there any one alive who has tasted Bath punch?

Kingston Overseas

While quieter times have descended upon Spanish Town and as Kingston bustles along, Jamaicans have continued to look beyond the island to kick-start new lives or to work temporarily in foreign economies before returning home. Many Jamaicans have emigrated, but few have left the island behind. As the poet A. L. Hendriks muses in "On This Mountain" (1965): "We are one people in one house and cannot leave it." Similarly, Michelle Cliff has skilfully outlined the unease of withdrawal and return in her collected thoughts, *If I Could Write This in Fire, I Would Write This in Fire* (1985):

> *I and Jamaica is who I am. No matter how far I travel—how deep the ambivalence I feel about ever returning. And Jamaica is a place in which we/they/I connect and disconnect—change place.*

Migration is not merely a modern matter. Kingston's harbour and airport have long been the gateway for ferrying people in and out of Jamaica, as forced labourers, adventurers or networking relatives. In the 1860s and 1870s, workers set sail in their thousands to Panama to construct a railroad and to take part in the ill-fated first attempt to build the canal. From the beginning of the last century, after the successful completion of the Panama Canal, many Jamaicans left for Central America to try to make their fortunes. In reality, few did, but the myth endured. Claude McKay paints an engaging picture of one such returned migrant in *Banana Bottom* (1933):

> *First among the rum-shop fellows was Tack Tally, proudly wearing his decorations from Panama: gold watch and chain of three strands, and a foreign gold coin attached to it as large as a florin, a gold stick-pin with a huge blue stone, and five gold rings flashing from his fingers. He had on a fine bottle-green tweed suit with the well-creased and deep-turned pantaloons called peg-top, the coat of long points and lapels known as American style. And wherever he went, he was accompanied by an admiring gang.*

Heavy gold chains remain *de rigueur*, but the tweeds have taken a back seat in the fashion displays of today's wealthy returnees. During the 1930s and 1940s, tens of thousands of Kingstonians left the island to find work in the United States, aiming to escape poverty, find excitement or rejoin already settled family. Immigration reforms in 1965 further swelled the Jamaican ranks Stateside as relatives were reunited and well-maintained family chains linked up across the waters. Over half a million people of Jamaican origin now live all across the US, but the majority are found in the large cities, in particular the Queens and Brooklyn boroughs of New York City. Eastern Parkway has been popularly renamed "Caribbean Parkway", while Fulton Street, writes Paule Marshall, has the all the visible hallmarks of the West Indian diaspora rooted in New York:

Fulton Street today is the aroma of our kitchen long ago when the bread was finally in the oven. And it's the sound of reggae and calypso and ska and the newest rage, soca, erupting from a hundred speakers outside the record stores. It's Rastas with their hennaed dreadlocks and the impassioned political debates of the rum shops back home brought out onto the street corners. It's Jamaican meat patties brought out and eaten on the run and fast food pulori, a Trinidadian East Indian pancake doused in pepper sauce that is guaranteed to clear your sinuses the moment that you bite into it.

Carnival events such as the parade celebrated on Labor Day in Brooklyn have pushed forward pan-Caribbean identities among migrants, although inter-island rivalries still flare up in the form of jovial barracking and occasionally more cutting taunts and injuries. The famous calypsonian, the Mighty Sparrow, nevertheless chose to celebrate this coming together of the islands in "Mas in Brooklyn" (1976):

You can be from St. Cleo, or from John John,
in New York, all that done.
They haven't to know who is who,
New York equalize you.

Within this overseas diaspora, Jamaicans and their offspring form the largest non-Hispanic Caribbean population living in the US.

Networks of commerce and family life connect "Jamericans" to Jamaica, and Kingston, on a daily basis. Hillside higglers have adopted a transnational market plan, buying and selling goods between Miami and Kingston. International shopping hauls filled the childhood of Jasmine in Patricia Powell's *Me Dying Trial* (1993), a Jamaican story of lives straddling two countries:

> ... *for Jasmine travel plenty since her mother is a higgler woman, travelling to Miami and New York two and three times a month, so she can buy sneakers and jeans and sweat-shirt and pants and blender and pressure-cooker and sell them in the market at more bargainable prices.*

Jasmine soon spoke with "an American twang and told that 'You wear any Jesus Christ thing you feel'" overseas. Kingston dress codes duly became sneakered and sports-suited. Returnees brought with them not only relative riches, but the "latest" cultural kudos, even if also bringing embarrassment to their uninitiated kin. In *Bella Makes Life* (1990), Lorna Goodison's returned heroine strides boldly into a new "Jamerican" fashion frontier when she is greeted at the airport by an astonished husband:

> *He wished he could have just disappeared into the crowd and kept on going as far away from Norman Manley airport as was possible. Bella returning. Bella come back from New York after a whole year. Bella dressed in some clothes which make her look like a chequer cab. What in God's name was a big forty-odd-year-old woman who was fat when she leave Jamaica, and get worse fat since she go to America, what was this woman doing dressed like this? Bella was wearing stretch-to-fit black pants, over that she had on a big yellow and black checked blouse, on her feet was a pair of yellow booties, in her hand was a big yellow handbag and she had on a pair of big pair of yellow framed glasses. See ya Jesus! Bella no done yet, she had dyed her hair with red oxide and Jerry curls it till it shine like it grease and spray. Oh Bella what happen to you? Joseph never ever bother to take in her anklet and her big bracelets and her gold chain with a pendant, big as a name plate on a lawyer's office, marked 'Material Girl'.*

Life overseas has always brought back far more than revamped wardrobes and much-needed cash; it has also offered a challenge to the all-too traditional domestic set-up. Gwennie, the wily heroine of *Me Dying Trial* (1993), leaves behind an abusive husband and sets forth to make good. Like many women she seeks not only to step out of poverty, but to break away from Jamaica's crushing machismo: "I didn't come all the way to Foreign to put up with the same damn foolishness." She heeds her aunt's warnings against the "plenty gunmen and drugs and informer, just like them bad parts out here," accompanied by the steadfast advice: "Don't walk about at night, have company at all times. Believe in you Maker, do to church and pray."

Kingstonians continue to cross continents. Hot FM links the capital live with "the tri-state" every Saturday evening. Newark, New Jersey, Connecticut and Kingston maintain a lively conversation across the radio waves. Even in the vast cities of the United States, Jamaican tastes and habits have taken root and brought jerk chicken to the national palate. Louise Bennett's "America" looks with amusement at the spreading frontier of the Jamaican demographic empire:

Jane sey she meet so much ole frien
Wen she strole dung New York,
Dat she feel like is dung King Street
Or Luke Lane she dah-walk.

The Gleaner on-line and chat groups link up virtual webs across the "Foreign", but despite the movement outside the island, old links die hard, even to a past that lingers eerily in streets, buildings, customs and psyche. Michelle Cliff reveals the legacy of a collective Jamaican memory in *The Store of a Million Items* (1998): "We live in America, as we always will call it, but are the children of the Empire, St. George is our patron, his cross our standard. We are triangular people, our feet on three islands."

One response is to try to pass unnoticed into "lighter" mainstream society. This attempted denial of the self creates an awkward unease, as outlined again by Michelle Cliff in "Claiming an Identity They Taught Me to Despise" (1981), who as a Jamaican living overseas, continues to write most sensitively on the experiences and discriminations of migration:

> *Isolate yourself. If they find out about you it's all over. Forget about your great-grandfather with the darkest skin—until you're back "home" where they joke about how he climbed a coconut tree when he was eighty. Go to college. Go to England to study. Learn about the Italian Renaissance and forget that they kept slaves. Ignore the teas of the Indias. Black Americans didn't understand us either. We are—after all—British. If anyone asks you, talk about sugar plantations and the Maroons—not the landscape of downtown Kingston or the children at the roadside. Be selective. Cultivate normalcy. Stress sameness. Blend in. For God's sake don't pile difference upon difference. It's not safe.*

Mother Country

While the majority of emigrating Jamaicans have landed in North America, many have followed the neo-colonial link to the United Kingdom. Rejection, difference and ignorance in the former so-called mother country left many Kingstonians aggrieved and others amused and bemused. Morris Cargill relates his experience:

> *When, in the early part of the Second World War, my wife and I went to England, the landlady of a rather shabby-genteel boarding house near Earl's Court station to whom we had applied for a room looked at us rather oddly and asked us whether we were comfortable in European clothes and expressed surprise that we spoke such fluent English.*

In most cases, emigration was a voyage into the unknown, despite the official anglo-centric bias in Jamaican education and social etiquette for three centuries. Hyacinth Sinclair migrated to Manchester and described her initial impressions in "When I Came to England":

> *I never knew that there were poor people in England.*
> *I thought that they were all tip-top people.*
> *I got to realise*
> *that other people in the world have poor people.*

Before also arriving in Manchester and similarly writing up the story of his travels for the Gatehouse Project, Livingstone migrated from Jamaica to Florida as a contract worker, cutting the sugar cane until dusk. His circuitous and tough migratory route led him initially up the East Coast of the United States. Constant displacement and upheaval is the foundation of many migrants' lives:

We were six months in Florida,
then the sugar cane finished,
so they transfer us to the North.
The North is a big place,
so everybody go to different countries.
Some go for apples,
flowers,
Some go for tobacco.
You go where work is.
You're on a contract.
They supply the work, say for three years.
If there's plenty of work you're O.K.
But you're moving around.
You don't stop one place.
If I travelled again
I wouldn't go on contract.
On contract you're like a slave.
You can't just walk out.
I'd rather go my own way.

Over a quarter of a million West Indians, mostly from Jamaica and many from Kingston have settled in Britain. The mass migration to post-war Britain awoke waning imperial links, useful or otherwise. Miss Lou first versed the irony of this "Colonisation in Reverse":

What joyful news, Miss Mattie;
Ah feel like me heart gwine burs—
Jamaica people colonizin
Englan in reverse.

The *Empire Windrush* set sail from Kingston and docked at Tilbury thirty days later on 22 June 1948 as the symbolic first trickle of the Jamaican arrival in cold Britannia. Grace Nichols recounts the displaced lives of the last century, linked way back in "Beverley's Saga":

> *Me good friend Beverley*
> *Come to England. She was three.*
> *She born in Jamaica, but seh,*
> *Dis ya she country.*
> *She ancestor blood help fe build it,*
> *Dat is history.*
> *Dih black presence go back*

Joan Riley expands on the story of Hyancinth in *The Unbelonging* (1985). Similarly born in Kingston and growing up as immigrant in Britain, she faces accusations of where she came from:

> *'I didn't come from no jungle,' Hyacinth defended warily, feeling hot and embarrassed by the other's assertion.*
> *'Yeah? Then where you come from, a mud hut?'*
> *A vision of tenements with their zinc fencing and old rusting shacks, some with holes eaten right through, flashed shamefully through her mind to be pushed back hastily. 'I come from a city,' she said breathlessly, a little desperately. 'A nice big city with lots of sunshine and grass to play on at school.'*

Kingstonians travelling to the "Mother Country" brought their labour and were granted abuse in return. Linton Kwesi Johnson, himself a childhood migrant, stamps on the pain in "It Dread inna Inglan", where "Maggi Tatcha on di go / wid a racist show / but a she haffi go." And so she went, but the racism remained. Meanwhile, Jamaica talk reshaped the popular language of Brixton and other inner-city areas and successfully sent out messages to stiff upper lips and ears, similar to John Agard's "Listen Mr Oxford Don":

> *Dem accuse me of assault*
> *on de Oxford dictionary*

imagin a concise peaceful man like me
dem want me serve time
for inciting rhyme to riot
but I tekking it quiet
down here in Clapham Common

Home Sweet Home

Exiled Kingstonians have changed the airwaves, social landscape and diet of the countries in which they have settled. But exile, through choice or force, involves a stark reminder of days gone by and a lost land:

It's den I miss me home sweet home
Me good ole rice an' peas
An' I say I is a fool fe come
To dis lan' of starve an' sneeze.

"Quashie Comes to London" by Una Marson (1937) is one of the earlier contemporary laments for transnational separation. The myth of return haunted migrants' experiences for many years—the thought of heading "home", wealthier, to set up a family, to live out a retirement package or to build anew. In the last decades, the myth has receded and plans have turned to action as Kingston and surrounding areas have received the first flow of returning exiles. James Berry, who migrated to England in 1948 at the age of twenty-four, celebrated this growing number of welcome return trips in "Back to Hometown Kingston" (1976):

These faces are true,
all dark with the sun.
No one is snow bled
into enmity. This place
exhibits a welcome.

This wind brushes a laughing
sun. It shatters me how
my muscles let go:

I startle no one
with my black face.

"An Amazing Island"

For centuries, Jamaican and foreign travellers have written lines of romanticized and real praise for "an amazing island", the title used by W. E. B. du Bois during his Kingston sojourn in 1915:

> ...*of the lands that I have looked upon hitherto Jamaica is the most startling. The ride from Spanishtown to the northwestern sea is one of the great rides of the world... The whole island is a mass of gray, green mountains thrown on the face of the sea with gash and shadow and veil. The rain of Jamaica is the maddest, wildest and wettest of rains and the sunshine is God's.*

Kenneth Pringle's prose burns as sense-heavy as the scent and "scarlet fire of poncianas" that frame his view of the city from the hills above: "One hears the awakening hubbub of the city loomed over by the blue enormous presence of the silent hills. At this first shock one's impression of Jamaica is of absolute difference. It is another world, gorgeous and strong." Equally lost in rapture, H. M. Tomlinson argues away any denial of the country's divine beauty: "It is a jewel which smells like a flower."

Given a tortuous past and an uncertain present, Kingston's defenders have learnt to praise the good points and be wary of romantic stereotypes, as Michelle Cliff noted in "Art History":

> *I always become wary when someone not of my ilk speaks of Jamaica, especially if I like the person. I wait for smiling or sullen natives, simple or crafty market women, paradise lost on its inhabitants.*
> *'It is a beautiful place,' I said.*

The charm of Kingston ultimately lies not in grand boulevards of rich design or opulent, ornate palaces. Corners of town offer diverse experiences, from seemingly threatening tracts of downtown chaos to airy uptown vistas and unexpected glimpses of beauty laced throughout. Each adds to the larger picture of the contradictory urban whole, just as Anthony Trollope was pointedly reminded by a Kingstonian shopkeeper:

> *"Four-and-sixpence for white gloves!" I said; "is that not high?" "Not at all, sir; by no means. We consider it rather cheap. But in Kingston, sir, you must not think about little economies."*

Further Reading

Politics and History

Abrahams, Peter, *Jamaica: An Island Mosaic*. London: Her Majesty's Stationary Office, 1957.

Alleyne, Mervyn, *Roots of Jamaican Culture*. London: Pluto Press, 1989.

Austin, Diane J., *Urban Life in Kingston, Jamaica: The Culture and Class Ideology of Two Neighbourhoods*. New York: Gordon and Breach, 1984.

Barrett, Leonard E., *Understanding the Rastafarians*. Wilmington: Scholarly Resources, 1995.

Beckford, George and Michael Witter, *Small Garden... Bitter Weed: The Political Economy of Struggle and Change in Jamaica*. London: Zed Books, 1982.

Brathwaite, Edward, *The Development of Creole Society in Jamaica 1770-1820*. Oxford: Clarendon Press, 1971.

Brodber, Erna, Eleanor Wint and Versada Campbell, *Street Foods of Kingston*. Kingston: UWI, 1990.

Bryan, Patrick, *The Jamaican People, 1880-1902: Race, Class and Social Control*. London: Macmillan, 1991.

Buisseret, David, *Historic Architecture of the Caribbean*. London: Heinemann, 1980.

Chevannes, Barry, *Rastafari: Roots and Ideology*. Syracuse: University of Syracuse Press, 1994.

Clarke, Colin G., *Kingston, Jamaica: Urban Development and Social Change, 1692-2002*. Kingston: Ian Randle, 2nd edition, 2002.

Cooper, Carolyn, *Noises in the Blood: Orality, Gender and the 'Vulgar' Body of Jamaican Popular Culture*. London: Macmillan, 1993.

Cundall, Frank, *Jamaica.* London: Kegan Paul, 1900.

Curtin, Philip D., *Two Jamaicas: The Role of Ideas in a Tropical Colony, 1830-1865.* Cambridge: Harvard University Press, 1955.

Foner, Nancy, *Jamaica Farewell: Jamaican Migrants in London.* Berkeley: University of California Press, 1978.

Gambrill, Linda (ed.), *A Tapestry of Jamaica: The Best of Skywritings, Air Jamaica's Inflight Magazine.* Oxford: Macmillan Caribbean, 2003.

Gunst, Laurie, *Born Fi' Dead: A Journey Through the Jamaican Posse Underworld.* Edinburgh: Payback Press, 1995.

Harrison, Michelle, *King Sugar: Jamaica, the Caribbean and the World Sugar Industry.* London: Latin America Bureau, 2000.

Hart, Richard, *Towards Decolonisation: Political, Labour and Economic Developments in Jamaica, 1938-1945.* Kingston: Canoe Press UWI, 1998.

Heuman, Gad J., *Between Black and White: Race, Politics, and the Free Coloreds in Jamaica, 1792-1865.* Oxford: Clio, 1981.

Manley, Michael, *Jamaica: Struggle in the Periphery.* London: Writers and Readers, 1982.

Manley, Michael, *Up the Down Escalator: Development and the International Economy, a Jamaican Case Study.* London: Andre Deutsch, 1987.

Manley, Rachel, *Drumblair: Memories of a Jamaican Childhood.* Kingston: Ian Randle, 1996.

Marx, Robert F., *Port Royal Rediscovered.* London: New English Library, 1973.

Murrell, N. Samuel, William D. Spencer and Adrian Anthony Mcfarlane, *Chanting Down Babylon: A Rastafari Reader.* Kingston: Ian Randle, 1998.

Nettleford, Rex, *Jamaica in Independence: Essays on the Early Years*. Oxford: James Currey, 1990.

Nettleford, Rex, *Mirror, Mirror: Identity, Race and Protest in Jamaica*. Kingston: William Collins and Sangster, 1970.

Norris, Katrin, *Jamaica: The Search for an Identity*. London: Oxford University Press, 1962.

Olivier, Sydney Haldane, *Jamaica: The Blessed Island*. London: Faber and Faber, 1936.

Payne, Anthony J., *Politics in Jamaica*. London: St. Martin's Press, 1989.

Pawson, Michael, *Port Royal, Jamaica*. Oxford: Clarendon Press, 1975.

Post, Ken, *Arise Ye Starvelings: the Jamaican Labour Rebellion of 1938 and its Aftermath*. The Hague: Martinus Nijhoff, 1978.

Rampini, Charles, *Letters from Jamaica: The Land of Streams and Woods*. Edinburgh: Edmonston and Douglas, 1873.

Rodney, Walter, *The Groundings with my Brothers*. London: Bogle-L'Ouverture Publications, 1969.

Sherlock, Philip and Hazel Bennett, *The Story of the Jamaica People*. Kingston: Ian Randle, 1998.

Small, Geoff, *Ruthless: The Global Rise of the Yardies*. London: Warner Books, 1995.

Smith, Michael, G., Roy Augier and Rex Nettleford, *Report on the Rastafari Movement in Kingston, Jamaica*, 1960.

Stone, Carl, *Class, Race and Political Behaviour in Urban Jamaica*. London: Praeger, 1986.

Taylor, Frank F., *To Hell with Paradise: A History of the Jamaican Tourist Industry*. Pittsburgh: University of Pittsburgh Press, 1993.

Turner, Mary, *Slaves and Missionaries: The Disintegration of Jamaican Slave Society, 1737-1834*. Urbana: University of Illinois Press, 1982.

Tyndale-Biscoe, Jack and David Buisseret, *Historic Jamaica from the Air*. Bridgetown: Caribbean Universities Press, 1969.

Wardle, Huon, *An Ethnography of Cosmopolitanism in Kingston, Jamaica*. Lampeter: Edwin Mellen Press, 2000.

Waters, Anita, *Race, Class and Political Symbols: Rastafari and Reggae in Jamaican Politics*. London: Transaction Publishers, 1989.

Arts and Travel

Archer Straw, Petrine, *Jamaican Art: An Overview—With a Focus on Fifty Artists*. Kingston: Kingston Publishers, 1990.

Barrow, Steve and Peter Dalton, *Reggae*. London: Rough Guides, 1997.

Boxer, David and Verle Poupeye, *Modern Jamaican Art*. Kingston: Ian Randle, 1998.

Clarke, Sebastian, *Jah Music: The Evolution of Popular Jamaica Song*. London: Heinemann, 1980.
Froude, James A., *The English in the West Indies; or the Bow of Ulysses*. London: Longmans, Green and Co., 1888.

Hebdige, Dick, *Cut'n Mix: Culture, Identity and Caribbean Music*. London: Methuen, 1987.

Hill, Errol, 1992, *The Jamaican Stage, 1655-1900: Profile of a Colonial Theatre*. Amherst: University of Massachusetts Press, 1992.

Hurston, Zora Neale, *Voodoo Gods: An Inquiry into Native Myths and Magic in Jamaica and Haiti*. London: Dent, 1939.

Leigh Fermor, Patrick, *The Traveller's Tree: A Journey Through the Caribbean Islands*. London: John Murray, 1950

Makin, William J., *Caribbean Nights*. London: Robert Hale, 1939.

Manley, Edna, *The Diaries*. London: Andre Deutsch, 1989.

Mordecai, Pamela, *From Our Yard: Jamaican Poetry Since Independence*. Kingston: Institute of Jamaica Publications, 1987.

Morrow, Chris, *Stir It Up! Reggae Album Cover Art.* London: Thames and Hudson, 1999.

Nettleford, Rex and Maria La Yacona, *Roots and Rhythms: Jamaica's National Dance Theatre.* London: André Deutsch, 1969

O'Brien-Chang, Kevin and Wayne Chen, *Reggae Routes: The Story of Jamaican Music.* Philadelphia/Kingston: Temple University Press/Ian Randle, 1998.

Pringle, Kenneth, *Waters of the West.* London: Allen and Unwin, 1938.

Salewicz, Chris, *Rude Boy: Once Upon a Time in Jamaica.* London: Victor Gollancz, 2000.

Salewicz, Chris and Adrian Boot, *Reggae Explosion: The Story of Jamaican Music.* Kingston: Ian Randle, 2001

Trollope, Anthony, *The West Indies and the Spanish Main.* London, 1859.

Winkler, Anthony, *Going Home to Teach.* Kingston: Kingston Publishers, 1995.

Poetry and Fiction

Breeze, Jean Binta, *Riddym Ravings and Other Poems.* London: Race Today Publications, 1988.

Cliff, Michelle, *The Land of Look Behind.* Ithaca: Firebrand Books, 1985.

Cliff, Michelle, *No Telephone to Heaven.* New York: Dutton, 1987.

Cliff, Michelle, *The Store of a Million Items.* New York: Houghton Mifflin Company, 1998.

Craig, Christine, *Mint Tea and Other Stories.* London: Heinemann, 1993.

Dawes, Kwame, *Wheel and Come Again.* Leeds: Peepal Tree, 1998.

De Lisser, Herbert G., *Jane's Career: A Story of Jamaica.* Kingston: The Gleaner Company, 1913.

Goodison, Lorna, *I Am Becoming My Mother.* London: Beacon Books, 1986.

Goodison, Lorna, *Baby Mother and the King of Swords.* Harlow: Longman, 1990.

Hearne, John, *Voices Under the Window.* London: Faber and Faber, 1955.
Mais, Roger, *Black Lightning.* London: Jonathan Cape, 1955.

Mais, Roger, *Brother Man.* London: Jonathan Cape, 1954.

Mais, Roger, *The Hills Were Joyful Together.* London: Jonathan Cape, 1953.

Patterson, Orlando, *The Children of Sisyphus.* London: Hutchinson, 1964.

Powell, Patricia, *A Small Gathering of Bones.* Oxford: Heinemann, 1994.

Powell, Patricia, *Me Dying Trial.* Oxford: Heinemann, 1993.

Reid, Victor S., *New Day.* New York: Knopf, 1949.

Rhys, Jean, *Wide Sargasso Sea.* London: Andre Deutsch, 1966.

Salkey, Andrew, *Earthquake.* London: Oxford University Press, 1965.

Salkey, Andrew, *Jamaica.* London: Hutchinson, 1973.

Scott, Michael, *Tom Cringle's Log.* Edinburgh, 1881.

Senior, Olive, *Summer Lightning and Other Stories.* Harlow: Longman, 1986

Spence, Vanessa, *The Roads Are Down.* Oxford: Heinemann, 1993.

Thelwell, Michael, *The Harder They Come.* New York: Grove Press, 1980.

Index of Literary and Historical Names

Index of Places and Landmarks